D0926272

KETTLE RIVER BOOKS

Mud Pony

Mud Pony

STEPHANIE BAKER

KETTLE RIVER BOOKS

Kettle River Books
499 Alabama Street, Ste. 321
San Francisco, CA 94110
kettleriverbooks.com

Mud Pony/Stephanie Baker. –1st ed.
ISBN 979-8-9860962-0-9 Paperback
ISBN 979-8-9860962-1-6 eBook
1. Bio/Autobiography/Personal Memoirs. 2. Pets/Horses.
3. Body, Mind & Spirit/Nature Therapy
Library of Congress Control Number: 2022915357

Publisher's Cataloging-in-Publication data
Names: Baker, Stephanie Jeanine, author.
Title: Mud Pony/Stephanie Baker.
Description: San Francisco, CA: Kettle River Books, 2022.
Identifiers: LCCN: 2022915357 | ISBN: 979-8-9860962-0-9 (paperback) | 979-8-9860962-1-6 (ebook)
Subjects: LCSH Baker, Stephanie Jeanine. | Horse trainers—Biography. | Horse whisperers—Biography. | Horsemanship—Therapeutic use. | Human-animal relationships. | BISAC BIOGRAPHY & AUTOBIOGRAPHY/Personal Memoirs | NATURE/Animals/Horses
Classification: LCC SF284.52. B35 2022 | DDC 636.1/0835092—dc23

Preliminary layout and design inspiration by Laurie Anderson
Book Design by Lars Kim
Cover Art by François Capehart

for David

El lodo, apartándolo del lodo, no es más lodo.
—Antonio Porchia

Mud, when it leaves the mud, stops being mud.
(trans. W. S. Merwin)

· One ·

I call him Mud Pony because he's small and dirty. He's a mutt, a mongrel, a mix of coastal scrub and soil, tule reed and cattail. He comes from accident and overpopulation, the human business of too many and too busy. Worms bloat his belly.

I get him for free from a rancher's wife who says she wants a child, not another horse. She stands with me, arms hugging her chest, as we watch three rancheros on foot separate him from the herd and usher him into a chute then into a borrowed trailer.

"Why is he so hard to catch? Is it because he's a mustang?"

"Oh no," she says, "his mama died when he was four months, so we set him loose with the others. Except for when he was gelded, nobody's touched him."

We haul him ten miles up the coast, open the door, watch him scramble out. He sniffs the base of a six-foot fence in a twenty-by-twenty-foot paddock then snorts at the trough in the loafing shed. Now that he can't hide behind the herd, I marvel at his big feet, feathered legs, and dark stripe down his back; I delight over his yellow belly and black tangle of mane and tail. I put a carrot in a bucket and stand outside the gate. Only then does he lower his head to snatch it. When the feed truck arrives with his evening hay, he bolts at the thud of a thrown flake.

I enter his enclosure and try to get close, but he skitters out of reach. I shrug, ignoring the voice of a cowboy I know, one who would say "not a good first horse."

My friend Patti says she'll work with us twice a week. On an evening in early fall when the summer fog has gone and the days are still long, we begin. Patti's hair and tanned arms are the same coppery hue; she wears boots, jeans, and a cowboy shirt, its sleeves cut at the shoulders. She points to a lanky palomino for me to catch and saddle. Then she tells me in her no-nonsense way to put on spurs and "Get some forward outta that mare."

The palomino and I get warm and dusty in the arena then return to Patti waiting outside Mud Pony's paddock. She coils a lariat and hands it to me with a pair of gloves. I shoot her a questioning look—she knows I couldn't lasso a house.

"Since he hasn't let anyone touch him," she says, "we'll chase him in here—his paddock has corners, but it can still be a round pen for training."

Astride the mare, I enter Mud Pony's enclosure, and he bolts to the far corner, kicking out his hind legs in my direction. Patti has positioned herself just inside the gate, where she can make a quick exit.

"Don't let him get away with that!" she yells. "Next time, you throw that rope at his rear!"

The stiff coil does the trick when I launch it at his next hind-end kick, extending the rope's full length and smacking the dock of his tail, causing him to skitter.

The mare and I press again, chasing him a few times around the enclosure with the lasso unfurled in sloppy fits. Finally, Mud Pony stops in the far corner, whirls, and faces us, nostrils pulsing.

"Now go slow," Patti directs. "See if you can get close. And if he needs to move, that's okay too. He'll just find a place to stop, and then you'll start over."

I nudge the mare toward him, but before we can even reach arm's length, he bursts from the corner, knocking into her and smashing my leg. As soon as he reaches the farthest possible spot, he turns and faces us, ears forward.

"He's gotta learn," Patti says. "Let him find out how much more difficult it is for him to have his way than go along with yours."

We drill this—press, pause, approach—or is it a dance? The mare absorbs each of his blows with a grunt. I worry more about him than her or me—perhaps he'll hurt himself in a desperate attempt to escape by clambering over the fence. But each time, Mud Pony stops unharmed and turns to face us, his breathing short and fast. He's stopped kicking out, so I toss the lariat outside the gate. Patti nods.

The next time we get close, he turns his back then lowers his nose to the ground as if asking Earth to disappear him.

"Go on up there," Patti whispers.

As we move in, he trembles. I lift my hand and stretch it toward him, but he leans away. And yet, with seemingly electrified volition, the topmost fuzz of his sprouting winter coat stands up and reaches for my fingers.

But too much, too close! He scrambles out of the pocket, again smashing my leg against the mare's belly. I ask the mare for a few steps to walk off the blow.

He's now closer to Patti than he is to me. From behind the gate, she produces the "flag," a plastic bag attached to a whip. She manages a slight rustle, and he races back to his corner.

"Okay, that's his safe spot as long as I'm out here by the gate with the scary noise. You get in there and wait. I won't move. I'll just be the pressure."

Patti gives the flag a bigger shake, and he scurries out, giving us the opportunity to move in. Then she flaps it again, and he bounces back to us. Now, there's just enough room in the corner for all three of us to squeeze in.

This time, I manage to get near enough to rest my hand on his withers—the bump of spine where back meets neck and an erogenous zone where horses groom each other. He's shaking, and I look to Patti.

"Go on!" she calls, "rub on him. He's figuring it out."

I'm amazed that he stays.

"Good!" she says. "Now get him used to feeling you. Tap him a few times with your toe."

I lay my hand on his back. Pause. Then I begin, slowly and gently, testing the pressure of my boot against his belly.

"Yeah! Now touch him again. But before he bolts—when you think you've found a good spot—walk away."

I follow her instructions, patting all the areas I've covered and giving Mud Pony one more toe-tap before turning the palomino's head in a single motion and retreating the opposite way. All the while, I resist the urge to look back—my predator gaze might inhibit any release he'd feel.

Patti holds the flag still and gives the play-by-play in a whisper behind me: "He's brought his head up... and he's looking at you... he seems to be saying, 'Is that all you wanted?'... Yes, he's really interested in you... he's watching... watching... not leaving... not leaving... good... that's the place to stop."

She opens the gate, and we exit the pen. I let go of my breath in a whoosh, feeling a rush in the wake of our first touch.

O

Everything feels like a gift when I'm with him—even the cold fog curling in from the Pacific and each day's increasingly early darkness. Several times a week, I leave the city and drive south to the coast to clean his paddock and work with Patti. In either direction, the thirty-minute commute is well worth the two hours of ocean air and aromas of eucalyptus and horse ranch.

I'd always dreamed my first horse would be a finely bred Arabian, not this mixed breed or mustaño, as the vaqueros would call him. But there he is, long-whiskered and warm, standing as far away as he can get. I squeeze inside the gate with a bucket of grain, pause to watch him watch me, set down the bucket and then exit. He rushes over for a quick bite and then retreats to a far corner. Even though Patti and I have worked diligently in the past few months, I still can't get near him without being mounted on another horse.

Still, he's a year old, and when I decided to adopt him, I knew it was for the long haul—some trainers won't even sit on a horse until it's three years old; most horses stop growing at five or six. My dream is to own a horse who lets me in to his deepest parts, who allows my two legs to become his four, who needs no words to be urged forward and stretch out underneath. There are few I can tell this to—fact is, I can barely say it to myself. *I want him to satisfy something in me so small, I've no words for it.*

I hover outside Mud Pony's gate as he eats, envisioning the brave, crazy, or creative human who first got the idea to get on a horse's back. Probably they were drawn to the primal sensation of a horse's large, warm presence. Carter, my husband, thinks the first human who rode a horse must have raised a foal and tamed it. "At least that's what I would do," he says.

But I imagine it a singular, spontaneous moment—private, quick, no witness—and only after much waiting and watching. What ground was broken with that first ride! The Indo-Europeans, Mongols, Romans, Spanish, Kiowa, Comanche, Sioux, and many others would invade, defend, or fall on horseback. I know something of the desire to be bigger and more powerful than I really am.

Mud Pony is now finished with his bucket and gives a relaxed, satisfied snuffle. Then he moves his lips and jaws in a lick-and-chew motion. I remain at the gate, eyes fixed on him while he holds his position; this would be a stare-down if he had my predator eyes on the front of his face. *Still, who will blink or move first?*

Whatever happened on that first ride, I'm sure that person fed the herd and slept with them. Horse and human. Together day and night, eating, standing, watching.

Now he moves away, ambling to the corner closest to the loafing shed, where his evening hay will soon appear through the feeder window. I stay put, admiring the feathers on his legs with their multicolor swirl of wild animal fur, and then congratulate him on his shiny coat and normal-size belly—the result of drenching his grain with worm medicine weeks ago.

Mud Pony must know I want something, maybe to eat him, but not in the way he thinks. I don't want to kill him for food but consume the knowledge that resides deep inside: how to cover great distances on foot; how to find the next mouthful; how to survive in the wet, dark, or cold; how to find safety in a herd. As a child, I dreamed of having the survival skills to escape my suburban neighborhood and live in the woods or mountains, but now I also want a feeling of lightness when I ride him—the ecstasy of my head touching the sky with seat and feet rooted in the ground.

At least, this is what I've read about and experienced while riding a few "finished" horses, where the combination of lightness and power feels like finding the balance point of forward thrust on a wave. This vaulted, airy feeling of being on the prow of a fast-moving ship comes from *bending* the horse, that is, asking him to lift through his belly and back from the slightest signal. I've read that the most accomplished riders just think it, and their horse responds. I've also studied videos, articles, and manuals, but training a horse to bend as a dance partner is nothing I can get from a book. Finding a master teacher is the best chance I've got.

Soon his dark outline will meld into the shadows. In the light that remains, I gaze at his beautifully set neck and short back; his shoulders have the pleasing slant of an Iberian horse, like the ones the Spanish conquistadors brought on their ships. With his confirmation and functional symmetry, he can easily become upright, shifting his weight to his hind end like those pony-size, muscled mounts ridden by Ancient Greek warriors on the Parthenon frieze.

Yes, the first rider must have seen the vast, grassy steppes and the horse's body as the same—the vertebrae ridges and hills, the belly earth. The first rider must have felt the horse's back as an offering, fed by the gut and muscled by human demand for weight and speed, or as a willing sacrifice from a nerve-rich plain. The horse's back became the rider's wide view of that grassland stretched before them.

As I drive home to our apartment that overlooks the lively, thronged plaza at 16th and Mission, I imagine riding Mud Pony. The coastal highway hugs the sea and follows a series of big and even bigger green hills that disappear into a gray blanket—mounting him means we become that mountain or hill. His back starts as a slow fall—from where the withers drop to just beyond the slope of the thirteenth vertebra—and becomes the face of the cliff against the sky when the fog is in, and the ocean is green. His back meets the sky precisely where the sky chooses to begin.

O

Mud Pony's evasions and explosions come less often after six months of helping him tolerate my touch from atop the palomino. Eventually, I'm able to leave the mare standing at the gate as he decides it's okay to be caught, haltered, and led, but only within the confines of his paddock. Then, one early spring morning, Patti announces, "It's time."

Swinging over her Appaloosa, she takes a position just outside the opening of his enclosure. I've often felt the weight of his resistance in my hands, so it's now strange to carry only the lightness of the rope knotted under his chin as we pass the threshold into an open and unfenced realm. He walks with ease behind me as we do a tour of the aisles; a few bored horses shove their heads out of feeder windows. Patti stays close, offering sporadic commentary. We've moved away from the paddocks and toward the pasture when something startles him.

The dirt comes first, then I'm gasping for air. Sure enough, he's loose and running to the far side of the ranch with Patti and the Appy on his tail, who deftly corral him between the round pen and a paddock. Once, I crossed a street in Paris without looking to my left and BASH!—got hurled to the street by a tiny, whizzing Le Car. And just like that, Mud Pony's bolt came out of nowhere. I keep still on the ground for a long minute, gently testing my limbs, then rise gingerly.

Months pass. We move him into a shared paddock with a gentle, older gelding to help him calm and settle. We continue to work on basic handling, such as being led and tied. Though the fear of getting trampled fades, it never fully leaves me. Even so, it takes a backseat to my ever-increasing pride and delight as I gain the tools I need to work safely with a fearful horse. In a year's time, I can lunge him at liberty or on a line, tie him to a post, and pick up his feet for cleaning and rasping.

I borrow the palomino to pony him off her on trails, making sure his nose stays at my right thigh. A lead mare, the palomino pins her ears whenever he shoves his whiskers past her shoulder. The mare has been trained to respond to leg cues, so she moves forward and sideways without my having to touch the reins. This comes in handy when I've got my hands full with holding his lead rope in one hand and a flag in the other to keep him moving forward. In this fashion, we walk, trot, and lope as a trio on trails. Calm, surefooted, and taller by at least four inches, the palomino is a perfect pleasure horse and foil to his feral nature and small stature. Alongside her, Mud Pony gains confidence when we cross other riders, packs of dogs and their dogwalkers, water crossings, hills, creaking trees, rusted and abandoned cars, bags of garbage. With each successful encounter, we get closer to the possibility of safely riding him.

The ranch owner notices our teamwork. At first, she offers me the mare as a monthly lease, but as she's got more horses than she knows what to do with, a proposal is soon floated.

"Twenty-five hundred is a steal," she says. Then, sotto voce, "If that horse wasn't a mare, I woulda kept her."

My breath empties as if I've been knocked to the ground. When I come to, I'm the owner of Mud Pony *and* a palomino mare.

· Two ·

To get to the ranch where my horses live, you drive twenty-five miles south on the coastal highway and then turn left onto a bumpy, mile-long dirt road, which runs next to a creek like the inside seam on a pair of pants. The road ends at the ranch gate and a stand of eucalyptus, but the creek continues and divides, splitting the property in two. An old barn sits at the crotch—it's the shell of a gutted church, framed by wooden planks with wide gaps between. Instead of pews, it's got eight box stalls and an owl family that lives in the rafters.

Two barns adjoin the larger one like a set of twins—they were painted brick red but are now weathered pink; the elderly farmer who manages the surrounding fields with his son was born in one of them. At any given time, at least fifty horses live in shared or single paddocks enclosed by electric fences, with a loafing shed for shelter during the rainy months. The herd in pasture, which includes my palomino mare and Mud Pony, has nothing but the scrub, a pine tree, and one another.

This pasture is mostly vertical—the herd walks up and down a hill on the leeward side of a ridge, a bump off the green slopes of Montara Mountain and the threshold to a little wilderness. If you walk one mile northeast, you'll meet the mountain. If you walk two miles west, you'll meet the Pacific Ocean. If you walk two miles southeast, you'll meet a forested watershed and, at its floor, Crystal Springs Reservoir, a tantalizing blue thumb of water, which holds the melted runoff from a High Sierra aqueduct.

From atop the pasture hill, a stream of cars on the coastal highway carries passengers who visit the beaches but rarely exit into the canyons. Here, farmers grow crops that prefer the cool and damp: artichokes, leeks, pumpkins, and Brussels sprouts. The first peoples built their villages in the sunniest pockets, feasted on an abundance of clams, mussels, and oysters, and left their shell mounds.

My horses live on land that bears the scars of modern human organization—invasion, persecution, plunder, and decimation. In the late 1700s, Franciscan missionaries from Spain, backed by leather-coated soldiers on horseback, imprisoned some of the Indigenous peoples, forcing them to build the priests' adobe structures, herd their livestock, and convert to Catholicism under threats of whippings and far worse. I'm not sure which came first, the failure of the mission system or Mexico's split from Spain, but the newly established government granted large rancho tracts to favored (Mexican) applicants and none to the surviving Ohlone, whose ancestral claims reached back many thousands of years. Our ranch sits on a parcel of one of those original land grants, which some locals still see as part of Mexico: my sister-in-law's cousins who migrated here call it "Oaxaca California."

All the recent settlers—Spanish, Mexicans, and Americans—transported and planted nonhuman species as they arrived: shrubs, plants, and trees such as French broom, oxalis, ice plant, pampas, and eucalyptus. These choked out the native grasses Indigenous peoples had once cultivated through controlled burning to harvest the seeds. Many of these invasive species are found in the hill pasture, but the herd avoids the weedy stands of eucalyptus, which creak in the wind or drop their branches without warning.

The region lost fauna at the top of the food chain as settlers and profiteers cut down old-growth flora, shipping the lumber to near and far-flung towns and cities. They forever changed the face of this watershed, clogging the creeks, so the steelhead trout and salmon that once spawned there disappeared. They also annihilated the wild pronghorn antelope, wolves, and grizzly bear populations, and proliferated herds of cattle or sheep. Although there are far fewer birds and animals than the Spanish colonizers from two hundred years ago described in their letters and logs, I often cross paths with hawks, owls, rabbits, quail, skunks, coyotes, and foxes. At dusk, deer and bobcats traverse the horse pasture, and at night, raccoons haunt the chicken coop. I've never actually seen a mountain lion, but I know they're there—on trails, I've stumbled upon paw prints and a dragged deer carcass. A few years ago, a juvenile lion attacked a thoroughbred in an adjoining pasture. The gelding still bears the marks on his neck and shoulder. Now, there are regular sightings in neighboring streets and backyards.

At the bottom of the hill pasture, the herd presses their feet into scabby ground that during the wet winter season becomes a gloppy mix of mud, manure, and sand, or in the summer months, a thin layer of dried droppings and dust. Each year, the hill erodes and becomes even steeper as winter rain washes the sandy soil into the creek. At varying speeds, according to their age or athleticism, the pasture horses run, slide, and deepen the grooves they've worn into its face. Herds confined to small spaces are heavy on the land. I shudder to think how the paddocks on the flat parts are sinking below sea level as the riparian corridor shrinks and the oceans rise. Instead, I focus on how the sea air and open sky oxygenate and refresh the soil and its inhabitants.

Riding out from the ranch, which is not a show barn but hangout for horse lovers and trail riders, I travel paths that extend and find their way back like a topographical circulatory system. One byway runs into a set of neglected cross-country jumps, part of a larger, show-focused equestrian center next door, which hosts English-style riding folks at one end and Western riders at the other. Over the past ten years, management has not collected manure for the local farmers, but spreads it in the dips between the hills. It's wise to replenish the soil in this fashion to counter the effects of erosion, but horse manure is full of weed seeds, and after the rainy season, I ride through head-high thickets of hemlock. Ticks cling loosely to their leaves, waiting for our warm bodies.

At the ranch's far edge, farmers access the fields by driving on an unpaved artery they call the PG&E road, which runs to the end of a box canyon bordered by pumpkin and Brussels sprouts fields. A green, windward ridge rises above it. I sometimes ride to the top where I gaze upon a small airport, the ocean, and a famous big-wave surfing spot.

My husband's sister first brought me here years ago—I found a good friend in her before I found the goodness in him. Jess was an accomplished rider who connected me with another boarder who didn't have time to ride her horse. With Jess's encouragement, I leased one and then a succession of steeds that offered their backs and feet for our adventuring. In the beginning, she'd simply asked me if I could ride—and when I mumbled half-a-yes, she put me on a stallion.

As a teenager, I'd experienced the thrill of riding on trails twice and only for an hour at a time, but Jess took me for epic rides—whole days that often became nights where we would wander, explore, and tell stories. We giggled as raptors and butterflies crossed our path, as we climbed ridges full of pine and eucalyptus and descended into meadows crisscrossed by enormous oak trees, as we waded creeks shaded by willows or trotted underneath second-growth redwoods. We rode on crisp, sunny, winter days and on foggy summer ones. We ventured out in the cold, rain, and wind, imagining ourselves gritty cowboys in B Westerns. The more miles in the saddle I accumulated, the more I hoped to become the riding companion Jess wanted.

Once a hailstorm caught us on horseback, and we found shelter with our mounts under a large tree as the pellets pelted our backs. We brushed the ice off our chaps and laughed at the storm.

Our favorite trail was a breathtaking stroll to the Gray Whale Cove parking lot above a section of the coastal highway called Devil's Slide, named for its history of collapses and car crashes. I often felt queasy riding above the moving cars and rolling waves but would soon forget in appreciation of the endless stretch of ocean below. At that moment, we'd take photos of each other on our horses, who stood at attention with arched necks against sky and sea.

Jess was the first person with enough chutzpah to urge me into a gallop and convince me that I could stay on. I remember her grin as she tossed me the challenge on a long uphill and then spurred her horse into a run. Perfectly balanced, she flung her arms behind her in a gesture of blissful release with the saddle horn loosely holding the reins. Jerked forward with no time to think, stop, or even steer, I went with the thrill of it, keeping my eyes on the bounding hind end that came in and out of view. Someone once told me *if your horse runs away and you can't stop him, keep your belly-button between his ears.* Maybe this advice saved me—but safety? *Forget that!* I cared only for the magic of becoming the horse I was riding—all muscle and wind.

○

Mud Pony is now three years old, the age that most of my ranch friends would deem appropriate to start a horse. On this first try, I know I'm not going to ask him to walk or move forward; I'll just sit.

He's without bridle or saddle, just a rope halter, after we've returned from a trail ride where I've ponied him off the palomino and enjoyed the view of a white-capped Pacific. I lead him to a stump, lay my belly over his back and throw my leg over.

Amazing! I sit and he stands still! Now I slip off, turn him around, and then, wanting more, position myself to mount from the right or "off" side. But as I swing over, my toe brushes his rump, and he leaps and runs to the other end of the ranch, leaving me to figure out how I landed in the dirt.

Patti, who has been casually watching while she mucks a stall, yells, "You better get back on!"

"I never even felt him under me!" I squawk.

She says nothing, puts her head down, finishes her chores. I fetch Mud Pony from the patch of grass he has tucked into, bring him back to the stump, gingerly lay my chest across his back and call that good enough.

At home, nursing my back and hip in a hot, salted bathtub, I think about the many times I've gotten hurt around horses. I often forget what preceded the blow or fall, but I vividly remember the sheepish feeling of asking someone to drive me home or being asked my name and the date in the emergency room. Falling off always seems both shameful and irresponsible, like I should have known or paid better attention, and now here I am inconveniencing someone. I wish Patti hadn't been watching today, but I also know she wouldn't want me to try it again without her.

More than hot water penetrates my joints. *If this part of me had a name, I'd call it wrong.* I sink into the water, stuffing it.

Later that week, I convince Patti to help me mount a saddled Mud Pony from the ground while she leads him from her Appy. This way, I can focus just on the desensitization or sacking out and—if we get that far—the riding. She agrees, but on the condition that I lay my belly across his back instead of swinging over. In this manner, we take a few steps at the walk and he seems fine, even placid. After letting him soak on this, I impulsively decide to throw my leg over, thinking the Appy's presence will help. It doesn't. My leg's sudden arrival on his right side provokes him, serpent-quick, to leap and jerk the rope out of Patti's hand.

At least this fall on my bum doesn't knock the wind out of me. As I take stock, Patti says that maybe my horse is so threatened by a human mounting on one side that he can't anticipate or tolerate something new coming at him on the other. While horses have a 350-degree field of vision, their brain registers separate pictures from eyes positioned on either side of their head. For humans to safely swing over, the horse must switch its focus from the side they are mounting (generally left) to the side where the other leg lands (generally right). A trained horse will make the connection, but an inexperienced one may see the landing (right) leg as not necessarily attached to the human on its left side. As a prey animal, they may see that encroaching leg as a lion leaping for the kill.

"Your horse," Patti says, "is what cowboys call a cold back... he needs to warm up to the idea of you getting on."

Also, she explains that my horse leans more heavily into the off, or right, side. Just as humans have a generally dominant right hand, most horses favor going left because as foals, they followed and leaned into their mother's right shoulder. Mud Pony, an orphan, never learned this. We now consider mounting from the right. On subsequent tries, we also pay more attention to warming him up in the round pen before the attempt.

Nothing seems to help. He remains tense, and I get more and more unsure about swinging over. And every time I groom him, I notice how he stiffens and freezes, ready to bolt whenever I approach his back—whether there's a brush in my hand, a carrot, or a flower.

○

Starting Mud Pony under saddle remains an unsolved mystery. I sense its solution must come unvoiced and invisible, not from words or thoughts but the heart or gut, so I reach through the dark for its shadowy shapes, the whiff of a hint or affirmation to piece together by instinct this inchoate puzzle. I envision these parts connecting to a larger, unnamed, still-obscured whole in a smooth, flat, and easeful way.

In a similar way over the years, I've learned to teach Humanities to classrooms full of high school students. Technique and preparation are essential, but first I must get to know who my students are under their defense of bravado or distance. I want to help them learn, but this desire needs to be reinforced by the structure of well-planned lessons and balanced with consistency and genuine caring—for teenagers (like horses) sense immediately if you like and want to be with them. It took me a while to understand this, and my first year of teaching was as difficult as everyone warned.

I got my first full-time position when a tenured teacher left on sabbatical the first week of the semester, and I was granted emergency teacher status by the district. As a newbie on a campus of five thousand, I was tested by more than one hundred and seventy teenagers five periods a day. In an overstuffed classroom and in the crowded hallways, at pep rallies and in the cafeteria, I absorbed the agitation and dispossession of trapped adolescents, and for the first few months, not a moment passed where I wasn't challenged by their refusals, scorn, or boredom. During my free period, I locked my classroom door, turned off the lights, and sat with my forehead on a desk. I avoided the main office and the staff lunchroom. Despite the response of those who seemed to be learning something, I had never worked so hard while feeling like such a failure, for I was compelled to create new curriculum for three different courses rather than just teaching from the textbook. And then there was the time-consuming task of organizing materials, grading weekly assessments, and contacting parents or the counseling office when students failed to turn in work or show up for class. I worked seven days and nights a week with rare breaks. At night, my overstimulated brain couldn't shut down—I felt like I was trying to sleep on the deck of a storm-tossed ship.

Early mornings before school, exhausted and frozen with panic, I couldn't step past the front door and worried I might black out if I left the cocoon of our apartment. My therapist encouraged me to call him at these times, and when he picked up, I could barely make sense of his words—it was his low, soothing tone that gave me the courage to teach my first-period class. Things generally got more easeful as I found my teaching rhythm, and finally, at 3:20 p.m., I exhaled in relief.

Even on antianxiety meds, I lost a significant amount of weight and went to see my doctor.

"What's that on your hands?" he asked.

I looked down and noticed clouds of green, black, brown, red, and blue markings all over my fingers and palms. They looked like bruises—only they were stains from writing on transparent sheets under the lamp of an overhead projector.

Now in my seventh year, after having been mentored by veteran teachers, it's still learn-as-I-go. Rarely do lessons go as smoothly as I'd like, since I'm always trying something new. Keeping the content engaging and at a decent pace is always tricky as is plowing through the mounds of writing that are so necessary to assign. "Every class is a dress rehearsal," one colleague used to announce cheerily in our shared classroom as she wrote the day's agenda on the whiteboard. Annoyed, I remember rolling my eyes at her banter, but she was right: teachers can never count on things going as planned, partly because adolescents are marvelously complex beings who are continually balancing their needs for structure and freedom.

To find the 'just right,' I've had to learn who they really are as individuals to uncover the strategies that best support their developing critical-thinking skills. When we find those openings of insight and understanding, there's a sudden, wondrous sense of hopeful energy in the classroom—an attentive silence, a pause to realize or process. When my students "own" a text they read or express pride in something they wrote, it's often because *they know I got them.*

Just as with my teenage students, I'm drawn to Mud Pony for the challenge of learning who he is. He's the most puzzling horse I've ever worked with because he may appear willing and attentive but can then flee in an instant, leaving me confused (and bruised) on the ground. Again and again, I think I get him, but then I don't. His calculus remains a mystery I'm not yet able to solve.

To ride him, I must learn to read him.

○

Driving south on Highway 1, I climb the precipice at Devil's Slide and then drop down alongside Montara Beach, where surly winds rough the sea. I imagine agitated creatures rising from below and breaking the surface, then diving down, leaving a gasp of foam. The shore break is a moiling wall of white, gray, and brown.

I muse about the years I surfed those waves and wonder if the real preparation for riding came from sitting on a surfboard or paddling through whitewater, getting tossed and tumbled, coming up for air, grabbing my surfboard and waiting for the next wave. Or has classroom teaching also prepared me? Long before I rode horses or taught teenagers, I rehearsed by bobbing beyond the shore break and lifting my board over the belly of each muscled roller. All the swimming in pools, lakes, bay, and ocean has prepared me too—a billion laps of breathing side to side, feeling the pull of my arm, the roll of my shoulder, the kick of my legs, the push of the current, or the lift of a swell. Perhaps it's no surprise that my best days of teaching are often preceded by a 6 a.m. swim.

I once watched a trainer prepare a young horse for riding without mounting by standing on the outside rail of a round pen and lining up the horse next to her. She could then keep one hand and boot on the rail while swinging her other leg over and off, or softly rest her weight on the horse's back. Either way, she could quickly exit onto the rail if the horse needed to leave. Over the last few months, as I've stood with Mud Pony at the rail, I've noticed he can leap like a bug when I lift my right leg near his back, his four feet springing exactly two feet parallel to where I cling to the rail. Despite countless rehearsals, I can't predict his sudden jumps, and this unnerves me. Fortunately, I've managed to cling safely to that rail every time.

Just this week, there's evidence of progress, as he hasn't suddenly fled as I begin to lift one leg. Perhaps he's begun to anticipate that my right and left limbs are somehow attached and one leg's motion follows the other.

Today I manage to sit on him for one hundred eighty triumphant seconds, my butt not quite yet in the saddle, one hand and one toe on the rails of the round pen, lead line within grasp. I stay with him, finding the fast rise and fall of his ribs, counting each second to myself, matching my inhalations and exhalations to his. Moving through that which is already moving, I find his breath like I would find the rhythm of swimming. And when his breath gets stuck, I let the wind out my nose and mouth. I ask him to breathe with me. Only then do I see movement at his lips, a lick and a chew. *Good, a release.* A few seconds pass. I touch his withers to try to soothe him, but he flinches—my well-intentioned petting is often not pleasing.

For millions of years, equines evolved to survive the lion that leaped on the back and clawed at the jugular, or the wolf pack that bit the belly and rump. I am awed by the permission he has given me to cross this line. I empty my lungs and pray I will not forget who he is.

○

Here we are again. I sigh and retreat, sitting safely on the rail as he remains lined up next to me, rigid and tense. I want to connect with him and listen; only then will I be able to anticipate the bolt.

But to do this, I first need to find a quiet place inside my exhaustion. *The energy of a hundred and seventy teenagers coursed through me today.* In the short space of that quiet, I try to give attention to my needs, not my students' or Mud Pony's.

I swing over again, but he snorts, and I promptly sit back on the rail. Now I want to give up or go get help. *Why can't he just let me do this? Maybe we both want to run!* I lean close to his cocked ear: "Listen, I'm still working on it myself, but someone once told me we are not our fear. We don't have to flee from our insides."

Last try. *We make it.*

I'm on for a few minutes, then his belly gives. A breath and a bit of let go. My two feet find the rail.

I can tie, lead, and pony him. I can trim his feet and he can wear a saddle. Sometimes when I find my nerve at the fence tail, I can sit on him. *Easier* and *tamer* are descriptors I usually shun, but after more than two years of lessons, after attending horsemanship clinics where everyone else is aboard their colts, and after watching videos where cowboys tame and ride wild mustangs in a scant three hours, I suspect Mud Pony won't outgrow his trouble.

Perhaps he's an outlier even among horses, for I can't hold his interest the way a snapped twig or sudden gust of wind can. I know I'm not the only one to notice, but at the same time, silent queries hover whenever ranch friends see me on the rail in the round pen. Maybe they're sorry for me, but at least they're too polite to ask, "What makes you think you can change him?" or "Why are you taking this on?"

I'm too embarrassed to offer my naked, honest answer: *Mud Pony is one of those teenagers who won't let me in yet gives me hope every time they respond. They may not share my passion for writing or reading, but they're beautiful and creative, shiny and wild.*

O

Awake at 3 a.m., brain churning. I know that when I've found a sweet spot of trust with a teenage student, it comes only after a stretch of time, a lot of work, and their testing of me. I think this might be possible with Mud Pony. Maybe he's waiting to see if I'll stick around. Plus, he's a perfect pasture horse, an easy-keeper who's well socialized after spending his first year in a large herd: now he asserts himself at the feeder to obtain the lion's share; he plays bitey-face all day with the other geldings; he gives and receives grooming from the herd. But when humans ask something of him, everything changes. While other horses dull themselves to the vibrations of domesticity, he lives at the very surface of his skin. In fact, he's tuned to a different frequency—one that doesn't include humans. Glumly, I realize that there was no trouble for him until I got troubled *about* him.

The sound of the fan, which usually drowns out street noise, is now the soundtrack for a new tumble of queries: *What's in it for him? Why would he ever want to leave the safety of the herd to join up with a human?*

I consider getting up and moving to the living room couch to distract myself with a book but decide to make another attempt at sleep, this time by counting to one hundred with slow exhalations... before I even start, my thoughts are off again, returning to a swirl I've more recently begun to consider.

Evolution. Weather. Desperation. These have brought us together. Before there was Mud Pony, according to fossil records, great herds of horses roamed the North American and Eurasian plains alongside the mastodon and mammoth—all hunted and eaten by the humans since the last Ice Age. Nonterritorial and perfectly adapted for the cold, they roamed thousands of miles, flourishing on the lowest-protein forage of stems and roughage, while their ruminant relative the aurochs (ancestor of the modern-day cow) ate the sweeter, less fibrous shoots. Over time, as the climate warmed, the forests spread, and the grasslands receded, the European herds retreated to the steppes north of the Black Sea (the American herds had already gone extinct). If it hadn't been for human need or desire, horses would likely have disappeared like the mammoth, mastodon, saber-toothed cat, giant elk, stag-moose, and other megafauna.

Horse skulls excavated at burial sites indicate that the herders who had already domesticated sheep and goats (between 11,000 and 8000 BCE) brought the horse into their fold. They probably fed the starving animals with the grain they had begun to cultivate. Around 4000 BCE, as sapiens discovered equines could be bitted and harnessed, the horse population dramatically increased across Eurasia. They began carrying us in treks across deserts and mountains, raids over plains, campaigns through swamps and forests. *Why do they do what we want?* The answer lies within their nature—to move and be moved, to be with a herd, whether it's horse or human.

Why doesn't Mud Pony want to do what I want? Does he not want to be with me?

Carter shifts at my side, his breaths now getting shallow and breaking in his throat. Then he raises his head from the pillow.

"Oh, you're awake," he murmurs.

I reach for him, say I'm worried I'm not going to be able to ride my horse—maybe he's too much for me.

"Oh...," then a long pause. "Well... what's the worst thing that could happen if you *can't* ride him?"

"He's not a horse you can sell. Maybe he'd live out his days as a pasture ornament, and then I'd have to content myself with walking him like a dog."

Silence. Carter will be happy to discuss my plight but not until his morning coffee is in hand. If I move into the living room, he will lie on his stomach and occupy the whole bed, with only his feet escaping the blankets. In moments like these I remember how, ten years ago, when we first met, he said gently, "You're touching me, but you're not really there. I've never been with anyone who lives at such a distance from herself."

This memory is more disturbing than my previous thoughts, and I can no longer tolerate the exposure of lying on my back. I get up and move into the living room, whose walls are illuminated with the movement of headlights and the reflection of streetlamps. I curl into a ball on the sofa and tell myself that I've come a long way with Mud Pony since he first scrambled out of that trailer. My need to soothe him or something inside transports me to a place *between*, one that's more tender...

Soon I will hear the early morning sounds of the city: traffic helicopters circling, BART trains whistling through the tunnel below us on Mission Street, buses motoring and braking, garbage trucks lifting and crashing trash containers. I envision the river of humanity at the intersection: street preachers, shoppers, addicts, anarchists, artists, hipsters, confidence men, commuters, tourists, techies, and the houseless, or those whom my students call "hoboes." Our one-bedroom apartment is on the second floor of an office building built in the late 1920s to house the Butchers Union. Rock bands, drag queens, squatters, and artists now occupy the offices on two floors and the meat lockers in the basement.

On our floor, a meeting hall was partitioned into offices and studios, and we now inhabit the one-bedroom apartment that was the original "Janitor's Quarters" (according to city records from the early 1940s). Later, I will spend most of the day at our kitchen table, grading essays and looking out the window where an empty schoolyard borders the brick face of the Armory in which the National Guard, often a union foe, once stored weapons.

For a period, when I felt frustrated about living so far from my horses, I'd bellyache to Carter about how dirty our street and building were, how awful the brokenness of its houseless, addicted, and poor. For a long time, he simply listened. Then he told me he was tired of me putting down our home: "Our *home*," he said, "*our* home." So I stopped. Every time I noticed a contraction or aversion arise—for our neighborhood, our building, our lives—I'd try to remember how it had hurt Carter.

Not long after, Carter found a prize in a stash of discarded furniture in our building basement: a wall-sized photograph of a herd of cows grazing on a sub-alpine meadow by a lake surrounded by snow-capped mountains and blue sky. Two cowboys on horseback watch over them. An old-timer at my ranch who'd known the head butcher said the photo was originally black-and-white and then colorized, as was the custom in an earlier era. He'd seen the photo a long time ago, said the photographer had gotten an aerial shot as they'd brought in the cows by helicopter. I can almost hear the shuffling and mooing as I look at it, echoes that celebrate the long-gone, massive cattle drives in the West. Each night, I close my eyes beneath a watchful cowboy riding a white horse. An unknown artist, probably from one of the basement studios, painted a pink scarf at the cowboy's neck.

On a hillside twenty miles south, my horses stand together with low-ered heads, their knees locked in the equine's natural, restful position while just outside the entrance to our building, street people wish they, too, could stand in their sleep. Deprived of ease ever since a city ordinance pro-hibited lying on sidewalks, they lean against walls or huddle over shopping carts. Before dawn arrives, they will wake and shuffle to a new spot, down the street or at the BART plaza, where they'll find benches, a public toilet, and a taco stand that'll open when it wants to.

O

Perhaps there's another way to approach my dilemma with Mud Pony: equines are herd and prey animals that communicate through physical and emotional energies. From ten feet, a horse can feel your heartbeat, and from close or far away, he can mirror your insides and reveal the feelings you didn't even know were there. The riders I most admire draw upon the equine's exquisite emotional and physical attunement, allowing room for the horse to respond with willingness and understanding. From the out-side, this appears as a partnership where the softest cue from the human results in a job getting done (sorting or cutting cows, hunting with a bow or rifle, jumping fences, carrying a beginner), not just safely, but with ease and athleticism. In this way, the horse is including the human in its herd, so the rider's cues appear magically unseen.

I've been inspired by the teachings of Tom Dorrance, a cowboy from Oregon who taught his students to work with horses by reaching inside themselves for something he called *feel*. Before he died in 2003, Dorrance worked cattle ranches for seven decades and taught horsemanship in the Salinas Valley. He famously modeled the concept of *feel*, so it became a way of being and moving in the world for those who could learn. I never met Tom or his brother Bill, also a master horseman and teacher, but I've read about how horses and students responded to them with willingness and moments of "True Unity." In transcribed words from a single, slim volume whose pages I've marked and dog-eared, he uses the phrases "feel the whole horse," "calm the innard part," and "comes from the inside of the one to the other." Dorrance tried to help his students understand the horse from the horse's point of view, "and when you think you're going slow," he said, "go even slower." This slowness allowed his students to look more fully at themselves and shift their perspective.

Tom Dorrance's ideas about *feel* were introduced to me by Harry and Roses—both of whom call Dorrance one of their teachers. After participating in several of Harry's clinics and taking lessons with Roses, I better understood the mindful, disciplined effort of looking at the horse without it being all about *me*, the human. The trick, as Roses and Harry learned it from Dorrance and his first generation of students, is to see them as fully horse, not human, to remove your ego from the situation, and to respect them as separate beings with an individual mind, body, and spirit.

However, as a beginning student, I struggled to see what Roses or Harry saw, and sometimes I didn't even understand what they said. I just knew that when they worked with the horse, everything got easier and better— for both the horse and the human. I began to consider the horse's unique qualities more deeply as a herd and prey animal and how it communicates with its body.

Equines express their own versions of frustration, defiance, boredom, depression, joy, excitement, or contentment. One animal scientist has recently categorized eighteen different emotional expressions that humans can recognize in horses. But to consider their point of view, you must read them without anthropomorphizing.

Just as a discerning parent or teacher sees the mind *behind* the behavior of a child or student and adjusts to meet their needs, so a master horseperson attunes to the horse and holds it accountable for its actions without a punishing attitude. To do this, she speaks with hands, seat, legs, whip, gesture, voice, energy, eyes, or whatever's available. By enlisting the *right amount* of pressure with the *right amount* of balance and proper timing, she can ask the horse to move in the desired shape, tempo, or direction. And the horse responds because it's both a flight and a herd animal—it wants to both move its feet and be safe in a group.

I know all this, and I've attempted it countless times on horseback to get my mount safely forward over a ditch or puddle, across a road, through a gate... but *feel* is still one of the most complex things I've ever attempted. There's no formula and it's not about technique. When I seek their guidance, Harry or Roses will often respond, "It depends." So that leaves me with experimenting on my own, making mistakes, and feeling my way through.

And to further clarify (or confound), while understanding your own feelings is corollary to a deeper connection with your horse, knowing and using feel is not about feelings! That said, if you're feeling angry or confused, or experiencing unsettled or deep internal conflict, a sensitive or frightened horse may mirror your energy in a variety of shapes—outbursts of kicking, striking, fleeing. Of course, this raises a question I shirk to answer: *Could Mud Pony be responding to what's inside me?*

Back on the rail, I'm playing with the flag above his saddle and crackling it as he stands lined up next to me. This is not the softness of *feel*, for Mud Pony has now produced a high-necked, pre-bolt, frozen stance.

"Don't use the flag to desensitize him," Harry might call to me if he were standing there outside the pen. "Make it meaningful. Don't do it for too long."

I lower the flag, ask him to face the opposite direction, and try the same thing, this time on the left side where he seems most wary.

I don't know how long we're there—five, ten, maybe fifteen minutes, then I begin to question if I should make this exercise more varied. Should I use the mounting block or the fence in a different arena? *Should I put my foot in the stirrup and launch my belly at his side?* I know Harry and Roses would tell me not to "drill him" but to get a "change," meaning a shift in demeanor that indicates processing (licking, chewing) or understanding (a softened, diminished physical presence; a big breath; a lowered head; a yawn). They would also tell me not to throw the leg over unless I've gotten some of these signs. And to slow down.

Feel now feels so far from me—and I'm failing to find my way out of this conundrum. *Mind, be there to guide, but let the shy parts of me speak as well.* The truth is I'm learning to feel *myself* as I sit on that fence rail.

O

It's been well over a month since I last trimmed his feet, the walls of which have thickened to a square shape. Luckily, the dead, peeling, stinky sole sloughs off easily, so I can see how much the walls should be rasped. I do this while he eats, expressing impatience as he tugs his foot away after finishing the grain in his bucket. Sometimes he moves so I can't reach the hoof I want to work on, or he grabs his foot back, causing me to strain my back. I try not to let go when he does this, holding on to his toe with my rubber gardening glove. I gently wiggle the foot side to side, and that seems to dissolve his tension. Since the rain has left his hooves soft and the horn is easy to work with, it takes me less than an hour to do all four feet—not counting conversations, bathroom breaks, and pauses to look at sky or pasture.

Today feels almost ceremonial, momentous, for I'm planning on presenting to Mud Pony the new, black leather Western saddle I've long saved for. Earlier today, I'd carried it down the steps to the first floor, then exited the gate and crossed the street with it slung over one hip, noting glances smiles from passersby.

As I smooth the blue Navajo saddle blanket over the saddle area, I ignore how he snorts and raises his head. Next, I lift the shining apparatus to meet its rug, swinging it from the side of my right hip in one motion. I have to move with him, since he sidles away, but the rope tying him to the post is on the short side so he'll not go too far.

Saddles, especially brand-new ones, aren't supposed to bite, but this one does, and he pulls back in alarm, hitting the back cinch, which latches onto his gut like the claw of an unearthed beast. The only place to go is up—so he does, crimping his middle, leaping vertically, and pulling tight the knot at the post. He falls to the ground on one side in an awful, contorted thwack, still tied. It's a strange sound when he lands—a crunch-grunt followed by a cry—*from him or me?!*

Then he scrambles to his feet, feels the back cinch grab his soft middle again, crimps and crow hops, falling to the other side. *Holy shit!* The force of his struggle has pulled the knot so tight I can't undo it. I stand at the post—dumb, frozen—my limbs and breath seem to have gone somewhere else. No one around to help... I can only stay out of his way and watch as he repeats the unnatural spectacle. *Oh god, oh god, he's on the ground again, then again, each side, still tied.*

Finally, heaving and trembling, he stops, yielding to the pressure at his head and belly. I am shaking, too, and whimpering. *How did he just now not snap his neck or land on the saddle horn and break his back? Will he ever be able to trust the saddle on his back, let alone a rider?*

I should know better: my first mistake was tightening the back cinch against his belly without first untying the knot at the post. As I tell this to Carter, he wonders aloud if Mud Pony sensed something in me that caused him to react. *Have I told him of my deepest fear?* Inside the echo chamber of memory, I'm taunted by the words of a trainer I once worked with, who called him "dangerous and unpredictable" and disparaged me for thinking I could ride him. "You're a teacher and a poet," she said, "not a horse trainer." Now her words stir inside my gut like a pile of poked worms. I push my doubt away, reminding myself what Roses once said.

"Would you tell me to give up if you didn't think I could do it?" I'd asked in a weak voice.

"Of course," she said.

"But it's been years!"

"It doesn't matter. This is who he is."

O

Megan's got muscled forearms like Popeye, and she's spent a lot of time sailing ships too. As a child growing up in Australia, she used to jump horses over fences so high you would hold your breath until they landed safely on the other side. Now she lives in Hawai'i and commutes to California for weeks at a time to massage and adjust horses. I trust her softness and strength, the way she walks over the ground as if she were thanking it for holding her upright. She wears a green polo shirt with the insignia of her business, INTERNATIONAL PONY RUBS, on the back, but it looks more like a beer can label than an advertisement for equine physical therapy. Though she's not a trainer like Roses or a clinician like Harry, I still think she uses "feel" every day in her work. There's nothing mechanical in her approach or movement, and she knows the horse's complex anatomy and techniques to help the body release.

The weekend after Mud Pony's mad pullback at the tie post, Megan arrives to massage and adjust at least a dozen horses, and I make sure my horse is on the list. Before she begins, she palps for the meeting point of each big bone or vertebra with flesh, finding the unaligned or tender spots. She asks me to note the following in her binder: atlas, TMJ, multiple cervical vertebrae, pectorals, left ribs, right ribs, left hip, right hip. Then she begins at the top of his skull, gently moving and massaging where the skull plates meet and where the jaw hinges. She presses her palm down the cartilaginous crest of his neck, and he begins to let go by sighing, chewing, dropping. She ends the session by adjusting his poll, and he sneezes and shakes his head. Relieved and thankful he can find relief after that terrible wrenching, I, too, enter an altered state.

I pull a plastic rain jacket out of a dark and cobwebbed corner of the tack room and find the shell of a brown spider in the sleeve. I shake the jacket, wondering where the soft, warm, live version lurks. Realizing there may be others, I decide not to wear it as a prop but use it like a flag. After thirty minutes of round penning at liberty, Mud Pony stands saddled, wearing what bit him a couple of weeks ago. After Megan's adjustment and some rest, he seems to have recovered. He watches my every move from the other side of the round pen. My plan is to work with a boot bag full of potatoes—it will sit on his back as a weighted object or be pushed over the other side in imitation of a rider falling off.

In a recent lesson, I watched Roses stumble, run, and fall in hilarious, spasmodic movements around the round pen, playing in quick succession what she called Drunken Sailor, Nine-Year-Old Boy, and Heart Attack Victim. With each lunge or spasm, Mud Pony would face and approach her before leaping away at the next herky-jerky movement.

I pick up where we left off with this, staggering stupidly toward him with outstretched arms. He maintains a safe distance as I continue with jumping jacks, marching up and down one side of the pen, and getting on my hands and knees in the sand to crawl toward him. Through this he stays alert and faces me, keeping at least ten feet between us. But when I move on to flapping the rain jacket, his gaze travels outside the round pen. Then he bolts with a powerful shove from his hind end, trotting in big, gulping strides around and around the pen. When he shows no sign of looking to me, I cease the pursuit. His circling continues, head high and body tense. I stop my playacting and stand in the middle. He pays me no heed. We could be in two different countries, on opposite sides of a border. As he circles, I wonder if I'm being wound by one long spun thread into a web I soon won't know how to exit.

I quit the exercise, unwrap the rain jacket from around my waist, and hang it on the rail. Only then does he turn and face me. *Finally.* I put the rope halter on and pet him. He softens under the reassurance, but his breath still comes in rapid puffs. I contemplate what Roses did in our lesson. *Her timing is better than mine. Maybe she established more of a connection. And she put the rope halter on too, so she could get hold of it and bring him back to her.* Now I can approach him with the scary jacket, and though he's wary, he stays at my side.

And then... a sigh and an unclenching of his jaw with a lick and chew. This is so much work for him, for me. And I want more than him just surviving or tolerating my presence. I want him to feel better *inside* about all the unknowns we might face together. *But how else except desensitizing him through playacting am I going to get him to stay with me when scary things happen?* I move to his left side with the plastic jacket and place it over the saddle. He casts a wary eye and again stands like a statue.

If Harry were here right now, he would tell me not to give up but to keep on learning and figuring it out. Roses would say the same.

I remove the jacket and offer the boot bag of potatoes, all the while keeping him close with the rope halter. He allows the potatoes to be placed over the saddle but leaps away when I push them off the other side. I pause and speak to him in a low voice as he leans his weight into me and his breath evens out. *Should I stop and fetch my gloves so the rope doesn't wear another raw, red line into my hand?* Still holding on to him, I again raise the bag of now-broken tubers, set them on his back, and let the weight fall a few inches to the other side. In response, he plants his front feet.

Christ, he's a statue again. I step away and allow the potatoes to balance themselves. Then I tug on his breast collar, asking for just one foot to come unstuck, but he's frozen, fixated on the potatoes bumping his other side.

I don't know where to go from here or how to get him back. After all these games—Crazy Clown, Scary Jacket, Boot Bag o' Potatoes—he barely tolerates the pressure.

Harry once said, "I'm so busy making new mistakes, I don't have time to make the old ones." Which mistake am I repeating? What am I not seeing? And whom can I trust to help us?

· Three ·

As a child, I was mad like a monkey for horses, to grasp, groom, and smell them—but they were always out of reach, belonging to someone else or standing on the other side of a fence I wasn't allowed to climb. To suit my rough imaginings, I played with plastic horse models whose legs invariably got broken and taped, then broken and taped again. All my pants had knees worn to a shine or single thread from romping across the family room rug. During the hours I spent at church, especially the extended services of the Advent and Lenten seasons, I recycled the priest's prayers into pleas for a living, breathing four-legged being: "Please, Lord. Give me one or make me one: a bigger body, four long legs, and an even longer spine that ends in a tail."

Neither the God I prayed to in church nor the Holy Mother we invoked during the rosaries recited at home granted my wish, but they did give me my best friend, Isabel, and her affectionate, fun-loving mother, Mrs. Burns. Their family lived across the street in a twin, two-story colonial in our housing development. Mrs. Burns called me her second daughter and invited me to watch Isabel's indoor weekly riding lesson by her side. A few times, I got to ride too, and it was a thrill to walk and trot endless circles in a group lesson. Unlike Isabel, I didn't know how to ease a bit into my pony's mouth or mount with grace. I couldn't keep my seat when the horse shied as I asked it to approach a jump. One time, I lost my balance and grabbed the arena fence instead of the mane, leaving me with large, splintery gashes in my hands, which I proudly bore as evidence of a real-life horse encounter.

Sitting in the back of the Burns' family station wagon on the drive home, I sighed with delight at the smell of horse dirt and sweat on my skin. For days after the event, I'd repeat to myself, "I went to the barn today." Then, for two blessed summers, I worked at Isabel's stable in exchange for riding lessons. This was real life, not the stuff I read about in borrowed books. I mucked stalls and groomed for the advanced riders when they trailered out to compete at shows; I went to auction with the barn manager on sticky summer mornings and helped her unload and stack a season's supply of hay. And when the stable hosted a show, I was part of the jump crew and ran around setting poles in their brackets as soon as they got knocked down. Afterward, we gorged ourselves on free hot dogs at the snack stand. To my mind, this haven attained new heights of wonder when a show rider outfitted in leather boots, gloves, and velvet helmet handed me their dirty, sweat-shiny steed to hose down at the wash rack. I'd get wet with the spray, scrape its rinsed coat, then wait for it to shake the excess water like a huge, feted poodle. If my charge relinquished a pile of steaming manure, that was a bonus, for then I could fetch a shovel to scoop it up.

Isabel eventually got her own horse, a peppery gelding named Rebel, and when I next received the sacrament of confession, I gave the priest every green detail of my envy: how Isabel had a saddle she brought home from the barn and lovingly cleaned in her room; how her tan breeches and black leather boots clung to her athletic legs; how Isabel walked assertively into the tack room with its walls of tack for dozens of horses and didn't have to stand there and wait for someone to tell her which saddle and bridle to use; how Isabel's mother watched her ride around an arena and then praised her for handling Rebel so well. As Isabel dismounted, her mom would hand her a cold soda!

To my confessor, I conceded that Isabel was kind and generous, a good friend, always willing to give me tips at the barn or tell stories about Rebel, but my stomach ached with envy. *Was this a sin? To have such desire for what others were so easily given? Or was the real sin God's silent refusal—how he had instead granted me this yearning?* I longed for the priest to bestow Christ's wisdom, to help me understand why my insides roiled, but he only nodded, made the sign of the cross, and instructed me to say ten Hail Marys.

Years later, I found my way west and discovered I didn't have to have money to ride horses—I just had to show up by train, bus, or borrowed car and work the same way I did as a kid. Over time, as I worked in exchange for riding time or leased a horse from those who no longer had time to ride, I took lessons, went to clinics, and learned how to load a horse into a trailer, turn him on his haunches, change my post on the diagonal without missing a beat, counter canter, leg yield, side pass, or keep my balance when the horse had a fit under me.

Now, with Mud Pony, who is still young, the full package I dreamed of as a child seems within reach—maybe he's the horse I can bond with, who will allow me to merge with his raw, untrammeled being, so I can become something one could only imagine: a centauress! My braver parts know that being with Mud Pony helps me access my most authentic, alive self. And yet... there's another voice I hear in my most honest moments: *I want to be held by your light. I want your power. You serve my end and my end only. If you could give me everything, I would take it. I would use you. I would use you up.*

O

At the ranch next door, a cremello horse with a wide white blaze on its face stands tied to a post like a soldier awaiting orders. An old man sits on a nearby mounting block.

"¿Está Rolando aquí?" I ask.

"What? Rolando?" he returns, and he points to a young, tall, square-shouldered man wearing a cowboy hat and cleaning a saddle. As I approach, Rolando meets my gaze with dark, unwavering eyes. Has my ranch friend Lottie, who knows him, already vouched for me and told him about Mud Pony?

"I'm wondering if you are training or starting any horses?"

No response after I offer my name. He looks down and continues his ministrations, massaging oil into saddle leather.

"Evenings are best." He says more, but never looks up as he speaks. Then he's quiet.

I wait but then realize I've been dismissed. I turn on one heel and head back to the city.

I'd signed up well over a year ago to take Mud Pony to Harry's clinic coming up in early fall, but after that pullback at the tie post, it's clear Mud Pony needs more than a weeklong series of one-hour lessons with Harry. Plus, Patti's got a new job and Roses is six months pregnant.

On separate occasions, three people at my ranch, including Jess, told me about a vaquero named Rolando—how sensitive he is and what a fine rider. My heart leaped—*could he be the teacher to help us?* Suddenly I was willing to jump in, but I still worried about the monstrous stories I'd heard from people who'd sent their horses away to trainers they initially trusted. The horses returned with physical or mental problems that took months or years to unravel due to too much asked too soon. I knew at least two women with horses they couldn't ride after sixty days of training.

Perhaps Rolando sensed my hesitation? He had gestured toward the cremello, describing in careful, barely accented English how he trained this gelding, how the owners couldn't handle him and were afraid. "These people don't believe me when I say a child can now ride the cremello."

I found his response compelling. Perhaps Rolando has the physical strength, experience, or fearlessness that Mud Pony requires for someone to ride him?

The next evening, I pull Mud Pony from his hay and lead him next door, where I linger in front of the tack room and wait for Rolando to appear. Three ranch hands sit on the steps of a trailer. There's a weedy roan running in circles inside a round pen. She calls to my horse, and he pricks his ears in response, raises his tail, and stretches his neck toward her. I pull him away and then pretend to read a ranch bulletin board nearby. Still no sign of Rolando, his horse, his tack, or the old man.

I finally decide to query the rancheros sitting on the steps. I recognize their faces but don't know their names, even though I see them almost every day. They are the factotums behind the scenes. Day in and day out, they feed the ranch, shovel manure, dig ditches, fill holes in the road, and drag the arenas.

I'm closest to José, who works full time at our ranch and whom I've known for years. He calls Jess *hermana* and me *amiga*. We speak easily and laugh at how his English is better than the Spanish he tries to teach me. But I wonder how the rancheros sitting on the steps see me. The cultural and socioeconomic divide suddenly appears a gaping ravine. No, they don't know where Rolando is or why he's not here.

"What does his truck look like?" They shake their heads. No truck. "Okay, what does his car look like?" No car.

For the third evening in a row, I summon the courage to walk next door. This time I spot Rolando, who offers no explanation—he simply nods his head, takes Mud Pony's rope, and goes to work, throwing on a saddle and tightening the cinch. He doesn't ask for my horse's name.

The first time Rolando tries to put his full weight in the stirrup, he doesn't anticipate the leap or jerk. Mud Pony rips the rope from his hands and bucks across the round pen. Rolando catches him up and talks softly to him in Spanish.

There are many things I want to explain to Rolando about my horse: his incredible survival instinct, spectacular athleticism, and great curiosity; how he's playful and sensitive; how he likes to be scratched on his neck and withers but is wary of being touched on his head. The web of skin between his belly and his flank is an especially vulnerable spot—he does not soften when you rub there. If you make a sudden movement, he will bolt, snort, jump, start, pull back, but he is not malicious or mean-spirited, and despite his fear, he has great courage and will try to do everything you ask...

But all of this remains an unspoken monologue, for there's no opening, and now Rolando has asked Mud Pony to stand while he pushes down forcefully on the stirrups. The saddle he's thrown on him looks like none I've seen: bone-white leather with a red cloth cinch and a wide, flat horn for dallying horses or cattle. Two flat animal bladders are attached to the cantle. The hoofed foreleg of a deer or goat hangs by a string to the bladders and dangles like a wand or medicine instrument over one flank. I doubt this saddle fits. If there's a next time, I'll make sure he's wearing his own light trail saddle.

Mud Pony moves away to avoid the sudden, forceful pressure on the stirrups, and Rolando growls deep in his throat. Then, to my surprise, he looks over and pronounces, "He will be easy." As Rolando's voice gets low at the end of every minimally constructed sentence, I must step closer to hear.

"Say it again?"

"He knows everything."

The fog swirls in on this chilly Sunday evening. Rolando, hatless, in his blue jeans, denim jacket, and cowboy boots seems the quiet, obvious an-swer to a question I've been struggling with for more than four years: *Who will ride Mud Pony if I can't?*

"I think he needs someone to hold him," says Rolando while I stand there, open-mouthed, blinking. "He's scared. He just wants to know about everything."

Day 1

I hear them before I see them: four laughing vaqueros on their dancing, muscled mounts, exiting the trail and entering a fenceless arena where Ro-lando points out each one of them to me. "Napoleon, Miguel, Guillermo... Diego."

The men acknowledge me briefly, nodding their heads. Napoleon, who rides the cremello, dismounts and hands him to Rolando, then stands and waits while the rest of the men and horses get into formation like a drill team, a pair on either side and one in front. Mud Pony's rope gets handed to Diego, and then Rolando mounts the cremello. Apparently, Rolando will lead from behind, as a bell mare would.

Yesterday, when he said my horse needed "someone to hold him," I thought he was speaking figuratively, as if he, Rolando, would somehow "hold" or soothe his worry. But now, ready to go to work with his crew, I see he meant it literally: he has assigned Diego the task of holding Mud Pony's lead rope.

The laughter has ended. None of the men speak, but they all seem to know what to do. I stand out of the way on a log with my hands curled into the long sleeves of my sweatshirt, relieved when Jess and her badass rodeo buddy Karie arrive on horseback. Napoleon, a wiry teen wearing baggy pants and a hoodie, disappears briefly behind a trailer and returns with a string of blue baling twine, which he pulls through his belt loops. He hitches up his pants, tightens the string, and approaches Mud Pony. Then, with the agility of a gymnast, he steps into the left stirrup and leans his full weight across the saddle. I inhale sharply.

When he swings over, Mud Pony, who seems to have deliberately waited for this moment, gathers everything inside him and springs straight up, then down, then straight up again, ripping the rope out of Diego's hands and knocking him off his mare. Napoleon, solo and with no reins, rides a leaping, bucking beast down the length of the field and then falls to the ground. Catlike, he's back on his feet in an instant, brushing the dirt off while Rolando fetches the runaway.

Once my horse is captured by the team on horseback, Rolando takes the line and ponies him from the cremello up and down a nearby hill until both horses come back hot and sweaty with foam between their hind legs. Meanwhile, someone catches Diego's loose mare, and the scattered crew returns to its original formation.

As this happens, no one seems surprised or looks to me for comment. I sort through my feelings. *Excitement? Trepidation?* I once watched Diego work a horse by tying the reins to the saddle horn on one side and letting the horse struggle until it gave in to the pressure and allowed its neck to hang twisted, slack, and tired. I've seen the bulging necks and rolling eyes of the vaqueros' jacked-up horses, how they make them dance and curvet with whips snapping at their feet. But something has shifted in me due to recent events: Mud Pony's leap like a bug at the round pen rail, his pullback at the post, my innumerable mistakes and failures on the ground. I'm not a strong or confident enough rider to stay on and show him that a human on his back isn't something he needs to flee. Maybe he will stop leaping from his rider if someone like Napoleon or Rolando can stay on long enough to prove he won't be eaten.

A woman could do this work too. Witness Karie, who has just now mounted the colt she's been ponying off her paint mare, deflecting a buck with her strong seat and firmly asking the young horse to stand with her. Nonetheless, there's the fact of testosterone, and the fraternal bonding between geldings and men, and now there's the historical conditioning of this team of men who first learned to break horses from their fathers, uncles, grandfathers, and the men before them who learned the conquistadors' methods, the same horsemen who, in turn, learned from their North African fathers, the Moors.

Hundreds of years later, the vaqueros still perform the springtime ritual of bringing down the wild horses from the mountains of Guadalajara, inviting them into the world of humans in the same way they are inviting my horse now. I don't know their plans for him, but at least there is no snubbing to a post, and no one dallies my horse from a saddle horn. Further,

Napoleon wears no spurs, and my horse carries no bit—only a rope halter and his Western saddle. This team of vaqueros simply asks for Mud Pony to move forward with their brother on his back.

Attempt number two. The crew seems prepared for an explosion, but it doesn't happen. Napoleon sticks to Mud Pony's back like a burr. Quickly, they move the pair forward without pause or comment, ushering Mud Pony off the field and out onto the trail like a pod of whales protecting a newborn calf. The vaqueros are shielding Napoleon, but they are also offering protection to Mud Pony on one condition—he must move forward *with* them. Karie catches my eye, hands me her paint mare, then legs me up. Off I go at a canter on the wrong lead, around the turn, up the hill to follow the crew until all return safely. My horse is sweaty, tired, but sound—and yes, still unbroken in spirit.

Later, I turn him out with his herd. Before pinning his ears at the other horses to chase them away from the feeder, he drops to the ground with a grunt and rolls. Dizzy, exhilarated, I wonder if I've given over my troubled young boy to the men who can help him grow up.

At night, after entering their world, I'm still riding with the vaqueros, tossing and turning, climbing and descending those hills. At first light, I'm excited to go there again, but there's my summer job teaching rising ninth graders. I ground myself in my routine, drinking water, eating eggs and potatoes, organizing my school bag and classroom materials. I ride my bike across the city, frequently glancing over my shoulder to see if an oversized human chariot is getting too close. I speak English with my students who mostly speak Spanish. My native language seems thick and awkward, my tongue flaps and curls clumsily. I resolve to improve my Spanish, so I may speak as my students do, and as Rolando does with my horse.

Day 2

I call Patti and tell her about the first day of work with Rolando, and she tacks up her Appaloosa and joins us.

"This is what Tomahawk needed," she says. We watch from outside the arena as the vaqueros surround him with their horses. "The cowboy who took him—this is exactly what he did."

I never met Patti's first horse, whose bucking fits so unnerved her she had to sell him, but I'm relieved she approves, and I'm even more relieved when my horse does not flee after Napoleon swings over. As the crew heads out on the PG&E road, I see Napoleon make the sign of the cross.

Patti raises her eyebrows. "They're just gonna take him directly out on trail? And why isn't Rolando riding him?"

"I don't know," I say, shrugging my shoulders. "I just do what he says."

I press the palomino forward—this is between Rolando and Mud Pony.

There's one fewer vaquero this evening on my horse's right side, and Diego rides his gray gelding, not the high-stepping bay mare that fled from the action last night. *Are they short-handed? Did his horse get hurt?* Diego holds the lead rope as Rolando follows directly behind. José, another spectator, whistles to me as we pass and gives two thumbs-up. Then Lottie, who has apprenticed with Diego as a shoer, appears on her bay mare, Tika. We three women on horseback hold up the back end of a parade on an empty PG&E road.

I observe Napoleon occasionally squeeze Mud Pony with his legs and tap one shoulder with a twig. Lottie rides beside me, proud and smiling, one of many who have witnessed my struggle.

"It takes a village," she says, and I reflect on the constellation of friends who brought us here: Patti, with her trailer, access to ranch horses, and the skills to get us started; the boarders who recommended Rolando; Lottie, who vouched for me to Rolando; and José, who told me to bring the vaqueros beer, not money ("because the job is not done"). Then there are all the friends I call to tell the good news, and Carter, who can't fall asleep with me at night because he's so excited too.

I snap photos atop the palomino, and as we go up a steep hill, I watch Napoleon's wiry build rise above Mud Pony's round, driving hindquarters. Rolando lingers behind and waits for me.

"Back home in Guadalajara, when we first ride the horses from the mountains," he says, "we ride to the next town. We rest, then we ride back at night and the horse is very calm."

I imagine the hot, dusty afternoon, the sun-browned men and drooping horses, cold cervezas in the adobe, and the starlit ride home—horses snorting, their heads hung low and relaxed, men laughing, singing, talking.

"Tomorrow we work the reins and see if he can be away from the rider. In a week you can get on him. Next year, we ride him in the parade."

My eyes shine with the image of riding Mud Pony at the front of a proud team, clomping down Main Street for the Ol' Fashioned Half Moon Bay 4th of July Parade. On my way down the ranch road that evening, I leave a cooler full of beer in front of Rolando's trailer.

Day 3

Working at carrying Napoleon, managing the sounds, sensations, and shifts in weight, blinking his eyes, swishing his tail, Mud Pony smacks his upper and lower lips together, reaching with his mouth the way colts mouth everything: hay, tack, human fingers. Once when he was two years old, he nuzzled a woman who was fawning over his head and, to her shock, grabbed her tit between his teeth.

After handing my horse over to Rolando, I watch them work for a few minutes and then leave to tack up the palomino. The ocean is a salted turquoise lake. No fog or wind. Much warmer than yesterday. But I'm too late to join the parade. Just as I'm getting on the palomino, they've already disbanded after a short ride on trail, and Rolando, Napoleon, and Lottie have come to find me.

"Anything happen?" I ask the group, but no one responds, as if they are all heeding Rolando's silent directive.

When Rolando and Napoleon finally speak, it's to each other. With my elementary Spanish and the speed at which they roll and trill their words, I don't get much and so tune them out to observe the dark, sweaty circles around my horse's eyes. I sense his great effort to process the dips and rises, the uneven footing, the bumping of Napoleon's legs, the surrounding sounds and peripheral distractions: a single-engine plane buzzing down in circles to the tiny airport and its landing strip across the highway; bees and flies and heat; a white cross-country jump; groups of horses behind fences; farm machines traveling on a dirt road. He's learning to filter all of this as a well-schooled horse must.

Napoleon dismounts too quickly, and Mud Pony bursts three steps forward, surprised by the sudden shift of weight. Rolando directs Napoleon to get back on again, and gestures for me to position the palomino's head over the neck and shoulder of his own horse to block Mud Pony so he can't move forward. This time, when Napoleon gets off, he stands still.

After they leave, I hose him down. He's looser now, more relaxed than before being ridden. I watch him rub his knee and nuzzle the dirt for stray wisps and oat kernels. His lips reach like antennae, bringing it all in, processing this meaningful routine, his wanting to know and see everything, just as Rolando said.

Day 7

Rolando, guide and ferryman, do you know this yearning as I do? Do you know what it means to ask every day for years and years with every cell of your being? There's something new inside me you are showing and helping me believe, just as you are helping Mud Pony find his feet underneath your weight. You know this as sure as the strength of your back and shoulders, your mountains of Guadalajara with their wild horses, your toddler son, your wife at the trailer door who accepts the morning pastries I bring her. "Trust your horse. Trust him," you say, as you cradle Mud Pony between your legs.

Today, as our humble parade wanders the hills, you pause to tell me my horse is "fine—when he trusts the person on his back." And that trust begins with me believing in him, and me believing in *me*.

"Just go slow," you say. "Breathe. Talk to him."

At first, when I step my full weight in that stirrup, I don't throw my leg over. I hesitate, then step down. You shake your head in disapproval, say something I can't hear. *Was it "go slow" or "just glow"?*

"Get on," he says.

Miguel holds the rope from atop his gray gelding and puts one hand over my horse's left eye.

And there I go, legging over and feeling his hind end leap forward then stop as if caught by an enormous hand. Only it's the body and neck of Miguel's horse that stopped him.

"He knows he's in his house," you say, and then we move forward.

I know you know that when he moves his feet, Mud Pony is more confident and more connected to his survival than when he's standing still. So I tell him: *"Move forward" means feel better, work together, get the job done.*

"Move forward" means safety, reassurance, action—not reaction or danger. "Move forward" means the great cat cannot surprise you. "Move forward" means the snake can't sink its fangs into you. "Move forward" means the human can't slit your throat.

Later, Patti will say she saw me sitting deep and centered on Mud Pony as you stood in the middle of the arena and directed us. I felt a sudden rise into flight like a goose lifting midair after a running start with feet pushing, wings flapping, leaving the lake body behind. We are in the sky together—I, you, Mud Pony—held by a thread to something called Earth.

Day 8

During the morning break between summer school classes, I want to sit in the car and nap for an hour, but instead I eat sweets and push through, teaching a listless group of students on a warm afternoon. I anticipate the adrenaline rush that seems to come at the same time every day for the last week and kick into gear by the time I reach the ranch at 4:45.

After it's over, I'll remember a strangeness all day that accompanied the fatigue and tickle in the back of my throat. Rolando rides Mud Pony confidently on the trail, and for some of the time, he tests him out, unattached to Napoleon, who rides Miguel's gray horse. For the first time, Mud Pony wears a snaffle bit in his mouth in addition to the bosal (a headstall with a thick piece of rawhide around the nose).

He doesn't know what to do with the snaffle bit, but he's not supposed to—that's the vaquero way when starting a colt, to direct him with pressure on the nose. The bosal is the primary rein, and the reins that are connected to the bit that rests on the bars (or diastema, the jaw space between incisors and molars) are merely for him to carry. Eventually, when he easily yields to the pressure of the bosal, he will carry only the bit.

We return to the round pen, perhaps a suggestion that this time is for me. Rolando dismounts and stands in the center, holding Mud Pony. Napoleon stands next to us, still mounted. He tells me to get on. I do what he says but sense only tension and rigidity in Mud Pony as I lift myself up. If we were at the fence rail, I would not swing over. His head is too high. He might bolt. I step down. Rolando frowns.

I stuff my disbelief and swing over. Then there's that magic power underneath me as we move forward, except he leans against Napoleon's horse to such a degree, my leg is squished against its flank. Rolando walks us around, holding both sets of reins, and I'm embarrassed, like a child riding a pony. *Is it okay that he's more with Napoleon's horse than me?* But I don't say it aloud. I do no more than raise my hand to wipe a drop of sweat trickling off the end of my nose, and Mud Pony surges forward.

"Hold him, hold him," I call shakily.

"Don't worry," Rolando says, then we move forward. I want to dismount but say nothing.

Minutes later, when I am safely on the ground, Rolando says he's been noticing Mud Pony "falling asleep" whenever someone is on his back.

"When he wakes up, he gets scared, so you have to keep him awake by letting him know you're there, singing to him, or touching him with your legs."

A deep sense of shame and disbelief in response to my horse's insecurity. A sudden desire to be swallowed by the ground. *We are such emotional creatures! What a short distance there is between feeling and fleeing and stopping to think!*

Patti, who has been watching from the rail, waits for the men to leave. "You were looking at him all the time when you were on him," she says. "Try less seeing and *feel* him instead."

This is helpful feedback, especially since Rolando has said my horse knows everything that's happening above him.

"Commit when you get on him," Patti continues. "Don't hesitate or question. He senses that and it might cause him to do the same."

But how do I not overwhelm Mud Pony with my intensity? What is the "just right" here? Again, that strange feeling: What ground can I stand on?

That night as we brush our teeth, I tell Carter what Patti said. He spits into the sink and says something about how committing to get on Mud Pony is no different than learning to commit to other parts of my life—people, plans, dates. He doesn't mention it, but I know he's referring to how I get overbooked and will sometimes break our plans and strand him. Plus, I know I am often late, disorganized, chaotically running from one thing to the next. I am reminded of my zigzag trajectory so far with Mud Pony, all the stops and starts, all the varied attempts to reach him.

Carter, a self-proclaimed relativist, has a knack for recasting negativity, and I love him for it. "What a great opportunity to see it in a whole new way," he says.

But I secretly dismiss this encouragement. *Why do I do this? Why would I rather destroy those parts of myself like the machine I saw today on a demolition site?* As I passed on my bicycle, I caught sight of this monster punching holes in the sides of a building, readying the structure for imminent collapse. I wonder if I can be as selectively destructive, ridding myself of the anxious or doubtful parts yet preserving my passion.

O

In the mornings, Carter and I look out our kitchen window. High, heavy fog for five days now. The sky a blank template. Likewise, the schoolyard below, which used to house the city's continuation high school, has been empty for over two years. Whenever classes were in session and I was home, I would hear the security guard ring an enormous brass bell to signal break time, and teenagers would pour out of the sagging portables onto the lumpy asphalt to play basketball, gather in pairs underneath an unused volleyball net, or disappear across the street. If they returned, they held cans of soda and bags of spicy Cheetos with tiny tubs of cream cheese.

Now the weeds grow tall through the cracked asphalt, and pigeons gather in the mornings to rest in the sun or peck the weed seeds. Carter and I see cats curl around the bungalow corners in full feral stalk. Sometimes I throw them chicken gizzards from the whole chickens I buy downstairs in Thai's market, a grocery store in our building's first-floor storefront. Someone else threw a tangle of old shoes on top of one of the portables, whose baby blue stairs are now peeling. New objects regularly appear in different parts of the yard: a pink blanket, bicycle seats, a La-Z-Boy chair. Recently, I saw an emaciated woman walk across the yard, enter the boys' bathroom, and shut it behind her. I never saw her emerge, and at certain moments the rest of the day, wondered for her. Yesterday, Carter saw a man lug an enormous bundle across the yard and then stash it under one of the bungalows.

My horse needs constancy and connection just as the students who occupied these classrooms needed someone to believe in them and give them structure and guidance. What happened to them when the doors were closed? Are they now loose in the world like those who drift in and out of the schoolyard?

Day 15

Rolando has thus far guided me to the threshold of learning how to bend Mud Pony. "But first," he says, "we will straighten him," and attaches two sets of lines to each ring of my horse's snaffle bit. One set is composed of short, elastic side reins that link to the stirrups and hold Mud Pony's head in a frame at medium height; the other lines are long, thirty-foot driving reins held by Rolando, who cues him from behind like a farmer behind a plow, clucking and asking Mud Pony to walk forward.

At first my horse doesn't know how to react to the restriction of the side reins. *Where should I go?* he seems to be asking. I wonder if he will try to flee by rearing, but Rolando keeps encouraging him to move and eventually he succumbs, allowing his head to be held straight and upright. Patti taught me to ground drive a few years ago, but I've never tried it with a bit—I'd been wary of him grabbing the lines from my hands or tearing the sides of his mouth if he decided to take off.

But Rolando is far more confident and able to direct Mud Pony without incident to the big arena with a long straightaway, where he asks for more forward and runs behind as my horse breaks into a trot. Rolando uses the line of the fence to keep him straight, turns him at the corners. When Rolando pants with effort, I ask if I can try.

It's much harder than it looks, and I somehow apply too much pressure, so Mud Pony gets crooked, stuck, confused, instead of straight. He turns in circles and wraps the lines around his legs, chest, and butt. Fortunately, he stands still for me to unwind the lines—as if he'd succumbed to our efforts.

Could I feel his mouth in a softer way? It seems all Rolando had to do was wiggle the line instead of pulling and tugging.

"You have to start soft so when you need to go strong, you can," Rolando says, echoing my query.

By the end of the session, Mud Pony can move on a straight line for a reasonable stretch without having to be lined up against the rail.

As we unhook the equipment, Rolando states, "He has learned every-thing we've taught him so far, and we'll do more of this tomorrow before we ride to see..."

I don't question this; in fact, I dismiss any prior thoughts I had about the vaqueros restricting my horse with mechanical means. *After all, the bosal and reins are mechanical.*

José has invited me to his daughter Josefina's quinceañera, and at the ranch later that night, I park behind a long line of trucks. Over a hun-dred people gather at a trailer where tables laden with delicious food await hungry guests—there are homemade salsas, mole, fried fish, tender pork, roasted turkey, tortillas, beans, salads. José buzzes about with a huge smile, handing out drinks. His shirt is knotted at his waist like a teenage girl's. Josefina has José's beautiful smile, and tonight she's the bella donna of her sweet fifteen.

A DJ plays a slow banda as the light begins to fade, and José dances the first dance with Josefina—they move their feet in rhythmic steps with tenderness and ease. Rolando and his vaquero crew stand on the edge of the party like a line of outlaws, the cool outsiders. I long for Rolando's attention and realize I've got a crush. Embarrassed by this realization, I'm now a teen at a teen's party, throwing glances at an unreachable love and jealous of anyone who talks with him. Am I falling in love with my horse or Rolando? Or am I just loving love and singing along with it?

I move onto the dance floor—beer and cake and mole and fried fish swirl in my belly. José introduces me to his cousin Armando who can real-ly dance, but I can tell he's holding back for me. I am special by virtue of my awkwardness, my willingness to be open and in love with everything I learn.

Day 18

Halfway down the PG&E road and mounted on my horse, Rolando sud-denly swings around with a gleam in his eye, "You want to ride?"

Miguel, mounted on the gray ex-racehorse he's been training, doesn't blink.

"Really? On the trail? Do you think I'm ready?"

"Watch my hands," he says.

For the third day in a row, my horse's head is fixed in place with the side reins. While he's being led by Miguel, Rolando is also using the regular reins, leveraging head and neck left and right and showing me how my horse refuses to go right. Without giving an answer, Rolando dismounts and indicates for me to hand him the palomino and then get on my horse. This time, I don't hesitate. Miguel laughs at Rolando, who is attempting to wedge the wide toe of his work boot into my English stirrup.

"Ándale," he calls.

I don't know as I swing over to sit on my horse that I will have no say about where we go. Led by a vaquero on an ex-racehorse who doesn't speak my language, I realize Rolando has set me up. Off we go, and immediately I sense my horse a different creature out of the confines of an arena or round pen, moving forward like a vessel taken by the strong current of a deep, narrow river. But this body of water is uncharted—I don't know its depths or shallows or even where the rocks are, and I don't know how to use the tools I've been given to navigate. *Am I floating over the border into a new country where Mud Pony must govern on his own? How can I help him with the reins and my seat while attached to a stranger holding his head?* Suddenly I don't want any of this newfound power.

"Work the reins," Rolando says from behind, "slowly."

I've been so focused I'm surprised to hear his voice. He cues me to pulse the reins in the same way he did while working my horse from the ground with driving lines. This pulsing is familiar to me—years ago when I rode a bullfighter's horse on a Baja vacation, the bullfighter told me to ride like I was playing a fast song slowly—so here I practice *feel and release* more than *pull and hold*, and all my years of riding lessons have taught me how to do this. It's a conscious, gentle redirecting, and I remember his words about starting soft, "so when you go hard they know it."

I try to talk to my horse as we trot and lope next to the Brussels sprouts fields, but I often find my mouth too dry to cluck or call. *I hope he can hear me. I hope he knows it's me.*

Miguel laughs and smiles, matching me tooth for tooth with his silver grill. I bump against his leg every other stride as I ask Mud Pony to turn into the gray's shoulder. When we encounter obstacles—farmworkers in a rattling truck hurriedly closing a gate—Mud Pony gets worried and wants to turn around, but I keep him forward by asking him to lean into Miguel. There's a woman on a paint horse walking in our direction, but her horse is ignoring her cues. She can't move him out of our way. Somehow, with Miguel's steady hand, I direct us away from a potential collision.

Maybe this is a good place to stop, and I motion to Miguel. Behind us, Rolando shakes his head, "No."

Laughing, Miguel mimics him, "Rolando. No." And we're off again at a rollicking canter, this time leaving Rolando behind.

I can't believe I'm here—in this strange, new land. I'm grateful it's not a hostile place, but tolerant, welcoming, full of energy, forward movement, strength. Or is it? Out of Rolando's sight, Miguel's cell phone rings, but he ignores it. Then again. Finally, he answers. Then hangs up, laughing. And now we go the opposite way, toward the coastal highway. *Seriously?!* I gesture to Miguel with wide, frightened eyes, and this time we slow to a walk, returning to the ranch entrance where Rolando waits on horseback. Ranch folks are at their usual spot, hanging out in front of the barn, and they whoop and holler when we come into view.

Hooray! Look at us! Later, when I'm safely on the ground, standing next to Mud Pony, I grab Miguel's hand and give it a vigorous shake. He offers a silver-plated grin.

"Happy?" Rolando asks.

"¡Sí! ¡Contenta!"

· Four ·

Few of my summer school students write well and some don't write at all, but if they know they have *something to say* rather than having to *say something*—this is what matters most.

"*Essayer*," I tell them as I write on the board, "is a verb in French which means 'to try.' The guy who invented what we now call the *essay* used this word to describe exactly what he was doing—trying to say something—and that's what we're also doing: writing to discover."

Teens perk up from sullen or tired poses as I switch on the projector to display the image of a veterinarian's invoice for treatment of a puncture wound Mud Pony sustained in his first year in pasture, something they've probably never seen: *The extensive depth of the laceration has filled in with a healthy bed of granulation tissue. The epithelial edge is pale pink and not raw, inflamed, or irritated. There is a necrotic odor of a Pseudomonas organism on the surface of the granulation bed.*

I project another photo, this time of Mud Pony, and pull a story from the past, describing how I once found him standing at the gate with a leg swollen like a stovepipe and a deep puncture wound near his hock.

"What's a hock?" they ask, and I draw the rough shape of a dog on the whiteboard and point to the part of its hind leg that sticks out at a backward angle. Then they ask about the vet's visit, the treatment, and practical considerations. Perhaps they are simply curious or conspiring to put off the writing task that awaits, but as questions are part of this process, I encourage the inquiry: "How long did the vet take to get there? Did he heal up? How long did that take? How much did it cost? How long did it take to pay off your credit card? Where does Mud Pony stay? When do you see him?"

I ask what they think about the veterinarian's use of language in her invoice: "What do words such as *laceration, granulation, epithelial,* or *necrotic* convey? Why has she chosen them? Is this an essay? Why or why not? What can we discover about the roots of the words she uses? When was the last time you or someone in your family went to a doctor? How were things communicated to you?"

Most students find they have something to say. After the discussion, I give them several options for a direction their essay might take.

I sit at my desk, giving them the space to attempt it on their own and listening to the scratch-scratch of pens and pencils. A few stare straight ahead or put heads on desks. I ease my way around the room to check in quietly, and if they can't get started, I say they can write whatever they want. I tell them I'm interested, that I care about their writing. Crouching beside their desk but keeping my eyes off their paper, I wonder aloud with them, offer suggestions. Gradually, they begin. Maybe they write a few sentences, or a paragraph emerges, but I don't care what they write if they know they have the safety and freedom to move their feet.

Day 21

I hear Napoleon mounted on Mud Pony call to him in a sweet singsong, emphasizing each syllable of an unknown phrase. Entering the round pen, Rolando suddenly motions that it's my turn and Napoleon swings off and offers me the reins. *Is this reality or a dream?* Exhausted from my day, I repeat the phrase several times before it sinks in: *I'm riding him.*

Rolando canters at my side to help pick up the pace. Underneath me, Mud Pony leans into the cremello in a fast, tight circle, and I worry that we are at such a steep angle, we will merge and topple over—but strangely, the faster Mud Pony moves, the more he seems to balance himself. *Is he now carrying me, or is Rolando carrying us? Would he tolerate this without Rolando or the cremello?*

I have a sudden urge to humble myself, to direct my thoughts and intentions toward Mud Pony in an unaggressive and respectful way, for I wouldn't try to fight an oncoming wave while paddling out with my surfboard, but duck under it. I dismount, mount, and walk him around the arena a few more times, softly repeating, "We are safe, we are okay."

Then I remount. Twice, Rolando and the cremello loom next to us then pivot, turning away. The deer leg attached to Rolando's saddle brushes against my horse's flank when he comes close.

"I have to go," he says, "but you want to keep riding?"

Afraid to be without him, I shake my head. He lifts his mustache and round cheeks into a smile. I dismount.

He nods, then says, "Do it again."

Mount. Dismount. On the ground at last, my heart pounds and my mouth goes cotton-dry.

"You want one?" Rolando says, pulling a can of Tecate from his saddle-bag. I shake my head. *Does he know how terrified I am?*

"You have to ride him more," he says, opening the can and punching the tab.

O

It was Carter who found our rent-controlled apartment decades ago, and with the astronomical rise of rent in the city that hosted the dot-com boom, we've been fortunate to live in a place where I can afford to have horses and he can make sculpture. As a result, we pay attention when people in suits visit the schoolyard below our kitchen—the city could make a huge profit by selling it to developers.

In recent years, unattractive, cheaply built condominiums have boxed us in, and our view of the stately Bay Bridge has disappeared. Opposite the schoolyard, we eye the new renters of high-priced condos who rise early, mount buses to Silicon Valley, and return late at night or not at all. Squatters, looters, and junkies move in and out of the schoolyard with the light as if night's high tide has regurgitated more wreckage during its ebb: pants, bicycle parts, needles. Someone must have alerted the supervising staff, because yesterday afternoon the gates opened and a team of white-uniformed workers with weed whackers buzzed and cut all the foot-high weeds growing up between the cracks. As they worked, suited officials and a cop walked around, inspecting the bathrooms and the classrooms, which had been slept in and stripped. They didn't take away the dozen or so bicycle wheels or the blue stool on one rooftop.

The chopped weeds are a sign, a stirring. We miss the pigeons that used to comb the cracked asphalt.

Day 23

On the way back from our ride today, Rolando, mounted on the cremello, states, "You will ride him in the parade."

As if in agreement, Mud Pony matches strides with Rolando's horse. Raising my eyebrows, I look incredulously at him.

He continues, "Columbus Day."

"He means the one in North Beach in San Francisco," Lottie calls. She's the length of a horse's tail behind us on her mare while Patti and Darcy follow. I've heard about the parade through North Beach, a touristy, Italian section of the city, but I have the day off in recognition of Indigenous Peoples, not Columbus.

"I thought when you said *parade* you meant next summer's Fourth of July." My mouth must be hanging open, for I see amusement dance behind a pair of dark, unyielding eyes. "Don't you mean that *you*, Rolando, will ride him?"

"No," he says, "I will ride my horse. You will ride him." A sudden rush of lightness, glee. Because Rolando says it could happen, somehow it will. I glance at Lottie, also smiling.

"You've got the day off, right?" Lottie coughs, slyly. "I sure feel it comin' on."

"Guess I'll have to call in sick too," Patti chimes.

Mud Pony and I are at the center of a great circle, held and watched closely with hearts, eyes, hands as I urge him in front of the others in our miniature parade on trail. Never in my life have I felt surrounded by such meaningful attention.

We ascend the steep, uneven portion of the hills above the ponds. I urge him into a canter, and it soon becomes a gallop. He grabs the hill with his front feet and pushes it away with his hind. We are running now as I've only felt in dreams—heady, floating, wild. As we descend at a slower pace single file on the downhill, I suddenly feel him startle and leap. My helmet wrenches loose under my chin, clatters to the ground, and scares him even more. Disoriented, he doesn't respond to my pulse or tug: his head and neck are hard, tense, upright. He plunges, scurries as if reaching for something to grasp, something solid.

How I keep my seat is a mystery. And then Rolando is there, moving the cremello's shoulder close to Mud Pony for comfort. He somehow catches hold of the lead rope and leads us away from the troubled spot to flat ground where Lottie dismounts and hands me my helmet. I'm shaking atop Mud Pony. As I grasp the helmet, its chinstrap swings against the base, making a hollow sound. Again, he startles and leaps, but this time Rolando is there to grab the reins. He motions me to get off, and now I can make it safely to the ground. Patti, Lottie, and Darcy all smile and congratulate me for staying on. They want to know what happened.

"He went to sleep," Rolando answers, "and then woke up when he heard the sound." Also, Rolando points out, he did the same thing in that spot last week with Napoleon, leaping and bolting at some seemingly invisible thing. "That is why you must sing to him, talk to him, keep him awake. Just like Napoleon does." After a pause, he adds, "Things happen with any horse. It's good this happened today."

I nod. "We have to be there for him," I say. "Teach him to think about it."

"Yes," Rolando nods, "it's good. He knows he can't get away with it."

Rolando then keeps me attached to him for at least one hundred yards before we ride down the switchback and through a busy ranch. My stomach is a tumble and I'm nervous about several blankets and buckets scattered on the ground. Mud Pony skitters away from an orange cat in a crouch at the wash rack.

Back at the ranch, he settles. We work in the sand arena next to the pasture.

"You can teach him whatever you want now," Rolando says, and I guess he means *right* now, but I have no idea what to teach him. "Two weeks more," Rolando says. "We do this every day, he's gonna be okay."

As I stand safely on the ground next to this man who is so at ease on his horse, my heart fills with gratitude for our safety. I lay my hand briefly on the cremello's sweaty neck and thank them both.

Day 25

I follow at a short distance over, up, down the hills. I predict the group will soon stop, and Napoleon will dismount, and Rolando will nod in my direction to exchange horses. But not today. They keep moving and Mud Pony seems to be troubled and working a lot harder than the other horses. He roots for the ground more than usual.

When we arrive back at my tack room and Napoleon prepares to dismount, I spy a four-inch gash on the back of Mud Pony's right foreleg. The skin flaps open to reveal blood and tissue—from that entry point, you could take a knife and skin the whole length of his leg.

"All this week," Rolando says, "you won't ride."

Suddenly I'm disarmed. What's under the lilt in his voice? Affection? Mockery?

"Just wrap it," he says. "I will call Lottie tomorrow."

The next day, Lottie says that Rolando told her Mud Pony needs the whole week to heal. Disappointed, I tack up the palomino and swing over with no tension, worry, or effort. She's so even-tempered and compliant, no challenge there. *Could I ever find a way to be satisfied with riding just her?*

On the trail, we come across a coyote—tall-legged, long-backed, gaunt—sitting upright on his haunches and staring at us. A typically calm and steady horse, my mare startles in place and I see the coyote's yellow eyes, which occupy most of the space on his narrow face. His gray coat is a speckled kaleidoscope of wild animal fur like the feathers on my horse's legs. Boarders bring their dogs to the ranch, and I've heard them describe the ones that got lost and what might have happened: a single coyote will act as a playful decoy, luring someone's pet to the pack to be killed and devoured. I consider the domesticated space of the ranch, how the coyote hovers at its edges like the street denizens in our neighborhood who wander in and out of the schoolyard. Urban or rural, the wild, raw hunger rises wherever it can.

Rolando remarked last week how he thinks Mud Pony, unhandled and feral for his first year, was also abused, because he's terrified of a twig Napoleon carried in his hand yesterday. I told Rolando what I know about his first year—the story of his mother breaking her legs in a cattle crossing, how he wasn't handled by humans but lived in a herd of wild horses that had been shipped in from some holding facility to be bred to the ranch stud for cow horses and rodeo broncs.

I used to think the herd a safe, comforting place for an orphaned foal, but when I witness the pasture dynamic—my horse pushing the other horses in a bullying way—I think he, too, must have been bullied. Probably that first herd didn't let him in to the hay. They must have kicked at him, flattened their ears, blocked him with their shoulders and hips. Newly orphaned, he had no mother mare to protect him. But now, in *his* herd, he eats first and as much as he wants. He will often be the only horse munching at the feeder while the others surround him like a group of seagulls, waiting for the alpha bird to drop bits from its mouth.

Day 28

I had no clue what to do with Mud Pony when Rolando suggested I "keep going" after our session last week, so I call Roses.

"Get a metronome," she says, "or sing a song with a steady beat." She wants me to use rhythm with every request—when we turn, stop, trot, and walk. "Set the rhythm for each gaits. Then ride that beat."

After Mud Pony's leg is sufficiently healed for him to work, I hum to him as I gather the reins. I become the metronome, clucking on the first beat of the 1-2-3-4 footfall of the walk. At the trot, I rise in rhythm to the march in my head, noting that if one ear turns back on the cluck, then he's awake and listening. I imagine the music we will ride to when we do more cantering—perhaps *The Galop Infernal* or the *Star Wars* theme song.

For now, we slow the metronome to a walking beat on the PG&E road next to the Brussels sprouts fields.

"Did you think two months back," Rolando says, riding next to me on the palomino, "you would be riding him?"

"No," I laugh, "and if you had told me two months ago that you would want me to ride him in the North Beach parade, I would have laughed even harder."

"So now you see," he smiles. "Anything is possible."

"Yes," I say, and gush inwardly, silently: *You have granted me one of the deepest wishes I have ever held in my body, to ride the horse of my dreams, the horse I fantasized about as a child. I invented stories about our adventures together, riding over mountains in great blowing storms, across rivers and meadows, traveling great distances, bringing food to refugees.*

Instead, I explain how the bullfighter in Mexico I once took a lesson from sharply corrected me for being too heavy on his horse: "You should ride a horse like you play an instrument."

I could understand the bullfighter's words but not execute them—I'd never ridden such lightness and sensitivity—and the bullfighter's fine-tuned performance steed got confused and speedy under my direction.

"I would love for my horse to be like that," I say, but *perhaps he already is, as he's now responding to the rhythm I set!*

"Sometime I will let you ride *my* horse," says Rolando, smiling. He means the cremello.

"Is he very light?"

"When he wants to be," Rolando laughs, and then indicates with his head that we've gone far enough and it's time to turn around. I ask Mud Pony to turn right and the opposite direction from the group, but he ignores me and turns left with them. I don't correct this but make a mental note to better prepare him the next time by asking for tiny serpentines or to walk at a short distance from the flank of the cremello. As if in reaction to my thought, Mud Pony increases his pace and roots his head toward the ground. Perhaps there's residual pain from the cut on his leg or maybe he's tired. Rolando doesn't seem concerned.

As we return through the gated entrance to the fields, I see a piece of paper on the ground. It brushes his hoof and he starts and snorts, but I keep my seat.

"Good riding!" I hear Lottie say behind me.

"He didn't see it," Rolando says.

Another mental note—keep him aware, get him to look at things on the ground, point stuff out to him instead of letting him be surprised, talk to him about it.

Back at the ranch, José sees me for the first time unattached to Rolando on my horse, and he hisses through his teeth, launching a huge grin and pointy finger. "Oooooo, Stephanie, muy bueno!"

I stick out my tongue.

Later, I'm not so sure. What if the goal of riding in the North Beach parade is too much to expect? What if I'm pushing for Rolando's vision mostly because I want to be seen as one of Rolando's crew?

Yesterday I called Patti and tried to predict with her everything Mud

Pony might experience in such a setting, and there was no end to the list: city streets filled with wind-crazy balloons and banners... roaring bus or truck engines and honking cars... restless, unpredictable crowds... the overhead crackling of electric lines... the random beer can or streamer that might be tossed at our feet... the cable car tracks on an unfamiliar and slippery surface...

Day 30

Rolando pulls a can of Modelo from his saddlebag but doesn't offer one to me or my friend Sarah, who has walked over the hill on her mare this foggy Sunday morning. I ride Mud Pony and Rolando rides Witch, the only horse I've heard the vaqueros assign a name to. We circle the farmer's fields, and the sky begins to clear as we enter the gate to the Brussels sprouts fields. Mud Pony wants to trot and push his nose in front of Witch. I have difficulty finding a consistent rhythm, and when he surges ahead, I try to make it his idea by asking him for a trot. But he careens to a walk when he gets too far in front, ignoring me and wanting to be back with Witch. When those behind us catch up, his jig begins again. What might happen if we got in trouble, and he really decided to shut me out?

Returning home on the single track of the PG&E road is even worse. We now canter next to Rolando and Witch—and the horses are getting jacked up. This could go bad.

"Make him calm on the way back," Rolando says.

Yeah right, how am I supposed to do that? After all, I've given myself over to Rolando's direction and so look to him for where we turn and how fast we go and when we stop. Mud Pony continues to ignore me when I ask him to walk.

"Make him stop," Rolando heeds, and he walks ahead on Witch.

I've lost contact with Sarah, who has been keeping a safe distance behind. Rolando halts, dismounts, and gestures for me to do the same. Then he hands me Witch's reins, and I clamber onto the white leather Mexican saddle with its big cow horn like a toddler's drum and the deer leg that dangles over the saddlebag. Underneath, I sense a horse that could go from zero to sixty in about four seconds. It has a huge, smooth walk, but there's tremendous power there too; the engine of a muscle car—Camaro or Corvette—lives in its hind end.

It's challenging to keep Witch at a walk—and Rolando, even as he's mounting and directing Mud Pony, tells me how to hold the reins. Again, I'm a child. "Like this," he says, demonstrating a single-handed grip, a fist with a thumb on top. "Then he will stop."

But Witch continues to dance underneath, and it's all I can do to focus on my seat—then my horse wants to match Witch's prance, and suddenly Rolando yanks two times on the right rein and pushes Mud Pony away from us and thirty meters up the embankment to its edge above. As if it's a cameo moment in a Western B-movie, he reins my horse back in and looks toward us. Right on cue, Mud Pony bolts and rears.

"Hold on!" I shout, and in mid-rear, Rolando clasps one hand to the top of his cowboy hat. He urges Mud Pony back down to the safety zone of our horses, and moves him ahead of the group, slapping the saddle and wiggling his seat, bending Mud Pony in serpentines, directing him way more aggressively than I've seen.

On our walk through the ranch, after all the horses have finally calmed themselves on home ground, Rolando asks, "Did you see?"

My reply exits my mouth as a squawk. "You gave him all kinds of things to do. You directed him every step."

"From now on," Rolando continues with low, measured volume, "whatever this horse does, it comes from the way you ride him. It's been a month. You know he can do it, so now you have to ride him how you want him."

I nod and gulp. Self-doubt and fear. Shadowy sensations too. Shudders.

A chapter has ended—the one where I get to be a passenger and be led around like a child on a pony ride.

As he dismounts Mud Pony, Rolando pronounces, "You have to ride your horse, not him ride you."

O

On the drive to church when I was a child, I pressed my face against the window of the family van to catch a glimpse of Afterdark, a thoroughbred who lived alone in a crummy paddock next to a three-hundred-year-old, stone-wrought mill. I dreamed of escaping with Afterdark to hidden meadows beyond the Church Farm School pond, across the hills of Valley Forge, through the abandoned orchard of the nearby corporate park.

The Lie was conceived over a series of Sundays while kneeling in church, closing my eyes, and pressing my forehead against the coolness of the wood pew as the priest prattled on, and I drifted to where I could be with Afterdark. At the time, I had not yet been granted Isabel and Mrs. Burns, so I prayed for Kelly Heck, Afterdark's teenage owner, to let me be her assistant.

On the day I returned to my third-grade class after weeks at home with a flu that had become an ear infection, my classmates surrounded me in welcome. Although the pain of a busted eardrum had made me sensitive to noise, I didn't mind their jumping or shouting. I'd brought a photo of Afterdark I'd snapped on a weekend walk during my recovery, and I showed it to my favorite classmate, a tall, brash smart aleck named Jackie who always talked back to our teacher, Mrs. Hawk. Although I was much shyer than Jackie, we'd become friends at recess, pretending our jump ropes wrapped around each other's waists were reins.

Suddenly emboldened, I told Jackie that Afterdark was my new horse, and that's where I'd been all this time.

"Well, how come you never show her to me?"

"She's pregnant," I said. "That's how I got her, and she can't stand a lot of excitement right now." I knew at the time that Afterdark was a gelding, but my imaginings knew no bounds of sex or reproduction.

Soon everyone in the class knew that I had a pregnant horse. Our teacher inquired about Afterdark's condition. Classmates who had never spoken to me before now approached my desk with questions.

A lie, however, has its own life (Carter calls it the Liar's Pond), and mine expanded into tales of riding bareback uphill, tales of "after dark" horse care ("That's how she got her name," I explained to my classmates, "I have to take care of her after dark all the time"), stories of galloping through fields of wildflowers and barely clearing barbed wire fences across our path. I told these fables mostly to Jackie, and I felt assured no one would find out because I didn't play outside of school with any of the kids in my class.

Two years passed and The Lie remained safe and unexposed. Any interest my classmates had expressed faded, and at the beginning of fourth grade, no one even asked me if I'd done any riding over the summer. By fifth grade, Jackie had changed the spelling of her name to Jacquie and become more interested in boys, while I was more interested in books. At recess, instead of playing with my classmates outside, I read in the library, a pleasurable and family-sanctioned escape. I consumed every horse title there was, cultivating a vocabulary of horse care, anatomy, and basic first aid for equines.

In sixth grade, I met up with Jacquie, who was now rumored to be smoking. "A pack a day," my classmates said, although I never smelled it on her. Jacquie now had a boyfriend and designer jeans. She also taunted the "preppies" in the Academically Talented class, making the pink-outfitted girls cry.

Jacquie made out with her boyfriend, Chuck, during recess. They'd walk hand in hand to a large bush outside the recess perimeter and hide themselves on the other side. While the girls dreamed of boys to go hide in the bushes with, I gazed longingly at the two horses in a paddock beyond where they kissed.

Sometime in our junior year of high school, Jacquie got pregnant. We hadn't been in the same classes since the sixth grade, but she'd been kind to me, adopting me as her "cool preppie." I remember how she waved me over from the student smoking lounge as I passed by on my way to class. In all that time, she had never once brought up our shared love of horses or Afterdark, but for some reason on that day she decided to ask, "Hey, did you ever *really* own a horse?"

My stomach flipped. It was like we had talked about it only yesterday. *Was I to be found out, mocked, and humiliated?* Jacquie's eyes narrowed. I remembered the pull of the jump rope around my waist as we galloped through the playground. Holding her gaze, I smiled. Not a word.

A week later, Jacquie left school, and The Lie was safe.

O

"Scientia potentia est. Knowledge is power. Agree, disagree, or qualify."

With this prompt on the whiteboard, I task my sixth-period students to find a partner and discuss its relevance to *Kaffir Boy*, a memoir written by Mark Mathabane, a man who grew up in the ghettoes of apartheid South Africa. To begin, I ask them to reflect on the experiences and circumstances that shaped Mathabane's response to the given situation. Was it his education, his mother's unflagging belief in his ability and her support, or his relationship with tennis professionals? I circulate as they share their thoughts, find quotes, and generate notes. Then they write silently and I write with them. After fifteen minutes, we discuss as a whole group, and discover that knowledge is power, but there are different kinds of knowledge and power that impact us. By the end, we've created a matrix with knowledge and power on one side and family support, education, political power, and luck on the other.

The plan was for me to offer my thoughts as a model, but I hold back. In my notes, I'd unexpectedly time-traveled to that Liar's Pond in second grade with Jacquie where respect, ownership, and, yes, power were granted me when I told my classmates about Afterdark. Applying the prompt to my journey with Mud Pony, I realize I have power but am still fearful *and* ignorant. I've foisted an apprenticeship upon Rolando the master horseman so I can ride Mud Pony to gain both the knowledge and the power I deeply long for.

I envision a follow-up prompt for my students: *What happens when you fake knowing what you know? Does that still grant you power?* Secretly, I hope their responses will inform something I might tell Rolando.

That evening, after roasted chicken from Thai's market and a bottle of wine from the liquor store across the street, I read to Carter what I couldn't share with the class, and I know he's listening not just to my writing but to himself as he quietly works a toothpick over his gums:

> If it's true that knowledge is power, then faking or lying about what you know is a superficial ownership, a claiming in name only, and a defense against the fragility of not knowing. As a child, I was determined to realize my imaginings and so stumbled upon the dizzying revelation of The Lie. If I could maintain its appearance, I could satisfy some of the longing, and my needy, splintered parts could

flourish in the fantasy world of horse ownership. Over the years with Mud Pony, I've earned respect from other boarders for taking on the challenge of starting a fearful and explosive horse, and I've gained some of the attention and recognition I so long for. Unlike with Afterdark, I've been *granted* the power to both name and own him. But is that really knowledge or power?

I look up from the page. Carter pushes away his empty dinner plate and gazes at the abandoned schoolyard. His pause allows me to fill the space, to enlarge:

I don't really *own* him because I don't really *know* him. And my palomino? Thing is, I already *know* her. She's push-button predictable, boring. Is it because Mud Pony has presented himself as *unknowable* that the prospect of *knowing him* is so enticing?

A creak from the wooden armchair as Carter shifts. He points out the window to an enormous crane on the top of a new high-rise. Its huge steel arm is frozen into a vertical position. An airplane's contrail has just floated into alignment with the limb, continuing the crane's gesture, like a giant finger pointing beyond to an even bigger giant or god.

O

Educational psychologists define learning as connecting what we don't know to what we already know. To learn therefore requires courage—to risk looking like a fool or being out of control by allowing someone to guide us into the unknown. As a teacher, I'm often reminded how vulnerable students are in a classroom and how risky it may be for some kids to even walk through the door or sit at a desk. Teenagers may say they know answers when they don't, or present the appearance of learning, so they won't seem stupid, vulnerable, or out of control. I tell myself it must be okay for them to fake it sometimes... as I have with Mud Pony, as I'm doing with Rolando.

But how do I consistently help my students get to the place where they are willing to risk crossing the threshold into the unknown? Some students do it naturally, but for many it seems as if I'm forever urging them to go where they may not want to go, driving them toward discomfort, corralling them to the places where they are vulnerable. *Is it really with their best interests in mind?* With Mud Pony, I know he will be better able to survive living in the world of humans if he can be ridden, if he can become a working horse. Then, if something ever happens to me...

Now I'm clearer about the knowledge I want to acquire from Rolando: *the experience of a deeper sense of ownership that can come only by working with feel.* I want Mud Pony to bend his body in a willing way, without being forced through mechanical means: ropes, tie-downs, cranked reins. For advanced riders, this is a deeply intimate and powerful connection. I've seen Rolando and riders like him. With a seemingly invisible stomach contraction or seat-bone shift, they cue a thousand pounds of horse flesh to leap, spin, or stop. To achieve this with the cremello, Rolando has spent years on the ground, teaching it to lift its back as an apprenticed dancer strengthens his core. Then the horse may round into the vaulted shape of a bottom-side-up boat.

Yes, Rolando is perhaps the teacher to give me this knowledge *and* power.

Day 31

¡Feliz cumpleaños, Alicia!

Rolando tells Lottie our ride is cancelled this evening and invites us to celebrate his wife's special day with tamales and cake. As we arrive at their trailer, there's banda blaring from a truck's speakers, and Rolando offers beer or wine, then shows us how to mix Alicia's homemade salsa into the pozole. Alicia and Allie, Diego's wife, sit at our table. Manolito, two years old and with Rolando's wide face and dimples, plays in front of the trailer where our party has set up, then gets passed from lap to lap. Older children kick a soccer ball in the yard. Napoleon, José, Diego, and other vaqueros sit at a table and talk. A woman I don't know sits with us and listens to our banter. Occasionally, she translates something into Spanish for Alicia, who smiles shyly.

Rolando brings me and Lottie more beer. He sets himself down. Across the table he says, "Now you have met and seen my people."

Rolando narrates his arrival in the US twelve years ago, how he worked as a wrangler in Texas and at a restaurant in Los Angeles. He says that everything I believe and know inside myself can be given to my horse.

"It's the rider, not the horse, who makes the horse," he says, "but you gotta believe—don't give up on something that doesn't work at first."

He takes two empty beer cans on the table, places his hands around their bases, shows me how he moves them, pulse by pulse, not pull. Out on trail, he tells me I have to be constantly working the reins like this.

When the fog rolls in and it gets dark and chilly, he invites us into the living room of the trailer to watch a video of a young horse he owns in Mexico, a gray Azteca colt being trained by a man who looks to be barely twenty. Sometime the horse will come here, he states. The trailer is warm and cozy even as the fog and darkness move in. There's a kitchenette with a table, a family room area with a rug, couch, and a floor full of Manolito's toys. CDs with proud horses on their covers stand displayed on a shelf. The blue ribbon won by Rolando and his men at the town's Ol' Fashioned 4th of July Parade hangs next to the TV. Rolando pushes the remote, showing us a clip from a rodeo in his hometown.

We watch a family gathering with bull riders, horses dancing to live music, and youth and adults dancing and drinking and eating. Rolando says the fiesta went on for days with people moving from dancing to riding to eating in a slow, relaxed way, no rush, no business, nothing to be accomplished or finished. The horses are shiny, magnificent, responsive to their riders. Rolando points out that they dance only when their rider asks them to, not at any random moment when the music is playing. I love watching the male riders move their hips in time with their horses.

The film moves to a group of teenage girls dancing. "That's my sister," Rolando says, and points to a lithe and laughing young woman. "All day and all night, people just dance and sing and drink and ride. You can talk to anyone. You can go to the next town."

I notice there's no central arena, loud announcer, rock music, or obnoxious advertisements like in the rodeos I've attended. This is non-commercial, a family gathering.

"You miss it, don't you?" I ask.

He nods with sadness and longing. Alicia, too, has the same look in her eyes as she holds her sleeping son and points out to us on the video in a soft voice, "Mis sobrinos."

Around eleven, when Rolando has finished showing us his video and we've drunk the last Modelo, we shake hands, and Lottie and I step down from the trailer where we walk the short road between the two ranches.

"Let's ride!" I shout. But Lottie has already hugged me good night. The sky is clear to the west and south—a sprinkling of stars dots a moonless night. To the north, a napkin of fog seems to have been tucked into heaven's high collar. My horses hear me call to them and emerge noiselessly from the darkness. I halter the palomino and tie a quick bridle out of her rope halter. Pleasantly buzzed on top of the picnic bench, I don't hesitate to straddle her strong back. She's as comfortable as a couch. I float on her back under the few stars I can see.

Day 32

Around the pumpkin fields on the flat trail, by the wooden racks of the beehives, I see discarded shells from a rifle. My eye catches the black feathers of a still mass on the side of the trail.

"I don't like that," Lottie says. "I've never seen a shot crow before. I want to bury it."

Witch won't walk. He prances and jigs even after Rolando growls at him. After we pass the dead crow, Mud Pony catches Witch's rhythm and can't be calmed by Napoleon's hands or seat. At these times, I'm reminded that sometimes it's okay for the bolt to be brought up and out, but only if the horse returns to its rider and the rider has enough skill to stay on. That way he'll be reminded of his job.

After we return from circling the fields, Napoleon gallops Mud Pony straight into the corners of the arena. "Ho!" he shouts and throws his weight back in the saddle and turns him abruptly into the fence, replaying the same moves until my horse is sweaty and foaming between his hind cheeks. Rolando hangs a white sweatshirt on the top rail and Napoleon runs him alongside and then aims him toward the prop, yanking on his mouth. These are exercises to teach a horse to work with cows. Secretly, I wish I could ride him like Napoleon does.

"¡Necesito vaca!" I call out, and Napoleon answers, "¡Vaca!" and begins mooing.

Later, we are standing around with my horse, Rolando, and Manolito. My disappointment about not riding my horse this week is tinged with fatigue and a strange, unfamiliar emptiness. I hardly know what to say when Rolando turns to me with Manolito in his arms and asks, "How do you feel?" I'm caught speechless by the question. Except for Carter and my therapist, I recall few people ever asking me this in such an honest, straightforward manner.

"Good," I tell him, frustrated at not being able to say what I really want. "He gets stuck," I say, shifting away from what seems too intimate to share about myself and reflecting on what I saw happen today during the training session. "His mind gets stuck."

Rolando nods.

Perhaps my mind is stuck as well? I'm obsessed with Rolando's approval. I have a hard time letting go of my own thoughts. *Does my horse sense my stuckness? Does he mirror me?*

Again, the niggling fear. Something is not right. I want Rolando to ask not "How do *you* feel?" but "How does *your horse* feel?"

Day 35

Napoleon rocks Mud Pony into a canter while growling to him in a low voice. He brings him down to a big trot then revs him back up to a canter, stops him at the gate and attempts a backup, but my horse freezes into an arch-backed, stiff-legged posture. Napoleon saws on the reins without response. He turns Mud Pony to one side, retries the backup, gets a backward shuffle, shrugs, and then dismounts, handing the reins to me. Lottie, who is standing at the opposite end of the round pen, already has a beer in her hand, and Rolando is on his way to the cooler to get another. This time I accept. We talk about the upcoming Harry Wittsom clinic less than three weeks away, what it will be like to work with my horse there.

"You gotta tell the cowboy how much he has been ridden. You gotta ride him by yourself before the clinic."

I know he means Harry, and I swallow nervously: we are entering a new realm, one where I dread the fact of no Rolando and no Napoleon.

"He's going to be a good show horse," says Rolando between sips. "Napoleon, he would buy him from you."

I'm stunned by the idea of selling my horse—and flattered, too, but I shake my head. "I've waited so long..."

Rolando doesn't miss a beat. The more he drinks, the more he talks. "One thing I gotta tell you about this horse. If you ask him to do something, he gotta do it."

I nod.

"We didn't do nothing special with him" he shrugs. "It's just what we do. He learns everything."

Again, I nod. Maybe he approves of my decision not to sell Mud Pony.

He puts a hand over his heart. "This horse. You gotta keep him in here."

Manolito appears at the open trailer door and holds out his arms. He tumbles down the steps into a fallen pile but rebounds for the launch. Rolando is waiting and scoops him up. One smiling, wide face pressed against another.

Day 38

A week later, the footing in the ranch arena next door is the pleasing texture of crushed chalk due to Rolando's effort to groom it daily with a tractor into a smooth, even plain. Watching, Rolando sits on the same mounting block just outside the arena where the old man sat when I first asked for Rolando over a month and a half ago. I trot and canter my horse across its blank face, leaving hoof prints. I dismount a short distance from Lottie and Tika.

"He's done," he says.

Afterward, I find a scrap of paper in the glove compartment of my car and make a list of what Rolando told me to remember:

"Don't get him mad."

"Go easy."

"Walk."

"To turn and go back, turn him on the left, not the right. Walking out, you stay on Lottie's right side. Coming back, you stay on Lottie's left side. Work him in the arena before and after."

"Keep him away from your mare. He's attached to her."

"Use the bosal for now. He doesn't respect the snaffle."

"If you ride with other horses, make sure they stay back from him."

"If you ask him to do something, make sure he does it."

And then, the one thing I don't note—his offer. "If you want, I would buy him from you."

Day 40

Lottie arrives, mounted on Tika, and they stand next to us in the arena for support, so I can more safely swing over. I texted her on the way down—"can you help us?"

Relax, I try to tell my arms and back and neck, but I can feel my tired, stiff body and the sweat trickling down my brow. I mount up safely and forget the fatigue as we head out on trail and up the big hill above the airport and highway.

I now know the solidity, squareness, strength beneath me. With a short back and gravity low to the ground, he's the perfect shape for climbing hills. But he's both small and big—in a second, he can shape-shift from a long-eared, sluggish burro to a prancing parade horse. And maybe that's why my arms and legs are beginning to tire again. I'm riding every step and ten feet in front of us—all at once anticipating, watching, listening to both him and myself. Perhaps he's doing the same? Perhaps we are still wary of each other, but still, we seem to be building trust. From here, who knows where we will go? To the beach? Camping trips? To the Sierras? To North Beach?

"Mama's little baby loves rhubarb, rhubarb, a-be-bop-a-re-bop rhubarb pie." I sing to him out on trail. His ears flip back to listen. Lottie smiles.

A two-hour ride today. Our longest yet. Napoleon gives us the thumbs-up sign as he passes us on the ranch road in his truck, merengue on the radio blasting through open windows. Tanned and lean, he's dressed for something other than ranch work today with his black cowboy hat, fitted black jeans, ornamented rodeo belt buckle, cowboy boots, and a collared shirt open at the neck. Perhaps he's on the way to a club or dance hall, a place he will be singing, but to someone else.

Day 41

Rolando works a yearling colt in the round pen close to his trailer. When I approach atop Mud Pony, he releases the colt and walks to the rail.

"I'm in love with my horse," I say. "And I won't sell him—to you, Napoleon, or anyone." Rolando smiles, says nothing, turns back to his yearling, and we float away to find Lottie and Tika.

Riding Mud Pony feels like a dream. We can do this only together—transport to another dimension, driven by his back, hind end, legs, and my seat. I long for a redo of childhood, one on horseback this carefree, where I listen forever to rhythms of comfort and rest on the currents of this gentle river. No longer magical thinking but a real sort of magic.

Day 42

I wait until he stops moving, then swing up and over, getting on him in the arena for the first time without Lottie next to us! Mud Pony and I find her and Tika in the parking lot and ride side by side in search of Rolando. Lottie's phone chirps in her belt pack. It's Rolando, directing our gaze to the ridge where he's holding his phone to his ear, mounted on the cremello and outlined against a darkening sky.

Glued to Lottie and Tika, Mud Pony and I run up the big hill toward Rolando, my horse on Tika's tail. He takes huge, gulping strides. The edge of my sweatshirt catches the horn and a tricky few seconds of panic overtake me before I manage to free myself. *What if Lottie lets her horse go, and he follows, but I can't stop him?*

"Easy," I call in a constricted tone.

Lottie doesn't answer but halts at the top. Rolando and the cremello have disappeared.

"Sorry 'bout that," I pant apologetically as we catch up to her. "I got scared."

Again, she says nothing, and I redden with embarrassment. I wish I could be as cool as Rolando and the vaqueros—I want Lottie to want to ride with me because I'm just like them. "I wish I was good about running him as fast as he can go," I tell her.

"You'll get there," she states. The view of the ocean with glassy sheets of blue is breathtaking with hills rippling out from the shoreline like lumps of green and brown dough.

"Okay, let's run," I say on impulse, letting go and giving both her and Tika permission to let go too. Amazingly, my horse stays with them. I can't believe how his feet eat up this trail with steep sides and uneven footing, but he's surefooted enough to stick to the narrow, flat portion as it dips and curves. We are running and racing so fast no bump could cause us to tumble. Instead, we lift off and up into the ether. We hover and float over green hills into the blue. We land with a laugh at the airport across the highway. Or we dip into the sea, get tossed by whitewater, roll in with the foam, then giggle as we get dumped in the sand.

I call out and we stop before the big stand of eucalyptus and its coat of dry, slippery leaves underneath.

Lottie teases, "Balls-out racing! Your heart pounding yet?!"

Breathless but cool, I'm amazed at what gets flushed out of me—disbelief, uncertainty, judgment. How everything gathers then rises and moves through the body without any seeming effort. *Trust this.* We won't fall and we can't fail. And there's no such thing as redemption because there's no sin and no shame, only the ecstatic flying moment.

Day 43

After Roses arrives for our once-every-other-month lesson, Rolando, Miguel, and Napoleon hover at the rail and watch on their mounts, but they don't stay for more than a few minutes. Manolito sits in front of Rolando on the wide, flat top of the saddle horn. I want to wave but also don't want to drop the reins, causing Mud Pony to startle.

"Um, do they want to ride with us?" Roses asks.

"No, I think they just want to hang out," I respond, but when I turn around, they're gone.

"Ask him to back up," Roses says, back to business, but I'm stuck on how I've cut my friends loose. Now Mud Pony won't move one centimeter.

Roses approaches and gently places her hands on three different regions of his neck and heart-girth area. "We want to relax him. Here, here, and here... To help unstick his feet, you're going to ask him to move his spine back and forth like a snake. Do zigzags, snake trails."

He responds well to my leg cue to go forward, and we undulate back and forth in S-curves, first at a walk, then the trot. Mud Pony softens in response, lifts his back, wants to stretch out a bit. I give him more float in the reins.

"All this will help you in your lateral work," she tells me, "half passes, side passes, opening gates."

To move Mud Pony out of his stuckness by working from a different, unstuck spot—Perhaps this is riding with feel?

"Use your calf more than your heel," she directs.

I ask in rhythm, pulsing my calf against his belly and using the length of my leg rather than poking him with my heel as has been my habit.

"Remember that a broken horse is not a horse broken in spirit but a horse that can bend at the ribs."

When Roses first told me this, it was a revelation: a "broken" Mud Pony would turn easily in both directions with cues from his rider, that is, his rider could bring his opposite eye around when cued off the leg. It would be an easeful exercise, without resistance. *But I want more: I want him to bend himself around my leg just as he might lean against a tree to scratch.*

After the zigzagging, Mud Pony responds to my cue for back up, shifting one hoof and then two, but I have to hold and wait for it, something I haven't played with much because I haven't wanted to get into a contest, as Rolando warned me.

"It's okay. That's something he doesn't know yet," says Roses. "Don't worry about it right now. Think four corners. You are working toward being able to move him off any leg. And don't forget to release as soon as he begins to give."

I ask for movement at a standstill to the left off the front: bend left, right leg. He turns on his haunches. Then the same thing to the right.

"Well, that's easy," she says. "He can already turn up front. His difficulty is planting those front feet and moving from his middle."

We walk around in between my requests to halt. Then I ask for a turn off the forehand (his front feet) as I gently press my left leg to his side, put pressure on the left rein, and look toward the left hip.

"Don't drop your shoulder!" she calls.

Mud Pony struggles to turn on his front end in the way I ask, actually spooking and skittering a few steps as he's still holding on to his right side and eye—he can't yet shift left from his middle.

"That's okay, that's just where he is right now."

I sigh, wanting to keep going. Now this is the knowledge (and empowerment) I've longed for, and maybe I wanted it from Rolando, or to skip all that and already know it myself. Of course, at the clinic next week, I'm hoping for even more.

"How should I use the week with Harry?" I ask Roses.

"Practice what we're doing now," she says and slides into her car at the gate.

After I release Mud Pony in pasture, I ride the palomino to compare her response off my leg to his. Forward and light, she bounces off my calf, moving all four corners with the slightest move. She backs up with ease like a champion and does everything he can't yet do. Why is this such a mystery for him? *Will he ever be able to understand how to move from my legs, hands, and seat—like her?*

Day 44

Rolando appears at his trailer door when I knock. The gulf between us has widened since Wednesday's lesson with Roses. Earlier this afternoon, Lottie instructed me on the phone to return Rolando's bosal to him. *Was he insulted because I chose to work with Roses that day instead of him?*

"How did it go?" he asks.

"How are you?" I ask.

"Tired," he says.

"I've got some cold beers for you and your bosal. Thank you so much for everything."

He ignores the card and wad of cash on top of the cooler. He never mentioned payment.

"You made one," Rolando says, indicating the returned bosal.

"No, I bought one. But it's not as nice as yours." His bosal—the one we've been using—is homemade and worked into softness, not hard Indian leather for eighty dollars at the local tack store.

The horses are beginning to hair up for winter. The days that felt so long and slow during the last month and a half get cut short. I probably shouldn't be so worried about separating from Rolando and moving on to work with Roses and Harry. The school year has begun. I will have to work diligently every day to establish classroom routines and get to know my students before I leave them for a week at Harry's clinic.

And there's another loss. For forty days "the posse" (as one boarder named us) were all there for support. Everyone's presence, especially Rolando, Napoleon, Lottie's, was crucial, but all those on the periphery—Jess, Karie, Patti, José, Miguel, Sarah, Diego, Roses, and others—were there too. At the beginning, Rolando said my horse just needed someone to hold him, and he was right. With his leadership, Rolando held all of us.

And what a gift Rolando has offered—today on our ride, I rejoice at my horse's eager, forward walk, his alert stance, his proud neck, his life under me. We canter up the hill above the airport to look at the ocean. We brush against the dry fans of pampas grass without him startling. "You are the dream of a dream come true," I tell him. I want to find Patti and Sarah and show off. I gulp down every stride like it's my last, precious mouthful of air. I love Mud Pony, and for once, I love myself too.

No words from Rolando as I turn to leave. On the envelope stuffed full with cash, I wrote this note:

Rolando mi amigo, Gracias por toda tu ayuda con mi caballo. He aprendido tanto de ti y de Napoleon.

Gracias por ser un maestro estupendo y ayudarme a poder montar mi caballo finalemente.

> *Un abrazo,*
> *Stephanie*

Day 45

I wash Mud Pony's blue cotton saddle blanket in our kitchen machine next to the stove. As it churns, I cook breakfast. I find several fine hairs from his summer coat in my scrambled eggs and rejoice.

Later that day, as Lottie and I ride together, he shies at a plastic bottle filled with water and cigarette butts at the gate of the big arena. I use my leg, asking him for snake trails while Lottie rides around us at a walk and canter. He veers toward Tika, leaning left with a hard slant.

Rolando's voice is less audible in my head today as we ride. Occasionally, I'll hear him say, "You have to work the reins." I question if I'm being unclear with Mud Pony, and if he needs more direction than I'm giving.

I want to find Patti and show her how independent we've become. I want some big-girl points to ease my doubt. And there she is, crouched over a broken solar panel next to an electric fence.

To her back, I say, "Hey Patti," keeping my voice low and no big deal. She turns around and flashes a wide, beautiful smile in surprise at seeing me atop Mud Pony. She tells me about her job, hand-raised ducklings, broken fence. For the first time ever, Mud Pony sighs underneath me, taking a deep breath.

Lottie and I trot next to the dahlias in the strawflower fields, and a blanket of multicolored pom-poms cheers us on. Both horses are occupied with all the stray objects in the field—water pipes, black plastic crates, rusting farm equipment. All these obstacles cheer for us, too, because when I ask he moves forward.

My friend Sarah has said I'm either brave or crazy to ride such a green horse in the flower fields. Last year she broke her kneecap coming off her young mare on a trail ride nearby—the X-ray image looked like a shattered sand dollar, and I remember the six weeks she spent on a couch, but I have a faith in myself now that I didn't have two months ago. "Now you can believe anything is possible," Rolando had said that first week.

"Things don't happen for millions of years in evolution's trajectory," Carter said at breakfast this morning, "and the creative process goes very slow. Then, the big stuff wrecks everything. Eruption and irruption. Destruction and creation. Revolutions and radical change. Volcanoes and earthquakes."

At the time I thought it was his second cup of coffee talking, but now I know.

Six years with my horse. Then all this.

Day 47

Riding on the ridge today I forget how to talk—language feels foreign, words seem strange, improbable. Is it necessary to spew a complex mix of vowels and consonants when all that is really needed is a jerk of the head or a nod? Long sentences are full of syntactical ornamentations that don't match the subtlety and variety of the coastal flora, the silence of the hawk, the scuttle of the lizard, the frozen stance of a deer. The pampas grass with its rattling, fingery stalks and drooping feather boas is perhaps the most outrageous statement on the trail. The narratives of nonnatives have taken over, and their seeds have spread like someone who talks too much. In contrast, we humans and horses conserve both words and phrases. The horses blow and snort only occasionally, and rarely will I offer a question or observation to Lottie. And if I launch into a lengthy explanation or rant, I suddenly get self-conscious, stop, and go quiet, interrupting the story in motion, which is really the Ride itself—its rhythms, the view of the ocean, the fog sweeping in, the cypress lining the streets of the town, the gullies and shaded canyons, the trails we can't find because they're overgrown with poison oak, the clop of horse feet on pavement, the passersby who nod and lift a hand in greeting, the dog walker who holds her dog's collar for us, the trot my horse does to keep up with Tika.

I used to wave to Rolando nearly every evening as I left the ranch. Now the trailer door is closed. He's not holding Manolito on the steps or watching him play on his toy tractor in the driveway. No men mounted on their horses or drinking beer near the round pen. It's as if they have all melted into the hills. But the horses get fed and boarders come and go. It's dark by seven thirty, but as I drive by, I spy a single light on inside Rolando's trailer but no one to wave to.

Day 49

Wildfires rage just thirty miles south in the Santa Cruz Mountains. Another fire burns to the east in the Sierras. As I drive to the ranch, a thick line of red hovers at the horizon, on the ocean's blue lip. A thicker, dusty gray layer floats above it.

Before riding out to the farmer's fields, I work Mud Pony in the sand arena, and he's stiff and heavy on his front end. He can bend around my leg when I press my calf to his ribs, but he has a hard time moving more than one step back or to the side. I ask him for the S-curves Roses suggested then ride to the gate. Our first one. He gets nervous when I lean over to unlatch it, perhaps distracted by my wobbly reach or its clank. I pet him. Walk away. Return. Pet him again. Lean over and shove it.

Dread arises in my gut as we walk through. Will he bolt? Will he forget I'm on his back and slam me into a tree? I brace against what I both imagine and know. A fall from horseback is like a sudden, sharp slap from a mother's hand. What once held you turns without warning. The ground, like that hand, always comes harder and faster than you think. Then, you lie there, waiting for your body to tell you how quickly it can reorganize. Should you get up and get back on? Hit that hard thing back? Sometimes you want to just curl up in the dirt and fall asleep.

These thoughts hover like the smoky air. I wave it away, ride forward, bury them.

After circling two irrigation ponds next to fields green with pumpkin leaves and leeks, we ride up the big hill south of the PG&E road. We haven't been here since another boarder got chased by yellow jackets last week and dumped by her thoroughbred. We keep an eye out for any stray bees or holes in the ground indicating a nest. It's so warm and still this evening, Lottie wears a tank top instead of her usual long sleeves. At the top of the hill, everything below, fields, highway, ocean, and clusters of houses, appears blurry and hazy.

Later, as I drive back up the coast, I see a group of officials and rescue workers at the cliff's edge with trucks, long ropes, and pulleys. One wears a bright yellow jacket with CORONER in black letters across the back. Carter tells me later he saw on the evening news how an empty car with the driver's door wide open was found parked next to the cliff. Someone sighted a body in the water below. When they finally pulled the dead man from the waves, his body was so disfigured by the fall, he wasn't recognizable.

Day 50

I exhale as Mud Pony finds an easy, nodding walk. No running up this hill. Just as Rolando taught me, I ask my horse for a slight bend of his neck, by pulsing one rein then the other. The trail narrows and becomes crumbly where a gopher has eaten the roots of the grass underneath and punctured the earth with its digging.

Today, Mud Pony and I rode out alone, calling to Lottie in the parking lot, where she prepared to mount Tika at her trailer, "Stay behind, but give us some distance, okay?"

They are soon behind us, moving purposefully in and out of sight. I ride with rhythm, ten feet in front then ten feet in front again, checking in to see if he's listening. We walk past the spot where Sarah fell. There's now a ditch to prevent dirt bikes from entering this section of trail. Up the hill, through the pines and pampas grass waving to us on the edge of the trail. Past the water tower, to the top of the hill above it, stop, turn around to take in the view of ocean, canyon, ridge, headlands, the nearby hills, the great blue bump of Montara Mountain, horse paddocks, and scattered houses. There's Lottie and Tika, trotting up the hill, halting and grinning.

"She got it! We were playing Spy 'n' Scout!"

I think we should go back. I'm tired and must get ready for our departure tomorrow, but I push through. Now he challenges me, rooting for the ground and wanting to cling to Tika even at a short distance. When we separate from her, he gets more troubled—his head comes up. But this is not unusual.

To Lottie, I suggest that we separate then meet up at the farmer's fields. She nods and takes the high road, disappearing over the hill above the ranch road. I flash on an object sitting in some knee-high weeds—maybe it's an old tire or a plastic box. And in this moment, I'm not riding ten feet in front of me like Roses says I should but looking at that object. And now so is he—leaping up and to the left, sighting it just after I do, surprised by it, and surprising me with his lurch, leap.

I don't move with him but continue the direction we were headed, over his right shoulder, hitting the dirt with my hip then helmet. I call to him, but he's running away, reins and stirrups flapping. Two seconds. That's all it took.

The fall isn't bad. I push myself to my feet, check in with my level of pain, and discover disappointment more than physical injury. I rally my bruised ego and walk in the direction he ran, calling his name.

"What happened?" a boarder asks as I reach the ranch gate.

"I got dumped and he ran off. Have you seen him?"

"Nope... no runaway came through. You okay?"

Another boarder approaches from the barn entrance, cell phone in hand. Diego found him and Lottie's got him next door. As I turn away, she murmurs, "Wow, I thought he looked pretty good. I wonder how you fix a horse who does that?"

Face burning, I can't help but echo what Harry once said at a clinic. "I have to understand what happened *before* what happened *happened...*"

"Huh?" she responds, but I've already turned away. I find Mud Pony and Lottie at the feed truck. Irritated, I take the reins and swing up and over. I push him to a fast walk to the spooky spot, and as soon as he sees the black plastic box, he surges in fear.

This time, however, I'm ready. I hang on, pulling him with one rein toward Tika, who's there at our side.

So what happened before what happened *happened?*

Six years ago, I was there when the rancheros separated him from the herd and chased him into Patti's trailer. He leaped into the new world of a pen, which he then didn't leave for months because we could barely touch him, let alone catch him. Whatever trouble he carried into that trailer from his first year, he carried when Napoleon rode him through that first bucking fit. He carried it when Rolando used the side reins to straighten him. He carried it every time I asked him to do something that was beyond what he could handle—being tied as I tightened his back cinch or straddling him in the arena with a stiff, board-like neck and scared, unblinking eyes. He carried it when he pushed through my hands and rooted for the ground. I prioritized starting him without making things better for him, for us. Not knowing *feel*, I made it worse.

"Whatever it was," Harry will say next week at the clinic, "at some point, this horse knew he was going to die."

· Five ·

Carter didn't go to school much past eighth grade, and at eighteen, he dropped out, finding jobs as a dishwasher, donut baker, gravedigger, bus driver, mechanic, auto body repairman, and gravel truck driver. He lived on a commune, fixed up Volkswagens, stacked bloody hides in a slaughterhouse, and drove long-haul semitrucks. He sold psilocybin to friends and then settled into city life, buying a warehouse, and running a small company that distributed adult magazines.

I first knew I wanted to be with Carter when I saw him pet his sister's pit bull. He was sprawled across the backseat of Jess's steel beast of a Buick with the dog in his arms, a black-and-white rescue that had chewed holes in the vintage vinyl.

After a lunch date, I invited him to sit in on a class I was taking in graduate school. My Poetics professor—an author, poet, and griot who also never had much to do with educational institutions—told tales of nineteenth-century England from fathoms-deep reading and study. He interwove myth, scholarship, and personal reflection on the long-lasting effects of the land enclosure acts, industrial revolutions, emergence of modern medicine, and with it—body snatchers.

"I never knew school could be like this," Carter told me after that class. "Everything he's saying makes so much sense." Soon after, he signed up to take the GED. "I'm going to college," he said with bashful triumph.

I soon discovered that Carter lived as comfortably in a city as he had in the redwood forest that had been his childhood playground. During long walks through our Mission neighborhood, we'd pause at donut shop storefronts to assess the display, fresh or day old, and he'd explain the multistep process for making apple fritters with layers of leftover dough, grease, and sugar. He'd revel in the variety of urban structures and spaces—Victorian houses and earthquake shacks, warehouses and factories, construction sites and boat docks, skyscrapers and weed-strewn empty lots. He showed me the places where he'd lived, each with its own story of roommates and relationships, nicknames, and rock bands. Every outing became an adventure as he led me through hidden alleys, and I took him swimming in the cold waters of San Francisco Bay. On my first swim from Alcatraz, we jumped off the boat next to the island at six in the morning and he paddled alongside on his surfboard, directing me against the current and through the gap in the seawall to a safe landing on the beach at Aquatic Park.

Having first arrived in the city to frequent the punk-rock scene, Carter loved hearing of my explorations when I'd first moved here. I was twenty-two and thrilled to escape my family and the East Coast. I'd also hoped things would work out with a boyfriend who'd been transferred west as a DEA agent but was forever "on assignment" (code for surveillance). I told Carter of exploring my new home on bicycle, bus, train, and ferry until the early hours of the morning. On one of those trips, I was the only passenger on a late-night bus and sat behind the driver, who asked me if I wanted to get a cup of coffee. She pulled into a bus stop on one of the Avenues, set the brake, and chatted as we walked into Zim's. We hovered over the pie case and a server brought us two steaming cups.

Over breakfast at that same Zim's, I told Carter how, after finishing our coffee, the driver detoured to drop me in front of the house where I lived in the Avenues. Carter described these cookie-cutter houses as "birthday cakes," an apt description, as they had been built atop sand dunes and shifting plates, then painted with bright pastels. I lived in a basement apartment, and the morning after that bus ride, my first earthquake knocked the walls out of square. I sat up terrified in bed as the layer-cake walls shifted and wobbled and the building roared. If I'd been on the roof, I would have ridden that house like a rocking horse.

○

As Patti unhitches her trailer and drives off, I now wish I could hold onto Carter for comfort, but I'm alone with my apprehension. I've got everything Mud Pony and I need for a week at Bible Horsemanship camp—hay, grain, tack, water bucket, camping equipment. The troupe of strangers (our camp hosts) bang open the porch door of the ranch house and spill out into the warm September afternoon with long strides and welcoming smiles. They wear Wrangler jeans, leather belts stamped with silver crosses, and T-shirts patterned with Bible quotes and cowboys on horseback. My sore right hip reminds me why I'm here: I want Harry to ride my horse.

A year ago, when I saw the advertisement on Harry's website, I'd spoken to Carol, the ranch owner, and asked if a "nonbeliever" could participate. She nearly scoffed at my query. "Of course! Everyone is welcome to join our Bible study, and we're not evangelists. Our focus is not conversion."

Relieved, I pushed away my misgivings about being proselytized to—I'd had enough of that as a kid. However, now I wish I had pressed Carol to tell me more about the "focus."

At the clinics I'd previously attended, including one at his ranch in Arizona, Harry struck me as a sincere yet private person, someone who lived his faith but didn't share the details with students. I'd researched bringing my horse to his ranch, but without my own truck and trailer to haul us across two states, the shipping costs turned out to be more than I could afford. And Harry's clinics, Bible study or no Bible study, fill up fast—he limits them to six participants. Rolando hadn't been in the picture when I sent my deposit, but even when he was, it didn't matter—I still longed for the benefit of Harry's teaching.

The sound of his Kansas twang and unaffected guffaw from inside the house is reassuring. With Harry here, I anticipate stories and jokes, soulful conversations with other students about what's happening on the inside of our horses, and a week of sinking into my study of *feel*.

The troupe of strangers (our camp hosts) are welcoming and gracious. They tell me which pipe corral to lead Mud Pony to and where I can fill his water bucket. They help pitch my brand-new tent, and as if on cue for an impromptu icebreaker, the tent collapses even after following the instructions. We joke about how many ranch hands it takes to set up a human's tent at a horse camp. All the while I'm eyeing the Bible quotes on their T-shirts.

I end up not skipping the Bible part. All participants and auditors sleep in a line of tents near the paddocks, tucked in close to one another and under the shade of five magnificent oak trees; we rotate in and out of the ranch house shower and sit at picnic tables to eat meals prepared by a furry-faced camp cook. The daily schedule includes two hours of Bible study—one session after breakfast and one after dinner. In between, there are six hours plus of one-on-one instruction with our horses. Our minister and Bible study leader for the week, Jimmy, is the same height as I am and younger. Stocky, with light-blue eyes, tanned skin, a full mustache, and dark waves of salt-and-pepper hair, Jimmy met Harry years ago on the rodeo circuit. They worked together as rodeo clowns, and I can see them paired in the arena as a cowboy version of Abbott and Costello in reverse—the tall, lanky goofball and the short, stout straight man.

Fortunately, the circle of the round pen—not Bible study—is our focus for the week. Growing up, I rode horses at show barns on the East Coast in large, rectangular arenas with jumps or dressage lettering. But out West, all clinicians who practice what they call Natural Horsemanship commit to a foundation that begins on the ground in the circular, enclosed space of the round pen, typically thirty meters in diameter. Its lack of corners fosters a practical and safe advantage: there's plenty of room for a horse to run around if it needs to—or for the rider to work on the ground without getting stepped on.

Natural Horsemanship practitioners begin their work with a green horse by practicing the seemingly magical ritual of join-up. This mimics what horses naturally do in a herd, where the more dominant personalities push around the more submissive ones. Within minutes or hours, each horse establishes or accepts its position. In the round pen, the human embodies the energy and presence of the dominant horse and becomes the leader. Standing in the center, she gets the horse's attention with a flag or rope halter and then directs her body energy (via the flag or rope) at the hind end of the horse, getting it to move forward and circle around her.

There are infinite variations of this dance, but once the horse moves on the edge of the circle, the human mimics what horses do in their herd—she steps in front of its shoulder and the horse stops, whirls, and walks/trots in the opposite direction. After a few more circles or changes, the horse may lick or chew and put its head to the ground, signaling a readiness to follow its new leader. The human can then ease the pressure and the horse will naturally stop, be drawn to the human, and follow her around like a large, submissive dog off its leash. This is the practice Patti and I repeated with Mud Pony in the first months of our work together—a calmer or more domesticated horse would have quickly accepted our leadership, but we had to go slow with him and break it down into small and smaller steps as we increased the pressure—leading him, tying him, flapping the intrusion of a flag over his body, asking him to relinquish a foot to be cleaned or his back to be saddled.

Some Natural Horsemanship clinicians use the round pen to showcase their talent or skills, but during his clinics, Harry steps aside and allows the round pen to become the classroom. At the center is not the clinician (Harry), but the horse (teacher) and the human (student). Each session begins with a horse at liberty and the rider on the ground, so Harry can see the horse move unencumbered and evaluate how the human might be helping or hindering its movement. Every horse-human pairing has its unique challenges to work through, and sometimes Harry will grumble but then lumber inside to demonstrate or model. This week, he will surely want to see me work Mud Pony in this way, but I'm hoping we won't have to spend too much time on the ground so we can get to the riding.

The round pen can be a place of frustration and rejection, revelation and joy. Sometimes it's a vortex toward which the seemingly opposed wills of horse and human swirl in confusion. I've experienced and observed both hubris and humility in myself and other students during our attempts to ask the horse for softness or imitate a so-called horse whisperer's way of working. I once worked a young mule at Harry's Arizona ranch that completely ignored my efforts to get his attention, and I couldn't see why. Upset, I slapped my thigh to get its attention, wanting it to follow me but following it instead. At one point, the mule kicked out at me.

Harry shook his head and the word *pitiful* escaped his lips. "What's the difference between outlaws and in-laws?" he asked. "Outlaws are always wanted!"

Hee-haw. This mule was clearly treating me like an in-law. Harry's cue:

Lighten up.

At another clinic, after a participant reached an impasse with her troubled horse (everyone watching outside the pen had their game faces on), he asked the person sitting next to him, "What do a hurricane in Texas, a tornado in Kansas, and a redneck couple in divorce court have in common?" Somehow, somewhere, someone is going to lose a trailer!" Our laughter eased the tense expectations that had inadvertently gotten pointed at the horse.

Later that day, a student asked, "If you were a horse, Harry, what kind of horse would you be?"

Harry took a long time to answer with a no-shit serious tone: "I'd be a horse in an Alpo can, because I'd kick and bite and fight back at all these humans, and then they'd shoot me and I'd be dog meat."

A long silence after—it emphasized his deep commitment to learn from our horses and shift our thinking to better understand *their* point of view.

Here's the best way to explain: the round pen can suddenly seem like a ditch or a canyon you've fallen into. You get disoriented, as if you've lost your way, but that's just because your perspective has shifted far from your own narrow view to something you couldn't see before. Of course, all this depends on how deeply you're willing to dive in and to look at yourself. The good news is this: as your guide, Harry's got lots of *space* inside. He allows room for waiting, watching, joking, listening, talking, holding, and directing while holding the mirror up so you can see how the horse's body reflects your own physical or emotional state.

When Harry gets in there and works with your horse, it seems like magic, and then when he doesn't rescue you by doing it *for* you, you wonder if it'll ever work out. With encouragement and guidance, he makes room for you to figure out how to be in this new space inside yourself. You begin to trust that it *will* work out.

By its very nature, much of this is hard to see (and Harry doesn't allow any video in his clinics for replays—too intrusive or too easily misinterpreted by someone who isn't there). The space of the round pen at Harry's clinic can be both main stage and therapy office.

But Harry can get cranky too. He expects a high standard of behavior and responsiveness from everyone, horse and human. Once, after he'd walked me through a session where I'd worked a fearful, recently injured horse, he scolded me for zoning out. The gelding had begun to fret and weave after we'd exited the round pen. *Of course, it would be anxious, it was an anxious horse to begin with. Plus, my lesson was over. So why was Harry getting on my case?*

"You just left him there," he snapped. "You may as well not even worked with him!"

I gulped. Harry was asking me to be present in real time—to understand what I did mattered—in each moment, inside and out—not just to him or me—but to the horse. And most importantly, he believed the horse could, in fact, change. Just because it had been anxious before didn't mean it had to remain anxious on my watch or anyone else's.

Just about every equine that comes to one of his clinics has trouble in them from humans, even if it's not obvious to the owner. I've watched Harry ride horses and help them find a place of release so deep, the body frees up, the tail unclamps from the rear, and bright, unworried life arises. They let go at the walk and swing with ease and relaxation. One time, I was so moved by this transformation, I wept silently by the side of the round pen and wished I, too, could be helped like that horse.

Day 1

After pancakes for breakfast, we gather at the back porch of the house to sit in a circle with pads, pens, and Bibles, some of which are marked with numerous colored tabs. Tents and trailers are lined up behind us; horses in portable paddocks gather in the shade, eat hay, and whisk flies away with their tails in the morning sun. My Bible was a gift from my father for my college graduation. He bound it for me with thick scraps of leather and wrote a short, formal dedication on the inside cover. The pages are tissue-thin, the spine uncracked. I have opened it twice in the past ten years to find the source of a biblical allusion for my students in a novel we're reading.

Jimmy asks us to open to Proverbs 1:2: "The fear of the Lord is the beginning of wisdom." He and Harry start with an antiphon while I do my own version inside my head. I concede the part fear played in my getting dumped two days ago when my horse leaped at that half-buried box on the ground.

"The main point of organized horsemanship," Harry calls, "is to protect the human from the direct essence of the horse."

"The main point of organized religion," Jimmy responds, "is to protect the human from the direct experience of God."

"What are horses saying?" poses Harry. "'Humans are nothing but a bunch of amateurs at being horses'... All the folks out there who hang out a shingle and who claim to be like Tom Dorrance... Most of us do such a sorry job at having a relationship with the horse."

"In the same way," Jimmy answers, "we are amateurs at being Christ-like. But unlike the horse, we are born with a sin nature."

"We have a view of the valley from the hill," continues Harry, "but we can see the valley only because we're on the hill. To see from the horse's point of view, you have to shift where you stand."

"Proverbs," asserts Jimmy, "is here to help us understand the ways of the wise. If you get rid of truth, you have no standard, no place to stand, no way to look. Sometimes I wondered, when my mother was whupping me, why she was doing it, but now I know the only mistake she ever made was *not* to set the standard higher, not to whup me enough... when she was whupping me, it was not *to* me, but *for* me."

"But maybe your mother whupping you, like making the feet of the horse come to you, violates free will?" queries Harry. "We want to draw their minds and have them come to us willingly."

"Man has always tried to put God in a box," Jimmy continues. "Horse-manship in a box equals submission and conformity, not free will and understanding."

Members of the circle nod their heads.

"Amen to that," someone says.

Later that morning we gather at the round pen in front of the house. A few auditors sit under a nearby tree for the shade; other students warm themselves in the sun; everyone has notebooks and pens. Harry sets up his portable speaker system, attaches a microphone to his collar, then sits in his director's chair at the rail. A big complainer about any weather that brings temperatures lower than 65 degrees, he chooses direct sunlight. He wears Wrangler jeans and jacket, leather chaps, sunglasses, and a cowboy hat.

It's an idyllic scene: the sky buzzes as an airplane hovers above a landing strip; ancient oak trees dot the dry, yellow grass of the foothills, which rise in the east to the high granite crest of the Sierra; the Old Salt Dam Road runs flat and straight in the near distance through the valley; enormous white puffballs travel across the blue like crumpled piles of laundry just out of the dryer. Seems I could reach up and bat one like a beach ball.

I'm the second rider, after the first has finished working a lanky Tennessee Walker on the ground. I walk Mud Pony into the round pen with his saddle on then remove his halter. He circles me at liberty and I get his attention in the center with the flag and then let up the pressure as he stops and turns in. I gather him to me, put his halter on, and ask him to bend in the middle of the circle as I drive him around. Harry says nothing. *Good sign. I must be doing something right.* Mud Pony walks next to me for a few more laps; I rest one hand on the saddle and notice how his whole body is counterbent, leaning away from me at a slant. *Okay, nothing unusual.* Harry yawns and looks out at the hills. "Is this the horse everyone's been warning me about? He seems pretty good to me." Not even a grunt in response. Everyone's sleepy and sugar crashed after pancakes.

Groundwork completed, I'm ready to mount.

My heart swells as I gather up the double reins in my left hand, put my right hand on the saddle's cantle, place my foot in the stirrup, lift myself up, and swing my leg over. I'm amazed how easy it all seems after all the years of yearning and the significant planning and effort to get here.

Without warning, Mud Pony leaps. I've got one foot in that left stirrup—and I grab his head with the reins but get no purchase—he runs through the bit like a rogue wave through a quiet cove—JOLT then CLANK!

"GET OFF! GET OFF!" Harry yells, leaping from his chair and awakening everyone, words amplified by the speaker. Time slows to nothing. Afterward, I realize that sound was my back caroming off the rail.

Somehow, I land on my feet as my horse runs to the other side of the round pen.

"Are you okay?" Harry asks, now standing at the gate. I nod, shaking. *I thought I knew my horse. I thought I knew what I was doing.* I want to cry but instead grab my horse by the reins and squeak, "I need someone to hold him while I get back on."

"I don't think you should get on." He turns off his mic, takes off the headset, opens the gate and enters, looking quizzically at me and Mud Pony, who has shape-shifted into a tight, troubled, heavy-breathing being, holding a wooden stance with his hind legs splayed out as if to say, "Please, don't hurt me."

"What happened?" Harry wonders aloud. The words that fall out of my mouth feel like someone else's.

"I think it's being in a new place... he got scared... and I wasn't there for him... plus my leg surprised him."

Harry pokes him in the girth with the flag and Mud Pony jumps, nearly bursting out of his skin.

Wallowing in disappointment, I can't listen to Harry while he works with my horse to figure out what's going on. *Maybe he couldn't read him either?*

I remember nothing else from the lesson.

I later lie in my tent, sleepless and slipping in and out of despair and resolve, confusion and false bravado. My fear of failure, of not being able to ride Mud Pony, gushes from some fissure. But are these feelings about the present or the past? And underneath this swirl, there's something else—a great, hot flush. I'm surprised to find a thick layer of shame and self-blame—*for my failure, for my despair.* And deeper still, that voice again, the one that says *it's your fault.*

I don't want to admit it, but after this latest crash, I can no longer deny the truth: the way my horse is on his outside is the way I often feel on my inside—anxious and fearful, sometimes desperate and trapped. Only he's more honest about it.

Failure Road could have been the name of the street I grew up on in my suburban neighborhood, for the feeling I internalized was often one of disappointing my mother. *Did she even like me? Want me?* I had been cute as a baby, but then I'd heard her say she liked kittens, not cats.

As the middle child of seven children, I kept a low profile amid the daily battles and arguments, both verbal and physical. I tried to gain approval by helping with household chores, but it was never enough to get the connection or attention from her I so longed for. Instead, she seemed to favor my five brothers and expressed her disapproval through sharp criticism or stony silence, which I thought was my fault. I felt too ashamed to invite Jacquie, Isabel, or any school friends to play. I was like a stranger in our house.

To stomach what felt like rejection, I disappeared into books and horse imaginings. At the same time, I still longed for contact, and I hid in closets or the onion tub in the garage to see if anyone would notice I was missing. Sometimes I practiced being mute, communicating with only a notepad.

In my twenties, as a beginning classroom teacher, I saw a therapist for anxiety and insomnia. As we uncovered the triggers, I realized that I couldn't recall anyone in my family ever having been curious or interested enough to ask in a genuine way how I was doing. *Did I give them no hints or reasons to ask? Did I ever share with anyone how I felt?* Each of the nine members in our family pod seemed to be spinning on separate planets at great distances from one another, though we ate dinner together every night, held hands as we said grace, watched TV, played sports, went to church and school. Aside from my father dutifully kissing my mother on the cheek when he got home from work, I never witnessed genuine warmth or physical affection between my parents.

Luckily, they were responsive in other ways. I remember my mother putting her hand on my forehead when I was sick; at those times, she expressed concern and blessed me by making the sign of the cross. My father once sat at the side of my bed at night when I feared skeletons and ghosts emerging from the closet. Another time, I vomited in the back of our station wagon during a camping trip, and he cleaned it up without a word.

I know now that my parents were struggling with the pressures of raising seven kids and with their relationship. But instead of finding meaningful connection within our immediate family, my mother turned to religion for comfort, and she thrust that upon us as moral obligation. My father followed.

It wasn't until I was in my thirties that I remembered my first panic attack. It happened in second grade toward the end of the school day. I had once or twice missed the bus, and my mother yelled at me because she had gone out of her way to pick me up. I was so terrified it would happen again, I conceived the strategy of locking eyes with my last-period teacher as the minute hand crept toward 3:00. This was so I could signal her to look at the clock and release us to the waiting buses.

What did I want more than anything? *To be seen, comforted, carried.* Instead, I froze, read my mother's face, followed her moves. When she grimaced, I felt my chest cave and my gut hollow. I remember listening for the timbre of her voice or her tread on the stairs to see if I should hide. *Was her mood light or dark? Should I keep silent or approach?* When she gave it, softness was the strangest thing.

Day 2

Six a.m.: the hills in the east a warm orange. I walk with Mud Pony and follow a mile-long driveway through a wrought iron gate fashioned into the image of a cowboy driving a herd of horses. I'm tired after tossing in my sleeping bag most of the night, but getting up and moving around with my horse soothes me. I choose the path next to the road, avoiding the sharp rocks on the worn cement. He walks next to me as if yesterday's fit never happened.

At the road's edge and in the open spaces between, star-shaped yellow blooms on tall, brown stalks. Tarweed, Carol called it yesterday at breakfast: "I spend hours rubbing that sticky mess off their faces."

What awaits us today in the round pen? Will Harry say he needs to be restarted? How many chances at starting a horse do you get? Yesterday, I overheard one of the clinic participants say to another in a low voice, "She's in denial. That horse is dangerous. She's going to get hurt."

I'm also mulling over something Harry said during yesterday's afternoon sessions to another rider at the round pen rail: "Anytime you leave a horse mentally confused, he feels abused." *Is this how I've left Mud Pony, again and again? And on a bad teaching day, have I left my students feeling like this too?*

As we gather for Bible study in our circle, Harry mentions the "relaxation that comes through voluntary submission and not conformity." I listen and copy down what Jimmy reads from Matthew (15:8), "These people honor me with their lips, but their hearts are far from it."

A couple of hours later, I enter the round pen with Mud Pony. No saddle, for there's no expectation of riding today. I remove the halter and he walks in the opposite direction, pausing to watch a horse in an adjoining paddock.

"Not much interest in Stephanie," observes Erica, a young trainer who has brought her client's horse to the clinic.

"I'd whack the ground," says Harry, but I'm too late. Mud Pony has already decided to turn in. He comes toward me into the center of the pen for a second then leaves on his own. I try again, slapping the ground with the rope halter. Again, he ignores me. Another whack. Now he turns, walks to me, and crowds me with his head held high, looking out at the hills.

"I saw conformity there," says Harry. "He walked to her because he was supposed to, and when he did, he walked over and into her space. His feet were there, but his mind and heart were gone."

I motion my horse away with my arm and he takes another walk, then returns, this time facing me.

"Pet him, pet him," says Harry, but Mud Pony leaves, turning away before I can offer my hand. "He may not feel the best with her... try asking again." He returns. "Good, now pet him, but *leave before he does.*"

I do, and this time, he follows. I'm amazed at the difference I sense from even a few moments ago. There's softness and he's more *there.*

"Pet him," calls Harry. "But again, leave before he does." Again, he follows. "Yeah, that feels better to him. Now walk beside him and pet on him... now walk off, come in on the other side, there you go."

Mud Pony stands with me and it's as if we were having *our first real conversation,* one with the give and take of listening, talking, responding—and I can tell that he wants to be near me because I'm not forcing him to be there with the rope halter.

How many cues we attend to in a single exchange with another being without even thinking! Some eye contact here and there, the positioning of the body at a diagonal to the listener, not pulled or turned away, a slight leaning in to them. And in a classroom full of teenagers—how much is happening between and among us...

Harry shifts in his director's chair at the rail. Everyone seems pensive. "See how it's easy for us to make things difficult for him, but much harder to make the right thing easy? You can't *make* a thought come into him just by being firm, but if you can discourage the thought he already has, there's room for others to come in... and pretty soon he'll think that new thought is *his* thought."

I keep petting him, stopping now and then, and just stand there, but I'm *with* him as I do so.

Harry continues, "A fly can make a horse's life difficult, but rarely does it *trouble* him. We forget how little we need to do to communicate with our horses, and we drill them and work them in the effort to make the wrong thing difficult. But then they end up troubled. When we go and offer what's easy, they can't find the easy part because they're carrying all that trouble. That's where the confusion is coming in."

I think I know what he means. I used to set a boot bag of potatoes on him and push them off the other side. To him, this must have felt something like a child banging on a table or drum to see how big a sound it might make. Mud Pony's probably still carrying all that trouble, but for now he's with me, bobbing his head from the flies in the late-morning sun.

"So now," says Harry, "see how little you can do to get him to walk off and then bring him back."

I barely move my hand as I direct my energy at his hind end, pointing with only my index finger. He moves off.

"I like it," says Harry. Mud Pony returns, crowds me, then moves past. "Now he's making plans to go somewhere if he needs to."

How does Harry know this? My horse seems present to me. Maybe I'm not as much in the conversation as I thought. I lift my hand, and before it's even at my chest, he turns away and leaves, confirming Harry's observation.

"Now see if you can help him find his way back..." Harry calls, and I quiet myself and step back. Mud Pony turns in from the far side and comes to me, but this time he doesn't crowd my space. "You're such a good child," croons Harry. "Now if he walks off, walk next to him. Do no more than a half lap with him—just enough to direct him, and then back off. Yes, yes, keep him moving even when you back off."

I go with him, but it's not long before Mud Pony decides to go in a different direction, and Harry tells me to draw him back.

Erica, watching from the outside, asks my own unvoiced question, "Harry, why wouldn't you walk next to this horse all the way around the pen?"

"He's fleeing," answers Harry. "But he needs to experiment with this. He's not even going around the pen but going all over the place. If she steps in there and continually directs him, she's going to block the possibility of any new, more willing thought or feeling in him." A small airplane interrupts with its buzz, crossing the sky just above us. "Just because something's not going to work out right now doesn't mean he's in trouble. He needs to get this sorted out on his own."

How does Harry know when to back off and give him the space to figure it out?

How does he know Mud Pony will come back? Maybe it's the same as when I ask students a question and make myself count to ten in silence, waiting for them to process and think about it on their own? I've learned this is a tried-and-true technique that gives them the space to think for themselves.

When I stop and Mud Pony turns in, his feet land more softly. I draw him to me by backing into the center. He enters my space, but almost on top of me.

Harry comments, "He's crowding her, but if she does too much about it, he may leave, so just wait a bit on that."

Again, the wait time after a question. How long should it be, and how often do I need to do this?

I pet him and Harry again directs me to ask him to leave, but this time, "very softly." Sure enough, he doesn't turn the other way or get confused; he comes to me when I walk with him only a quarter lap before stepping back.

"Yep. Not quite the crowding this time," Harry states. "That's even without working on it because we *have* been working on it the whole time. Sometimes it troubles them more to make a big to-do about it... we often don't wait long enough to see what they were going to do." I keep petting him. Harry reports on the shift in Mud Pony's expression. "Ah, did you feel that? Now he's anticipating about leaving. If every time you pet him two strokes and send him, he will anticipate it."

As if Mud Pony were a comic-strip character, we see the thought bubble over his head!

Harry has observed something I didn't see until he pointed it out—an imperceptible shift, a slight raising of the head, rigidity. Mud Pony's gaze was focused not outside me but *inside himself*, as if he were waiting for something to happen, perhaps something to attack. *Did he smell or hear something I couldn't?* Confirming this, my horse walks away. I comment to Harry how every time he's left me, he's consistently turned right.

"Good observation, so next time, have your left hand up to block that thought of going right." I do, and when I put my hand up, he reacts with a raised head and worried look. "See, his anxiety came up there," Harry calls. "Pet beside him on his right. He's trying to protect himself there. These are the tiny yet very important things. We all get so focused on getting performance out of their feet. But we need them to not be troubled."

We've gotten this as good as we can for now, so I catch him up with the rope halter and lead him to where the blue saddle blanket hangs on the round pen rail. Strangely, my horse appears diminished, almost foal-size. I follow Harry's step-by-step instructions, rubbing him with the blanket, laying it across him cleanly, then walking off—all the while the line from the rope halter is gently draped across my left arm, but with no pressure or direction to his head. It's there just in case I need to draw him back immediately.

In reaction to my ministrations, Mud Pony puffs up and snorts, but the reaction is noticeably less than before. I exhale in relief.

"We want him feeling good enough that when we get to the spot that troubles him, he'll have the confidence to deal with it."

I wish Harry could tell me how I'm going to explain that to Rolando or anyone at my ranch when we return home. *Roses or Patti would see this, but who else?*

Now it's time for the saddle. He's still loosely tethered to me by the rope yet I'm able to rest the cantle on my right hip and approach. It's an effort to attend to both sides, switching arms and hips, throwing it on, off, then on again, and I break into a sweat. Each time I swing it over onto his back, his head rises. When I take it off, his head lowers. Harry says nothing. "Now put the cinch on him and bother him a bit. It doesn't matter which side you saddle him on." I unroll the cinch, pull it through, and tighten it slightly. He tenses.

"Ask him forward a step or two," calls Harry, "without tightening it." The movement seems to help Mud Pony release a tiny bit, and I gradually tighten it, walking him in between the adjustments. *If I had known this much a year ago, maybe we could have avoided that awful, body-wrenching pullback at the tie post.*

I then direct him on a circle around me with my left arm pointing and my right arm driving. Harry observes, "He's bending away from you to the outside instead of correctly bending toward you to the inside." *This must be meaningful, but how much can I even expect from him? And he often bent the wrong way when I rode him with Rolando.*

"I would probably work that pretty hard," continues Harry, "so get him farther from you and see if you can keep the head turned in... good... now see if you can get more speed and keep the bend without him getting boardlike."

Mud Pony does fine at the walk, but as soon as he increases in speed, he bends his head to the outside, away from me. "Give him more rope," says Harry. "This is a good goal for you—to not have him pull away from you at the trot like he's gotta go somewhere else. See, this horse can't separate 'flee' from 'go.' Soon as he goes to hurry, his mind goes outside the circle to be somewhere else. By the way he's breathing, you can tell he's worried… these are spots that have so much meaning to the horse and so little meaning to the human. And those spots don't seem like anything until you put your foot in the stirrup."

Harry gets up out of his chair, picks up the flag, enters the round pen. He moves the flag around my horse's back, legs, and shoulder. Mud Pony reacts with worry, tension, defense, a raised head. Harry stops and looks at me. "What do you know about whatever has scared him?" Of course, he means not just yesterday or today.

I tell him all I know: the sudden death of his mother when he was three months and still nursing and no handling his first year. The only humans he experienced during that time were cowboys who roped him and laid him down in pasture to be castrated without anesthesia (a standard practice with livestock).

Then a long pause as we all look at my horse, who exhibits a prickly tension through his body like a crackling electric wire. "Whatever it was," Harry says, shaking his head, "at some point, this horse knew he was going to die."

This statement wrenches my gut. No comments from the group.

Harry turns to me, "See I'd like to bring this flag out after twenty minutes and have him get like he was… then I'd be more confident about getting back on him."

So there it is. Harry's not going to allow me to get back on him until we've gotten the change that signals more understanding and willingness, not just the conformity we've been talking about in Bible study. I tell him how Rolando, Napoleon, and I rode him every day for a month and a half. "Well, just because you get some rides on him doesn't mean the understanding is there."

"So what happened when he leaped on trail and dumped me last weekend? Why didn't that happen before?" As the question leaves my mouth, I know I can answer it myself: *It did happen before that incident—and many* times, too, over those forty-nine days. He fled a bunch of times, but we were able to ride it, since we always had the support of another horse at his side. Napoleon and Rolando could stay on even when he fled because of their riding abilities. All this helped Mud Pony on trails and in the arena, but the understanding that comes with willingness wasn't there. He conformed to Rolando's wishes as did I, and I mistook his conformity for willingness and understanding. I'm suddenly deflated, as if everything we did were a fake, a ruse, a trick.

I've got more questions, but Harry's already launched into a story to illustrate the reason my horse leaped and dumped me twice in the past week, and it wasn't because of being in a strange place or glimpsing the half-buried box on the ground.

"You're all alone in your house at night," he says, turning to the group, "and suddenly all the lights go out, and you get concerned when you look out the window and no one else in your neighborhood has the same problem—their lights are all on. Then your heart begins to race when the phone rings, and you pick it up, and there's all this heavy breathing on the other line. Your heart races even faster. You decide to make your way to the fuse box down the basement stairs, but on the way there, something grabs your leg and you panic and fall down the basement stairs. Now it was your playful cat that grabbed your leg, but was it the cat's fault that you panicked and fell, or was it everything that came before that made you panic?"

I know the story of what happened before what happened *happened*—my horse was fleeing with his mind, if not his body—for all the days we rode him, but I just couldn't see it... then it all built up in him and when he got close to the edge, he fell over and took me with him.

"You want to get some of these spots cleared up so that he doesn't wish he could be gone," Harry says, ending the session. "Don't miss these many little things... Yep..." he nods, turning to Erica, who sits next to him in a lawn chair with her notebook still open. "Guess what I hope they put on my gravestone?"

She raises an eyebrow, "Here lies a stubborn old man?"

Harry snorts, "Why no, I hope they put 'He was picky' on my gravestone." He adjusts the microphone and turns to the group. "See, I'm going to be particular but not demanding with a horse. I'm going to have a standard of how these things are going to be between us because I want the very best he has to offer. When I ask for something here, even the tiniest thing, I mean it. You got that, Erica? Gee whiz, stubborn old man, thanks a lot, girl."

I walk away from the round pen with Mud Pony, my brain in a tumble. *What is sinking into me or what am I sinking into? What do I have to stand on?* It's as if I were in a dream where I'm falling off him, but I keep falling, never hitting the ground. I saw him feel better for a short while today—can I trust enough to find this again?

After returning Mud Pony to his corral, I stare at the morning's cold, leftover pancakes in the camp kitchen. I'm alone except for Laura, an auditor who also has a troubled horse.

"Don't give up," she says. "Sometimes when you're making progress, those darker places come up big. What I've learned from Harry is not to leave my horse in trouble. If I get into something I don't know how to get out of, I wait for the support I need."

I'm grateful for her encouragement but wonder about the last two months—it had felt so right. *And what if the help he needs isn't available?* "If you ever work through this with him, you'll have an amazing companion," Laura says.

But how can I know if he's really with me? How can I tell when he's not just conforming, but understanding? *Wasn't Rolando saying the same thing when he placed his hand over his heart and said that's where I should keep him?*

Day 3

Roused in my tent by the rustlings of other campers, I snuggle deep inside my sleeping bag for a few more moments, grateful I don't have to get up for work. Some mornings before school, I drive in darkness to a city pool, its chlorine fumes not strong enough to overpower the stench from the wastewater treatment plant nearby. The team arrives suited but must wait poolside until Coach gets on deck. Men in Speedo suits jump up and down while women cross their chests and rub their arms. At his signal, we slip in, the water cold and foreign, but soon, after I've been commanded to chop lap after lap, I wear it like a shiny, wet, magical cloak.

Tingling and red-faced, with goggle imprints around my eyes, I arrive at school and collect my mail in the main office. Sleepy or grumbling teens wait outside my classroom. I welcome them inside. These are my best days, the ones when I can do what Harry talked about yesterday—pay attention to the details that mean so much. Energized by the swim, my brain moves over the text and through the lesson like a seal or porpoise playing in a set of waves. I lead a whole-class discussion and wait ten seconds after I pose a question. I check for understanding and challenge them to dive deep.

All the clinic participants, both riders and auditors, are at the edges of their seats, leaning in to the circle of the round pen to see if there will be a change in Mud Pony. Rotating through yesterday's exercise (move him at liberty, draw him to me, leave before he does), I'm amazed how he no longer crowds me. Others observe he's also not making plans to leave. I ignore how the other riders have moved on from groundwork and are now receiving mounted instruction.

I catch him up, tighten the rope halter, and move him on the circle with one arm directing, one arm driving, the line there to guide him. *Here we are. On the ground. Together.*

As I fix the saddle into place, smooth the blanket, and pull up the cinch, his expression changes. Big worry. Ears sweep backward. He wants to leave.

"Just walk with him a bit. Go slow... and gentle," Harry heeds.

As we move together, Mud Pony's tension lessens, but I notice just like yesterday how he tries to keep me on his right side and away from his left (where he knows I mount from). Tightening the cinch one hole at a time and taking a few steps with him after each adjustment, I then pick up the flag, which has been leaning on the outside of the rail, but I don't rub it on him without thinking. Instead, I tap the end with my hand. He jumps sideways.

"What happened?" Erica calls from the fence.

"She bumped his stirrup," Harry responds.

"Oops," I say, "that's right where my toe goes."

"Try to do just enough to get his feet moving by touching him at the cinch behind his elbows," Harry calls out. "How he moves tells you a lot about how he feels."

I lead him toward the center to give him plenty of room and touch him with the flag at his shoulder, then at the saddle horn. The line remains draped across my left arm as I pet his face with the flag and notice his belly skin stretched drum-tight. He hasn't yet released a visible breath by sighing or sneezing. *Maybe he's learning to be with me, breathing and releasing his fear. These must become one and the same if we are to be safe together.*

Harry directs four clinic participants to get up and enter the round pen, assigning each an umbrella, flag, or chair. They blink into the sun, awaiting instructions and holding their objects uncomfortably at arm's length.

"Now," he directs from his chair, "set Mud Pony loose. All four of you, go to different corners of the pen. Now, walk counterclockwise... okay, keep walking."

I take off the rope halter. He's concerned about the increased activity in the round pen, but instead of fleeing, he chooses to walk *toward* me, even though I'm holding a flag. *Maybe he feels safe—with me?!*

"Do ya think he knows who his mother is?" chortles Erica.

"Pet him there," says Harry. "On his shoulder. Very good. Now walk toward the middle. Everyone else keep walking and give him plenty of room."

He follows, again at liberty. I'm amazed at how he stays with me. "Now pet him there with your flag... there you go," says Harry. "Very good. Now put the rope halter on."

I tighten the rope against his cheek just behind his left eye and then gather up the lead line.

"Now you four," Harry says, motioning to the participants with their props, "come out from the rail a good ten to twelve feet." Harry directs me to take Mud Pony for a hike and weave in and out of where they stand. Then, he tells them to walk as he and I continue to weave.

"Now stand in the middle as each person approaches with their object. I want you all to walk up to him with confidence," says Harry, "and expect him to be able to handle it."

Someone pets his shoulder with a flag.

"Keep touching him," says Harry. "Laura, you come in with the other flag and pet him too, but stay away from his front in case he moves forward." Now two flags move in sync on each shoulder.

"In unison," Harry directs, "go back and pet his hips with both flags... good... come back to his shoulder... both of you back away... good... pause for a moment... now come back in and see if you can arrive at the same time at his shoulders... Erica, go in front with the chair. Close it up... see if you can walk up and pet his face... now the umbrella."

Four people with flags, a chair, and an umbrella surround Mud Pony as if they were guests at a pony-petting party! He's not being pushed around, manhandled, or asked to do something he can't manage.

Harry tips his chair back. I can't see his eyes through the dark lenses of his Ray Bans, but I know he's pleased. "If he was getting a glazed-over look, I would shut it down," he says. "But he's aware of everything... and if he needs to go, you let him go."

We end there—with each person and their object leaving *him* rather than him leaving *them*.

After dinner, as the darkness settles, in cozy fashion, we gather for our Bible study circle, and Jimmy reads several psalms. To my surprise, I find one that lands:

Out of the depths I cry to you, O Lord;
   Lord, hear my voice!
Let your ears be attentive
   To my voice in supplication;

If you, O Lord, mark iniquities,
   Lord, who can stand?
But with you is forgiveness,
   That you may be revered.

I trust in the Lord;
   My soul trusts in his word.
My soul waits for the Lord
   More than sentinels wait for the dawn.

As Jimmy talks, I write in the margins of my Bible: *I can wait for my horse to find that trust.* Then, I remember an image from an early-morning dream: untacking Mud Pony after a long trail ride, I lift the saddle blanket and discover, on either side of his spine, two oozing tokens, like small cups of crushed raspberries.

I realized with astonishment that even as we rode uphill and down, my seat bones pressed into those wounds. With every step, he felt the pain but carried me anyway.

Day 4

Away from both city and classroom, I'm able to find a quiet place inside. Both human and horse herds seem to have settled into the rhythm of the clinic. We go to bed just after dark, rise before the sun, throw hay to our horses and check their water, find tea or coffee in the kitchen, gather breakfast and our Bibles, wait for everyone to arrive at the circle. It's been only a few days, but seems so much longer. Without any cell phone coverage or Internet, my jam-packed days of driving, working, and having to be somewhere at every minute are blissfully distant. The only thing I miss is Carter, so I write everything down to tell him when I get home.

O

As a sixth grader, I learned about the US-Soviet nuclear arms race, and found myself in incessant, free-floating ruminations: if the atomic bombs dropped on Japan during World War II were modest compared to the nuclear weapons now being built and stockpiled like the Lincoln Logs in our basement, what was next? I kept at it long after school was over, into the night, and as I sat in church, all that worry wrapped around what my mother had told me about the end of the world: *the Virgin Mary appeared to a group of children in Europe and told them it would happen in our lifetime.*

My mother mail-ordered stacks of pamphlets with the Virgin's translated messages and placed them in strategic locations—doctor's and dentist's offices, the waiting room at the car mechanic—where she hoped others, both believers and nonbelievers, would find them. In the summers, when lightning flashed against a green sky and great gusts of wind arose, she herded her brood into the basement, where we lit candles and prayed on our knees. We also said the rosary in the car on trips home from the beach, on First Fridays, and during the Advent and Lenten seasons. I dreaded having to give myself over to these recitations—"Say it like you mean it," my mother would urge, so I learned to fake it.

Did my mother find refuge in religion but then leave me to deal with my fear and insecurity? What about horses? Are they my refuge? I consider the strength

I garner from riding: a horse's big movement moves through me, massages my internal organs, rocks my body in a steady rhythm, connects both sides of my body, softens that hard ball inside. I am lucky to have the comfort of these beings that willingly carry my weight and worry. They have been my refuge—save for Mud Pony, who's now an assigned koan. *Perhaps I am using him to help me face my fears?*

So often, he's an old-school Zen master hitting me with a stick to wake me up during zazen—but for what? My own redemption or release? To reify everything I would rather hold, contain, or hoard? To awaken? *No matter what, Mud Pony spills it all out of me. He helps me see it.*

○

Just after sunrise, we again walk the long, empty stretch of the Salt Dam Road. The sun has not yet risen above the mountains to the east. It's impossible to avoid stepping on the encrusted, ping-pong-size pods scattered on the shoulder. My horse lowers his head and searches for grass among them.

What will happen when we get home if I can't get back on him this week with Harry's guidance? How much more trouble needs to arise before I can get on him again? *Can I find the nerve to ask Harry to ride him? I can't ask Rolando now, not this week.* During our morning Bible study, Jimmy says, "God looks at the heart, not at the accomplishment."

In the round pen a few hours later, I lay saddle and blanket on the rail and lead Mud Pony to the center. Nervous with everyone's gaze pointed at us, I pause, take a breath, and ask Harry if he will ride my horse.

"Well," Harry responds, "I won't take that risk yet. I'd like to see a whole lot of things more solid... getting off and on, standing still, getting him to move forward without so much worry. If he were a young horse, it'd happen faster, but with the baggage he's got... he's one that's not going to fill in for you. But if you could get on and get two quiet spots..." His voice trails off. He must see the disappointment in my face. "If we had another horse to give him support, we might try, but the support of another horse hasn't helped him and nothing was fixed. Getting on him might mean we just sneak in another ride. To the best of my ability to see what's taking place and to keep you from getting killed—at least while I'm watching—we may *not* get him ridden, but we might play with *acting* like we'll get on. But first, we need to see where he's at."

I resign myself to Harry's wisdom and set Mud Pony loose. He trots away to the other side of the round pen without a backward glance. *Oh Rolando, it was all too easy. What confidence you tried to give me.*

"Just stand still and see if he doesn't make it around," calls Harry. "Now do something, slap your chaps or move the flag... more."

Mud Pony makes it around and then I draw him to me with a single step backward. Cool! *He comes to me more quickly than yesterday, even though I've got the flag in my hand.*

"Very good," says Harry. "Pet on him and let him come with you like that before you ask him to move off."

I stroke his neck and shoulder. From heckling distance, someone I can't identify makes a crack, "Hey Harry, I paid all that money just so I could learn how to pet my horse?!" Everyone ignores them.

Off the line, Mud Pony has become a model student, now choosing to receive my touch. I think of my mother and how she would sit in church. While running a busy household, she made time most days to get quiet in this way. I often saw her unhappy and troubled, but I could always count on a positive shift in her demeanor when she came home from morning Mass. *Maybe Mud Pony and I are now feeling soothed in a similar way with each other.*

"See, it's never his idea to have you on his back," says Harry. "It's his idea to cooperate with that. Same with the flag. I've seen people do something like what we have here. They say, 'We're getting the horse to get used to the flag,' but this is NOT desensitizing. We want the flag to have *meaning*. Mud Pony hasn't much security within himself. We need to build that in him. We need to teach him how to learn and think about new things... How he responds to something he's aware of is a big issue with him. I see a lot of people discouraging the horse from searching for an answer—they're going to whack him—but I'm promoting *his* search for the right answer. I want to change how he responds... I want him to never have to fly backward."

After more work with the flag, we reenact yesterday's pony-petting party. This time, five clinic participants scatter to different points on the round pen's circumference, creating concentric and clockwise circles. We walk counter to their clockwise. Harry calls to the participants like it's a square dance: "Walk faster, skip one step, now three steps! Now change direction and skip three more. Now stop!"

Then he asks each to enter our space in the middle. Two at a time pet him then skip away. Two more arrive by hopping then pet him.

For the "Ring around the Rosie" finale, all five pet him at once, then skip away and encircle him. Harry directs me to weave with my horse through the circle as they move, getting touched by each as we pass. Through it all, Mud Pony is attentive and unworried. Finally, after all participants have exited the round pen, saddling him seems easy, natural, relaxed. I put on my helmet.

"Move your feet with his if you need to," Harry calls, as I tighten the cinch and lead him a few steps forward. "Bounce around next to him and flounder. Be sloppy."

His tension returns. I pet him.

"See how the tail got tight, how his head came up?"

I move close to his shoulder and stay there, again petting.

"There, there, it went away... if there is any opportunity to hold that up position, you can try it."

I put one foot in the left stirrup, lay my left hand with the rope held loosely in my fingers on the crest of his neck, and place my right hand on the cantle. He doesn't move. I pull myself up for one second: twelve inches. Again, he doesn't move. I can't see what his eyes look like—are they soft or scared? But his head stays level. *Maybe all of him—not just one ear, eye, or side—is listening to me, seeing me.*

"Yeah! Very good!" says Harry. "Now take a break and lead him off somewhere."

Soon we are playing on the right side and following Harry's instructions to get sloppy with my foot near the stirrup.

"Do something obnoxious," he calls, so I swing the stirrup fenders and slap the saddle. "Good job! Notice how he's not as troubled on the right side, and you might go up a bit more. Pet him. Good. Walk off. Okay, now come in on the left again. See how this side has a different feel to it?"

"Should I go for the left side again?"

"Yup, but with no real intent to get on, just to get him ready. You can raise up farther... there... there... he was worried enough to move his feet."

I find the ground with my feet and pet him.

"I would advise doing things above him and getting on the fence to do that." Harry nods "Yep, this is the most relaxed I've seen this horse in a human's presence."

O

In the warm, woozy afternoon, I'm suddenly exhausted and fall asleep without bothering to close the screen door of my tent. I can see my horse standing in the pipe corral next to the other horses. I dream that he's back home in the hill pasture. He descends to the flat area at the bottom where a large puddle awaits. He steps in and, as his hooves touch the water, it widens, becoming a deep pool with a sparkling surface of iridescent swirls. Mud Pony sinks into the water, disappearing into a portal called "St. John's Magic Hole." He's gone for a long time, but I rejoice, knowing he's safe on the other side.

That evening, the one before our last full day together, we gather around the fire and Jimmy, Heidi, and Steve break out their guitars. We sing pop tunes, ballads, even "Row, Row, Row Your Boat." It's my mother's birthday, and I request the birthday song. Harry's in rare form with his jokes. Tomorrow evening after dinner, he'll ask each of us to share what we liked and learned this week. Then on Saturday morning, we'll trailer out early and Harry will head back to his ranch in Arizona after having been on the road for over four months, teaching clinics cross-country. He seems both relieved and exhausted.

Have I ever enjoyed sitting around a campfire and singing songs in this way? A sudden wave of gratitude for everyone in this circle sweeps over me—how they have supported and witnessed my process, how we share a passion for finding an authentic relationship with our horses. Amazingly, I'm more accepting of the connections that have been made this week between the Bible and horsemanship. I know I will never belong to a church again, but there's a word to describe something we can all belong to: *feel.*

Day 5

Our last morning at Bible study, Jimmy asks us to open to Galatians: "For you were called for freedom, brothers. But do not use this freedom as an opportunity for the flesh; rather, serve one another through love. For the whole law is fulfilled in one statement, namely, 'You shall love your neighbor as yourself.' But if you go on biting and devouring one another, beware that you are not consumed by one another."

My thoughts wander a different path: *release and freedom come from concentration and connection.*

Soon after, I saddle Mud Pony and walk him to the round pen. Will this be the day I get on with Harry to guide me? *Stop it! That's exactly what's gotten me into trouble before.* No longer can I allow the aggressive parts of me to cause Mud Pony to flee.

I lead him to the center of the round pen and take the rope halter off just to see what he will do without being attached to me. He walks away then returns with heavy feet. "He's not as connected as I'd like to see," says Harry after a long minute, "but it is better than it was."

"Should I get big and drive him around the pen?"

"I wouldn't change much," he responds, "because he's feeling better. But I might do something to brighten him up."

Mud Pony appears less worried than the past four days, but I wonder how much of what we've done has sunk in. As he stands next to me, I kick up some sand. His head comes up and he leaves.

"See, there's a borderline," says Harry. "Do much more than you did there and he'll be upset."

After an untethered half-circle, he returns to my orbit. I pet him and he lowers his head. Harry directs me to halter him and play with him on the line, asking him to circle around me with a bend toward the inside. As he moves off more comfortably, without reaction, I increase the pressure by using the flag—but the worry returns.

"Stop," says Harry. "Now pet him every so often."

I do, but I see no change. And when he moves bigger and faster on the rope, from walk to trot, his tension increases.

"A horse will tolerate a lot standing still," says Harry, "but what's crucial is how they feel when they are moving. Prey animals may disassociate to be detached from pain, but he can't disassociate from these things when his feet are moving. How he deals with it when he's moving is a thousand times different than when he's still."

Where are we going with this, Harry?

As if in answer to my question, he gets up out of his chair, takes the rope, and stands on the outside of the rail. At six foot three, he's so tall he can have one boot on the second rung and still tower over a small horse like Mud Pony.

Harry plays with the flag, moving it above his head and over the length of my horse's body, then he puts it down and places one hand on the top of Mud Pony's poll, between the ears, asking him to yield.

"My goodness, he's braced up!"

Then Mud Pony licks and chews, offers a softer look. Harry takes his hat off to brush away a fly, and my horse reacts, suddenly launching himself backward but stopping when he hits a firm grip on the rope halter.

"Does it matter during training if he's in a pasture with other horses or in a stall by himself?" an auditor asks. "I've heard horses will be more responsive to training if they're separated from the herd and can rely only on their human."

"No," he responds, "it makes no difference; it's the work you do with them that will cause them to bond with you."

Harry hands me the rope and directs me to continue. He comments how the right side is so much better than the left. Unlike most horses, Mud Pony favors right over left. Both Patti and Roses have observed similarly. Perhaps it's the developmental deficit of an orphan colt that never leaned into the right shoulder of his mother.

As soon as the flag moves to that left side, I can see the gauge on the barometer rise—an alert head and neck. There's a worried look too.

"If his left side looked as good as his right," Harry says, "I'd say put a leg over him. This horse, his cup is so full. If he had a way of looking at things differently, he could take in some more without slopping all over the place. But with all the vaqueros got done with him and you getting him to feel good about things, you just may get on and ride off one of these days."

Hallelujah! Three days ago, I wanted to throw Rolando and everything we accomplished under the bus! I'm most relieved that my gut didn't betray me: I was right about Rolando's intentions and know-how, but maybe Mud Pony is a special case, or maybe he just doesn't know as much as Harry.

"It's true," I say. "He didn't feel shut down to me when we worked. We had lots of good moments. But on the days when I wasn't so confident, could you say he was filling in for me?"

"I don't know if I would word it quite that way. When I say, 'filling in,' I mean if a horse doesn't feel so good, he can still hold it together okay. *This* horse, when he doesn't feel good, *can't* hold it together."

Mud Pony didn't seem so good when he was surrounded by Rolando's men on horseback that first day, but perhaps I underestimated the support and presence of the other horses. Maybe by moving his feet with the others, he was safe enough to withstand the pressure of a rider.

"All this time," Harry says, "you've been able to get some rides on him... take advantage of that experience on the trail you had. Not all of it was so bad. Some people just miss things. They get the horse *tolerant* instead of feeling *good*. Now get him to feel good. You are so close!"

I want to leap off the rail and dance! But a voice creeps in, minimizing the celebration: *How can I trust that it's true? How can I get him to feel good when it's just me?*

Mud Pony thrusts his head in my lap as I sit on the top rail and loosely hold him with the rope. He doesn't like the flag in my other hand, but he's not fleeing from it. This behavior is super cute, but he could also push me off the rail. I anticipate leaving tomorrow and am suddenly desperate at the thought. I want to get everything I can from Harry while I've still got his attention. "I shouldn't let him be like this, should I?"

"Don't be too critical of that," Harry says, directing me to get my helmet and put a toe in the stirrup. I look at Mud Pony's left eye. It's soft, half-closed, with a dark, kohl-like line on his inner lids. I place my left hand on his neck with the rope, my right on the pommel, and I lift myself up less than a foot. He stands.

"That was pretty good," says Harry. "Fact, that was *real* good. Quite a change in his tension when you put your toe in that stirrup. Did you see, top of his tail just loosened up too." Mud Pony wears no bridle or bit, just the rope halter, and I've got it long and loose. Harry directs me to shorten it and bend his head in my direction. "Be ready to step off," he heeds.

I lift myself higher, nearly halfway.

"I'd be looking for the day when I could do that and his head not come up and he's not looking to leave... now, try again, raise yourself up with a bit more commitment, but still be ready to get off. Allow him to move his feet if he needs. Just stay with him there by that stirrup."

Just before I place the foot in the stirrup, he takes one step, then another. Then, he stops, as if to test his trust of me.

"You want me to go up higher!?" I ask, feeling a thrill.

Harry nods. "When you do, reach over and pet him on the other side. Don't go that far if it doesn't feel right. See how you are feeling of your horse here? You are not doing something *regardless* of him."

Here I go, lifting up and up—mere inches compared to the heights we reached with Rolando, but no less exhilarating. I gently touch the right side of his neck.

"Good! Excellent!" Harry contains a shout. "That has meaning to him... If you can keep him feeling good... you'll be legging over in no time."

I'm floating so high, it's tempting to stay there, but I step down.

"If you got that leg over and he had to squirt away, don't grab the reins too quick. Enjoy the ride for a few steps and *then* ask him for something."

My heart is back in this, big and eager for more, busted wide open like a piece of ripe fruit fallen to the ground. Together we've found comfort and safety, a soothing connection after so much uncertainty. Sometimes my horse can *tolerate* being ridden, especially by an expert rider like Rolando—but that's often not safe for me, and it's not helping him in the deep way of feel.

And I want more than Mud Pony just going through the motions—I want him to feel good. Earlier this week, Harry said, "If you've ever ridden a horse whose feelings have been taken into consideration, you won't want any less."

In the dark, as I zip up the door of my tent, I notice him standing apart from the other horses, as close as he can get to me at the fence—only six feet or so separates us. When I peek out at sunrise, I see the shape of a relaxed body and lowered head. He never moved. My heart does backflips at the thought: *for one night, we rested together in each other's herd.*

· Six ·

The once-promised parade through North Beach has come and gone. I saw the horse trailers leave that morning from the ranch but heard nothing of how it went. I envision Rolando maneuvering his horse over the cable-car tracks and worn pavement of Columbus Avenue. Surely the cremello snorted in fear as silver balloons bounced in a street vendor's helium pileup or trembled when the Blue Angels cracked the city sky with their jet engines, flying in diamond formation within a few deadly inches of each other, commemorating a holiday that is no holiday.

I'm on my own. No Harry. No Rolando. No Patti. No Roses. I try to be brave, to think I know what I think I know.

The first time I go to Mud Pony after the clinic, he puts his head over the fence where he's been quarantined for ten days upon our return (a standard ranch practice) and issues a high, insistent whinny that makes my heart leap. By his side, walking through the ranch and on trails, I focus solely on him, matching each one of his steps with my own.

I set him loose in the back arena. He covers its length at a full gallop, tail lifted like a banner announcing his arrival. The fog blew in low to the ground last night, and there's a thin layer of wet dirt on top of the dust. When he turns in to face me, I halter him and then bring him to the gate for the saddle. No riding, but lots of petting. I let go of all my previous notions of cowboy machismo—how he's supposed to work *for* me without being comforted. I go to him any time his head goes up, his skin gets prickly, or there's a worried look. *Even before Rolando, why was it such a challenge to attend in this way?*

I stroke him between his eyes, offer soft words, rub his shoulder, wait for his neck to lower, his eye to soften. I note how he protects his left side, how when he's at liberty in the round pen, if I walk behind and approach the left side, he leaves. I remember what Roses once said: "You are always riding two horses: the horse that looks out at the world from the right side and the horse that looks out from the left."

Doubt arrives as the days pass, and I retreat from social interactions at the ranch. I want to focus just on us, but I worry I've let Lottie down by abandoning our trail rides. And what will I say to Rolando the next time we cross paths?

Fortunately, both Lottie and Rolando seem to avoid my orbit. I'm met only by the questions of a few ranch friends: "After all that work with Rolando, how come you're not riding him?"

"My horse and I have pro-*re*-gressed," I say, knowing my answer won't meet the expectation. "This summer we made a lot of progress, but now we have to back up a bit because we missed some things."

I've utilized loose justifications as a strategy my whole life, like when I told The Lie as a second grader, said prayers in church, or as an adult entered a classroom without a solid lesson plan. *If you say it like you believe it, they will believe it too.* Yet, there's what I can't say without fear of being mocked: *I want a horse whose feelings have been taken into consideration. I want a soft, willing partner who turns to me for comfort.*

○

A few weeks after our quarantine has ended, I pony Mud Pony off the palomino and then work him in the round pen near the PG&E road, hoisting myself up on his left side just as I did at the clinic by putting one arm across the pommel and the other on his neck. He seems relaxed, skin not prickly, neck lower than usual. But I don't swing the leg over—at least, not yet.

José has just finished repairing a fence and brings his truck to a stop near the rail, waving me over. "You rode him today?"

"No."

He clucks disapprovingly. "Mira, you've gone back to what you used to do all the time, you're not doing anything with him."

I half-listen as he tells me about some rider at another ranch who could show me what to do. José wants me to succeed and honor the hard work of Rolando and his crew. I know this but can't suppress my reaction: *I don't need this. I've already put so much pressure on myself and my horse.*

With José facing me like judge and jury, I defend everything I've learned about Mud Pony. I get blustery and break it down, emphasizing each point by pushing down a finger.

He shakes his head. "But this can happen to anyone on any horse. You are making too big a deal. You should push on, push ahead." He shoves a hand toward me as he speaks.

"Amigo, let me show you how quickly it comes up in him and how different he is than other horses."

Standing next to José's driver's-side window, with the palomino in tow and Mud Pony several feet behind her on a long line, I make a quick, aggressive gesture with my hands at the palomino. She remains still, indifferent, practically yawning in response. But when I've barely begun the same motion toward Mud Pony, he snorts and snaps his head backward, so the rope meets his poll. If I got any bigger, he would rear and rip free. José shrugs and drives off to mend a broken fence.

How do I defend myself against these voices that criticize or challenge? Ranch folks have good intentions, but their questions help me realize I need to counter these voices before the questions even get asked. *If only I could learn to connect my horse's outside with my own insides.* And after Harry's clinic, I know that achieving this will ultimately be more fulfilling than any mindless ride on a checked-out, conforming animal.

I create a list of cues as reminders, so I can remember the details before I swing over.

Observing Mud Pony, inside and out:
1. Is his head level with his withers and his neck soft? If his neck is not level and instead raised slightly, how high is the pressure of his defense barometer—is this an understandable alertness or the prelude to a leap or bolt?

2. What is the look in his eye—troubled, fearful, distant? Does he allow me to touch him between his eyes with a relaxed drop of the head, or does he avoid my hand? And what happens when I touch him—does his eye soften and get half closed and sleepy?

3. What level of tension does he hold in his skin? Tail clamped tight to his butt? If I bump my toe against his heart-girth area—does he recoil? Is the skin of his belly reactive and prickly, or is it loose?

4. When I take off the rope halter and set him loose, where does his attention go? Does he walk away from me without a glance to the other side of the arena or round pen? Does he come to me because he's following with his heart or conforming to my wishes?

5. Does he crowd my space when I ask him to enter my circle? Does he offer me one side but not the other?

6. Do his feet fall hard as they meet the ground, indicating resistance or tension?

7. When I put him on the line, is he able to circle with a slight bend, eyes coming around, or is he looking outside with stiffness through his body? What happens when I ask for more speed?

8. When I tighten the cinch, walk him a few steps, bring him back, put my toe in the stirrup, and bump up and down, does his head suddenly come up or does he seem accepting of this task?

9. Is he making plans to be elsewhere? Does he leave before I do? How does he respond to something he's unsure of?

Self-observation, inside and out:

1. Was I happy to see my horse today, or does being with him seem like a chore? Do I feel light and joyful in this work?

2. Am I so concerned about others watching that I have a hard time focusing on him?

3. Have I eaten something nourishing today? When was the last time I drank water?

4. Do I have the support I need to finish what we started—when and if I bring up the trouble in him? Am I willing to end sooner than later—in a better place than where we started—rather than pushing for more?

5. Am I using pressure (my presence, the flag, the whip) in a way that has meaning, that is not about punishment or scaring him in the attempt to "desensitize"? Can I get creative and change things up enough so we're not just going through the motions of drill and kill?

6. Am I aware of my surroundings and asking him to be aware too? Do I check in with him to see if he's listening and awake?

7. Do I notice when he checks in with a look or listening ear? Can I pause and offer him the space to search for the right answer? Can I hold back and wait that extra five or ten seconds so he can find it?

8. Do I believe in this work we are doing together? Am I committed to the adventure, our connection, and our process? Do I believe in the power of my own intuition, feeling, and judgment as well as his generosity, strength, and willingness?

9. Can I get him to feel good in my presence, or is he simply tolerating me?

Later, I discover I don't even need to bring these notes with me to the ranch because I can condense everything into three questions: *Is he listening to me? Am I listening to him? Are we together?*

○

Who are our greatest teachers? Other humans and the discoveries they share? Friends who care about us enough to say the things that are hard for us to hear? Or our own insides in response to the world around us—what we can see, touch, smell, or study? And how do we know we've missed something except to listen deeply to others or ourselves? What about the big picture of the past? Doesn't history give us knowledge about the present we wouldn't otherwise have? What about our dreams—do they teach us too?

As a Humanities teacher, I bask in the revelations of historical research and fossil record, as I read about Dawn Horse, an early mammal, and the Eocene prototype of Mud Pony, who scrambled through the primeval forests that once covered the high plains of what's now Polecat, Wyoming. There, our primate progenitors emerged at the same time as these dog-sized creatures.

I'm amazed at the synchronicity. *Who could have predicted how the horse-human relationship would shape history... and my life?* I imagine two skeletons: a tiny monkey in a crouch on Dawn Horse. Then I recall a story that Harry once told about a student who'd had several pet monkeys living in her horse barn. The monkeys helped sack out a herd of yearling colts by repeatedly, in fits and starts, sitting on their backs and launching themselves in carnivalesque romps in the upper reaches of the barn structure. "Those horses were practically rideable afterward," pronounced Harry. "Monkeys get a lot done."

○

I spend more time with my nose in a book than in a toolbox, but after watching a farrier work on my horses' feet, I became determined to trim them on my own. As a beginning horse owner, I wanted to save money, but working on their feet was a whole new endeavor. I spent months plying a barefoot trimmer with questions as he trimmed my horses. He called me a shoulder monkey and suggested I learn from *his* teacher. To shape the contours of my horses' unshod feet, I had to learn where and what and how deep I could go.

At her Church of Barefoot Trimming, Dora Lynn, a gravelly voiced East Texan, begins her teaching with awe and reverence, explaining how, when balanced, a horse's hoof is a sacred geometry of three shapes—a truncated cone for the hoof wall, a dome for the sole, and a triangular frog. The frog is a rubbery, nerveless cushion, while the other parts have the hardness of horn and human toenails. In the wild, horses wear their feet to perfect proportions due to a constant search for food, and the horn becomes hard or soft, depending on the season and terrain.

Without knowing enough to name them, I'd seen these shapes reveal their colors after hours of walking at the beach or on a rain-soaked, forested trail: the palomino's hooves became buffed pink, gray, and blue like the insides of shells, while the horn of Mud Pony's feet revealed a ring pattern around the perimeter like the undulating grains of the wood fungus I stumbled upon that attached itself to fallen trees.

No hoof, no horse goes the saying, and for good reason. A hoof is more flesh and skin than wood or bone, and when it becomes constricted, broken, or sore, the horse becomes understandably irritable or shut down, but will keep working anyway.

"I hope you have strong stomachs," Dora Lynn says, pulling a garbage bag from a cooler filled with ice. She opens it to reveal a collection of freshly severed horse legs, cut just above the bony fetlock then selects a furry, white specimen with a tendon hanging from one end like a protracted tongue. "Each hoof has a story to tell. In fact, each hoof has two stories, an inside and an outside story. The shape and form of the outside affects the inside."

She begins the dissection in crude fashion, with knife and saw, showing us how the hard skin or horn on the outside is the hoof's own shoe, housing the coffin bone at its center in a blood-rich cavity, while the inside of the hoof's mechanism functions like a pump subjected to gravity—the motion of the horse lifting then setting down the foot. The navicular bone, poised at the top of the hoof-pump, is a hinge bone (like the human knee), which acts as a valve, allowing blood to fill the foot when it's lifted off the ground and shutting off the flow when it falls. There's an exchange of about a quarter-cup of blood each time the horse picks up the foot and puts it down. Blood and bone are protected by the growth of sole and walls. Wild horses are constantly on the move and cover five to fifty miles a day in search of food and water, enabling blood to circulate through the hoof. Domesticated horses don't have that need, so the human must help the domesticated hoof imitate the shape it would take in the wild by rasping, trimming, shaping.

To my astonishment, Dora Lynn reveals that when a metal shoe is nailed onto a horse's foot, it decreases the circulation in the hoof—80 percent by her estimate. This can cause the observable, outer shape to contract and shrink. On the inside, the healthy, circulating tissue becomes whitened and misshapen. Often, the semiporous coffin bone at the hoof's core tips at a sharp angle within the hoof itself, causing lameness and, ultimately, death. Farriers and vets call this condition coffin bone rotation. The analogy can be made to a person who walks in nothing but ridiculously high-heeled shoes.

Luckily, Mud Pony and my palomino have always been barefoot. "Many of the horses at our ranch have shoes, and they seem fine," I query.

Dora Lynn scoffs, "Horses are herd and prey animals built to hide their distress—otherwise, they are vulnerable to attack. The key phrase is *over time*—shod horses die younger and develop more joint, hoof, spine, and body ailments. This was documented in the mid-1800s by Bracy Clark, one of the first modern veterinarians. *Over time,* they lose their muscle tone and become unhappy when asked to work." I question Dora Lynn's absolute stance as I know horses that seem to function well when the farrier is knowledgeable and consistent. At the same time, I'm fascinated by the argument she offers.

Researchers have used the ninth century as their date of origin for horseshoes because carbon dating of excavated metal traces them to this time. Plus, any mention or depiction of metal shoeing is absent from the writings or artwork of Ancient Greece, Rome, and Classical Asia. As far as we know, horseshoes first appeared in Europe during the feudal age, when nobility lived in castles on hilltops and used horses to carry their riders or haul their loads. The aristocracy no longer kept their horses in fields and open areas but stabled them in enclosures where their horses' feet deteriorated from long stretches of standing around during the winter months. It seems likely that horseshoes were invented to keep the hoof intact during lengthy confinements: perhaps an enterprising groom experimented with nailing a piece of metal into the hoof horn between two ragged or torn spots.

As shoeing became more accepted, only the privileged few could afford to pay a blacksmith, but the sight of a noble on a huge animal clattering on cobblestones or a troop of soldiers deafening passersby with their iron-shod footfall likely inspired both awe and fear and made the usage of horseshoes more attractive to aristocracy and the growing merchant class.

In contrast, Xenophon, the Ancient Greek historian, general, and horseman who wrote *The Art of Horsemanship*, maintained that his horses worked until age thirty-five and died at forty to fifty years. Dora Lynn assumes those horses moved constantly and never wore shoes. I thought of all the senior horses I'd known. I couldn't think of one who had lived (let alone *worked*) much past thirty.

On day two of the clinic, I raise the severed end of my cadaver hoof to my nose. No smell—just like fresh meat from the butcher. My friend Sarah and two students each sit with a black-haired foot in their laps. This set of four feet is now complete.

Dora Lynn watches as we dig in, pointing out the significance of a too-thick sole, too-long toe, or contracted heel—how this is reflected on the inside of the hoof. I whittle and crunch apart the dead horn in chunks with my knife and nippers and find the blood-rich inside of the hoof, the laminae—and where it separates from the hoof wall, like a toenail being pulled away from its bed of flesh underneath.

Founder, or laminitis (inflammation of the lamina), can happen to well-meaning horse owners who allow their herd too much sugar-loaded grass or feed, often in combination with insufficient movement. I discover founder in my cadaver hoof, which could have occurred years before the horse's death. With proper trimming, Dora Lynn heeds, this horse could have recovered instead of suffering a slow and painful decline.

My classmates and I acknowledge this is sad to hear, but we're grateful for the opportunity to delve into the hoof's interior.

I find the navicular bone, wiggle its hinge, and see how it allows blood to move in and out of the hoof like a door into a chamber. I find the septoid bones and marvel at the rounded mechanisms held in soft chambers of tissue. Dora Lynn points out the hard, bumpy accumulation of calcium around the top of the horn (ringbone). By the end of the afternoon, a pile of bones, hair, and tissue lie at my feet.

I'd heard ranch friends shake their heads at the bad news—*founder, ringbone, navicular, coffin bone rotation*. But not even an image in a book could help me comprehend what I was now sensing, a strange intimacy with this animal and its ancestors. In a previous lifetime, it lifted its hoof and the navicular bone swung open, allowing a quarter cup of blood to wash over the coffin bone and feathery laminae that attach to the horn. Blood-filled gills fed callused skin. The hoof hit the ground and the navicular hinge swung closed: the blood stayed pooled in the hoof. And so it went. The pumping action as the animal walked—open, release, land, close, lift, open, release, land, close...

Might I bring this knowledge—practical know-how, anatomy, empathy, history—into my classroom? How might I share this with my students? How might they write about something that inspired them from the inside out?

Each of Dawn Horse's feet ended in three functional toes, and millions of years later, as the climate cooled and the great forests receded, these early equines became travelers across open spaces—grasslands, savannahs, glacial valleys, or high deserts. Eventually, their toes merged into a single hoof, giving them great bursts of speed and agility to outmaneuver predators. Their hooves also evolved to grip, push, suck, and dig into earth's surfaces with traction at both sprints and slow ambles—up and down hills and mountains, across plains and glaciers, or any place the search for food, water, and safety led them.

Primates also inhabited the savannahs but developed a gradually more erect posture. Their front paws stretched wide to house the hominids' opposable thumbs, giving them the ability to skin hides, push needles, grind seeds, flint stones, weave fronds, reap and thresh grain, twist udders, and forge metal.

The night after the dissection, I sleep fitfully with moving-picture dreams of galloping horses, one whose legs and feet I enter in a fantasia, sliding down tendons, gripping ligaments, and seeing the foot bathed in blood's heat as the navicular hinge opens. A surge and splash as the capsule fills with blood. I'm entering the heart of the hoof!

When I wake, the pads on the ends of my own fingers are as sensitive to touch as a horse's hoof. *Equus* and I possess equally agile, sensorial organs—my own opposable thumbs an adaptation that give my species the ability to survive and thrive... or defend and conquer. My thumb and fingers manipulate rasp, nippers, and knives, while the hoof pulls, contracts, extends, and digs into the ground. But while I can learn to function without my thumbs, the heart of *Equus* beats only because their feet do.

○

On a soft, warm evening a few weeks after returning from Harry's clinic, I realize I've neglected the palomino. I leave Mud Pony in pasture and wince at her walk as we move through the gate—short, painful steps on her front end. As she trots in the sand arena, I can't discern any head bobbing or obvious lameness. Perhaps the short steps are a combination of sore muscles and arthritis? There's a fresh pattern of bite marks on her hind end, and lately, she's had to maneuver quickly at feeding time because of a new, more dominant horse in pasture.

Getting her blood moving is good for both of us. I mount and leave her girth comfortably loose, so she doesn't protest at its tightening. As she warms up at a slow walk, I adore this sturdy mare who has never kicked, bucked, or left me doubting and fearful. Her presence is safe and comforting, especially on an evening where I wear only a T-shirt, where barn swallows slice the sky and skim the farmer's irrigation ponds, where the sun casts red, pink, and orange rays on darkening clouds, lighting them up in the shape of a fist.

By seven o'clock what's left of the day? Dust and alfalfa splinters from the remainders of thrown hay. Mud Pony calls out to us when we return in the dark. I feel sated, yet I want him more than the sure bet I now unsaddle outside the pasture fence. *I want to ride that uncertain edge.*

○

I love him and I'm afraid of him, yet I can't choose what I fear. I can't choose what I love. My conundrum and maybe my failure, but I don't have to despair because I can still find a hundred things to celebrate—a crow cawing in a street tree, a pasture horse ambling to the water trough, a student smiling shyly at me in the hallway between classes... all this, both inside and out.

One morning, a month after the Bible Horsemanship clinic, it happens just as Harry said. I swing over and he just stands there, waiting, ears back, listening. I swing off. Suddenly the world teems with possibility. *I can ride this Mud Pony.*

· Seven ·

I find a stool in the corner of Carter's sculpture studio and watch as he works with ease and absorption. He straightens burned coat hanger wire by hammering it against a steel slab on his workbench. Then he bends it with his hands, playing and experimenting with the shape it might take. At this stage, he doesn't know what it will look like, but as he fills the negative spaces with plaster and then carves its surface, he's listening and attending to every dip, curve, and contour. He's told me that his art practice is so much more rewarding than washing dishes in a restaurant, digging trenches, baking donuts, repairing dents in a car, or moving pixels on a screen: each moment of making is full of possibility, mystery, the unknown.

I'm fascinated by how he brings life to these shapes, which is how he is with everything. He sincerely enjoys pushing a broom, soaping dirty dishes, rasping hardened plaster, pocketing a flattened battery or other object he's spotted in the gutter.

"Carter, why are you so kind? Where did you get that?"

He pauses straightening a wire to puzzle over my question, which hangs as disembodied as the ideas I like to pluck from books or thought wanderings.

"Why do you even notice that I'm kind? Where can you find that in yourself?"

He lays it flat on the workbench and somehow manages to hammer gently, not a pound but a blunt staccato, as if he's playing an instrument. Unlike me, Carter would probably not need Harry's help to learn how to pet his horse.

"I'm not being rhetorical," he says. "You wouldn't be able to see it in me if you couldn't find it in yourself."

I watch Carter in his studio and see myself looking straight into my own stink eye. *But this time, I look not from the outside in but from the inside out.* I'm not building a wall around my heart to feel safe. I'm not looking at anyone or anything as plan, thought, or other.

O

"I got on him," I tell Roses on the phone. "Once. By myself. Can you... ?"

"Yes," she says. After giving birth to a baby girl a few months ago, she's ready to return.

I swing the saddle onto my horse and pull down the latigo as Roses emerges from the chemical toilet and the door slams behind her. I startle at the sound. "Must be nervous," I giggle.

Roses is a tall, thoughtful, quiet person with a bright, winning smile that betrays the joy underneath a quiet exterior. She doesn't take up space unless she needs to, so she laughs when I suggest that her presence is causing me to jump.

We get to work, and I show Roses how he walks away and then approaches me without much life in him, as if he's sleepwalking.

"Yep, you got it. He's pulled into himself, a dissociation, not soft. Notice how he's breathing shallow and how tight his skin is. He might flee even if all you did was blow on his tail."

The horse-body never lies. On the left, he leans the shoulder into me when I tighten the cinch, putting his full weight behind it. I've seen him assert himself in the pasture herd in this way—despite his pony size, he's able to stand his ground at the feed trough against much bigger animals with the force of that shoulder. Once I even saw him confront José on the tractor as he moved a load of wood chips into the pasture.

"Did Rolando use side reins with him?" she asks. "He looks like he's holding tension in his neck and poll."

"Yes," I say and recount the ground-driving sessions with Rolando where he showed me how to straighten Mud Pony along the fence line. "When we did that, it seemed to help him pay attention to the bit."

Roses shakes her head. "Even a few days of that will force him into a frame without any real give in his body," she responds.

Oh, so that's why he's been pushing into the bit and not yielding. I shove the thought away and conjure Carter's kindness and connection to things. I trust Mud Pony's big heart, what others have called his single greatest talent, his "try."

Working on the ground in the round pen, Roses helps me see how much better Mud Pony feels when we encourage him on the line to release the base of his neck. "Can you find the rhythm in his body?" and "Can you match your stride to his?"

I know this. But the reminders help. And when he wants to move away from me, I bring him back with the rope by cueing him in the opposite direction. *Zigzags. Just like redirecting one of my students whose attention has trailed away while I'm talking.*

"Get in there and touch him, maybe throw the rope over his back or flap a stirrup and pet him to let him know it's okay," calls Roses. "All with rhythm."

It's a relief to have Roses walk me through it, to not be alone. As I prepare to mount, she calls out, "Bend him slightly toward you as you put your toe in the stirrup. Stay with him if he tenses against it, ask in rhythm for that thought to come around."

I have told her about all our mishaps, the fear that lurks in my belly. *I hope I don't clamp down on his sides and startle him when I swing over. I hope I give no voice to a scream.* I resolve to move slowly, thoughtfully, to check in with him... remember my list.

"Two of my own horses are flighty, and I don't commit to swinging over until I know they're with me," Roses says. "But when you do get on, move off with a bend, and bring your hand wide to bring his attention around. Remember, his body goes where his mind goes."

I get on. Safely. No eruption. No scream.

By the end of our session, he's released a single, brief snort. I would have preferred a yawn, sigh, or sneeze. That said, I'm riding. Mud Pony's head is more level now. We can build on this.

O

At breakfast, watching one of our neighbors walk down the street with his new rescue dog, I ask Carter what he thinks about us adopting one. He says certainly not, confident that with the amount of time I devote to two horses, he'd end up as the primary caretaker. For him, animal ownership is palpable, not a weight but a real presence, like his relationship with me or one of his sculptures. I tease him about his "kid animal sins," how he gained a reputation for taming wild animals when a neighbor delivered to their doorstep a wild raccoon that had wandered into a Havahart trap. He spent months teaching the raccoon (first with a glove on a stick and then finally with a gloved hand) to pry open his closed fingers and take a shelled peanut. He eventually released it but then set his own traps. A possum with a horde of pink babies in her pouch wandered in, and after the little ones were older, he set them and their mother free, keeping "Diddletoes," for himself.

During the day, the possum slept in his arms on the couch in front of the fire, and then it crept into darker nooks when Carter was off playing. In the evenings, visitors startled to see a rat-tailed, pink-nosed thing crawl from under the cushions. After a year or so, Diddletoes lost her hair and died (probably from a diet of dry dog food), but then someone from church presented Carter with a pigeon fledgling. Carter fed the bird, which found a safe spot on the dresser in his room where it roosted at night. After some months, he'd leave the window open, and "Henry" (later "Henrietta" when she laid an egg) would wait for him every day at the bus stop. This went on for some time until one afternoon, a dog from the family pack gobbled up Henrietta on the back porch.

When Carter was eleven, his mother resolved to fulfill a childhood dream after finding an ad in the local paper: *Free to good home, pony mare and colt.* Carter and his father were assigned the task of driving down the mountain to the Redwood City flats, where a Shetland and her colt were ushered up a wooden plank into their rear-engine family van. It was Carter's job to secure the mare with a string attached to her halter as she stood in the front-end dip of the Corvair, to prevent her from leaping into the driver and passenger seats. But as the van began to move, the mare thrashed like a netted shark, and they turned around to find another mode of transport.

Back at home in their gravel driveway, his mother directed him to get on the pony, who had never been ridden. "Hold on to the mane," she said.

Red bucked and kicked and leaped a hundred times, and Carter fell off and got back on again and again until it stopped. This was the end of riding horses for Carter but the beginning for his sisters, who rode bareback through wooded hills.

Carter says he feels horrible for torturing animals as a kid—and not just those with hooves, paws, beaks, and claws. His father built him a terrarium to hold captured snakes and frogs, the latter of which screeched in protest as they were eaten by the snakes, while his sisters watched in horror. This didn't faze his mother, who showed him how to put worms or other live bait on a hook and fish for trout in the creeks or jacksmelt and rock cod off the Santa Cruz pier.

As an adult, Carter can't stand for fish to be in tanks, and he rarely visits the ranch with me. After breaking Red, he had no interest in riding, and he feels sad for the horses that spend their lives confined to stalls or paddocks when they should be roaming over vast ranges. Further, he can't tolerate the idea of a dog in the city being left alone in an apartment. "They have no idea if you're ever coming back," he grimaces, haunted by the memories of dogs who looked at him with longing as he exited the house.

When one of my students presented me with two of her prized pet rats, I brought them home. Carter was amenable but insisted their cage remain open so the rats could be "free-range." "At least in the kitchen," he said, "where we can close the doors when we need to."

This worked for us both, and we enjoyed feeding the pair table scraps and watching them explore, sniff, and crawl into every nook—until they began gnawing on electrical cords. I suggested they go back to their cage, but Carter requested they be returned to my student.

A few months later, perhaps as consolation, he brought home a pigeon with clipped wings that he found fluttering in a gutter. She had a metal bracelet around one of her legs with a number on it, and we traced her origins to a registered breeder who'd gotten evicted, along with all his rooftop pigeons. Carter named her Chad.

At first, Chad wouldn't allow us near her but then found a safe place on a built-in floor shelf in our kitchen. This allowed us to give her a wide berth, and every morning, Carter would sit on the floor and lure her to his big toe with a trail of cracked corn and sunflower seeds. After a month or two, she finally became comfortable eating out of his hand. On the weekends, when we had time to clean up the mess (which included vacuuming her dried scat on the floor), we'd set out a basin of water and Chad would hop in and fling drops all over the floor. Then she would find a patch of sun and lie on her side, lifting one wing then the other to dry.

When her wing feathers grew back, Carter wanted to see what would happen if we left the window open: would Chad leave and then return to roost in the kitchen, just like Henrietta did when he was a kid? It took Chad a day or two to find the open window, but one evening, when we returned from the movies, the kitchen was empty. Carter walked the surrounding streets, peering closely at flocks on wires and sidewalks. He even visited the gutter spot where he first found Chad, but she never appeared.

Drawing upon his experiences with animals, Carter happily consults with me about my horse adventures. Lately, I tell him, even after the infrequent lessons with Roses, Mud Pony seems sleepy when we work, as if in a dream or a stupor. I'm not "sneaking rides" on him, as Harry cautioned. I've paid attention each time to see if he's really with me. I've offered reassurance when he gets concerned. I've taken his halter off when we enter the arena and given him the choice of being with me or somewhere else. I've followed Roses' instructions each time I get up the courage to ride him. And at least twice, I've refrained from swinging my leg over when he it didn't seem right.

"Maybe it's self-protection?" suggests Carter. Perhaps Mud Pony could be shutting down in self-defense as he learned to do in his first year—after the cowboys roped his feet and neck, laid him on the ground, and castrated him. Then, he could only surrender and suffer the entrapment without anesthesia. And maybe the same thing happened when he was chased into a chute, which became the confines of a trailer, which then became a roaring floor underneath his hooves as we drove him to another box (a paddock) from which he didn't emerge for many months.

Observers at the ranch say that since Rolando worked with us this summer, Mud Pony's changed; he's become calmer, more accepting. "That makes sense," says Carter. "Does he chase the other horses in pasture as much or startle like he used to? Maybe he goes back to his old ways when he needs them. More importantly, it seems like you are teaching yourself how to see this in him."

Yes, perhaps I've gained more confidence in my intuition. Others may have observed my horse to be tamer—seeing this as evidence of a job well done—but I think he's drawn further into himself.

Post-Rolando training and Harry Wittsom clinic, I evaluate his sleepiness in combination with a hard, slow footfall as we work at liberty in the sand arena next to the pasture. When I ask, *are you listening to me? Am I listening? Are we together?* his walk is not an easy, swinging shuffle but a stiff pound. He places his front feet on the ground like he's bracing against it. Around humans, there's little he trusts, not even the ground underneath his feet.

With support and guidance from Carter, perhaps the best I can offer is a compromise: whenever I go to Mud Pony, I will more consciously work to honor the part of him that can't be tamed; I will remember he's more feral than domesticated. I will remind myself that I don't want to oppress but grant him the freedom to safely move his feet.

I leave school just as it's getting dark and take a detour to sit in an empty movie theatre and watch *Into the Wild*. We've reached the halfway point of the semester, and I estimate being a month behind where we should be in the semester's curriculum. As well, parents, students, and school administrators have been demanding more time and energy than I can muster. I could've called Carter to join me for the film—we usually go to the movies together—but today I seek relief in solitude by crawling inside the story of a young man who finds his life's meaning in the most honest, clean, and raw form he can manage. He wanders as a mendicant, committed to a mystical vision of the wild, ecstatic moment. Traveling the western United States and working odd jobs, he prepares to fulfill a dream of moving to Alaska and living off the land. The end is painful, tragic—he dies alone and from starvation just a few miles from the civilization he sought to transcend.

Later, as I ride my bike down the hill toward our intersection, I sense the uneven weight of books and student papers in the stuffed panniers on both sides of my bike rack. My chain is dry; the brakes are worn. I fear the proximity of cars even in the wide, city-designated bike lane and move onto the sidewalk, where I dismount and walk the remaining blocks.

Like the film's protagonist, who ditched his family and rejected their middle-class norms, I responded to my controlling parents by moving to the West Coast. Did they realize, too late, how they trapped me? I used to think if I got far away from them, they could no longer tell me what to do or make me feel wrong. But here I am, riding and corralling other beings— my horses, my students.

I hope I'm not like them. I hope I don't need to control Mud Pony, a horse without the complications of being human, a being with a mind and spirit different from my own.

A woman on the street in front of our building's gate reads something in my face as I fumble with the keys. "Hey baby, it's okay, no worries," she calls, and holds open the door. Her kindness disarms me. Might she want to know that I carry a weight greater than that of the bags and bike I'm about to haul up the stairs? Might she listen while I tell her of a boy who left home, went into the wild, and died young because he figured out too late that what he could feel with others was more important than feeling it alone? He thought he had to go *out there*, where no one was, to figure it out. Am I doing the same by trying to live inside the wild part of Mud Pony? Could I do this in an easier, safer way by connecting with humans? Why do I keep throwing myself at this being? *Do I need him so I can access the deeper parts of myself I can't explain?*

The next day I'm still in the film. As I stand with Mud Pony, I wonder how he might forgive me and what that might look like. In my head, I hear both Roses and Harry: *His body shows it through its give whenever he yields to hand, leg, or rein. He blows and snorts and relaxes his jaw. He lowers his head, lifts his back, and sighs. He brings his eye around when you ask—he does not roll it back and keep looking out the opposite side. He does not flee. He does not smash his shoulder into your path.*

If I stand the saddle upright on its horn in the center of the arena; if I bring him to the saddle and then lift it onto him in the arena instead of at the tie post; if I work him in squiggly lines and ask him to release the base of his neck and level his head, he's less tense. "It's these many little things," said Harry.

I ignore the darkening sky and the increasing wind. The first storm of the season. In the short window of time we've got, I notice that he checks out a lot less since the lesson with Roses. I follow her pre-ride instructions and swing over. In the saddle, I look for the tiniest try to bring his thought around. I observe (once again) how going left is difficult for him—he crashes on that shoulder with a hard step, and after I've brought him around, he moves off to the right, which means that he wasn't ever going left. I ask again, and when I release the rein, he sustains the movement to his left. This one subtle thing, this slender nibble of a try in the direction I ask for. I'll take it.

After I swing off, I place the reins on the horn and turn away. He follows. I open the gate, and he walks behind me. When I turn around, he stops and doesn't defend against my approach on his left by blocking with his head but allows me to get in close, undo the throatlatch and chinstrap, lift the bridle off, and put the halter on his face.

Done with our work session, I sense the tension release through my own body. "It's okay," I say, as he eats his scoop of forage and the wind kicks up leaves and dirt and blows his mane and tail. I finish chores with the light I have left—sweep the rubber mats outside the tack room, pull a protruding screw out of the wall, toss into the garbage the rubber garden gloves I use for trimming with ragged holes at the knuckles and fingertips—"It's okay." When he's finished eating, I stand next to him and push down the ground with my feet. I place my hands on his ribs, on his heart-girth area, on his belly. I conjure warmth, expansion, and safety: the image of a sun-drenched, grassy meadow rimmed by pine trees.

"It's okay," I say again, but I'm telling myself as much as I'm telling him. I go back to the meadow and its grass and the soil it's rooted to, pull it up instead of pushing it around. My feet swell inside my boots, the wind throws itself against me, the damp sea air weighs down my hair, my eyeballs press against the backs of their sockets into my skull. Now I'm connecting with the source of it all, the light as well as the dark, its damp swirl. The wind picks up the air around us and offers it to my lungs. Mud Pony's rib cage releases slightly. His breathing is shallower than mine, but I can match it and then ask him to deepen it as I deepen my own.

"It's okay," I say, then I step back and give him space. "It's okay," and he drops his head and unlocks his jaw, opens his mouth. "It's okay." I'm believing now and growing stronger, even as large drops of rain start their splatter. "It's okay."

Then a breath comes, and with it, forgiveness. "Thank you," I tell him, "for allowing me to work through all this with you. Thank you for tolerating my clumsiness and surviving my aggression. Thank you for your wild parts that drive you to preserve body and spirit, no matter what mistakes I make. Thank you for sharing whatever part of this world you can. Thank you for giving me the parts of you I can never tame."

○

Winter begins. The days get shorter and steal the scant hours I have after school during the week to drive to the ranch. It will take so long to come out of that darkness—and where will Mud Pony and I be at that point? My visits are already infrequent. And now I have a strained lower back, which flares painfully when I sit for long periods at my desk, along with a dry cough and sore throat that doesn't leave. Each night I am awake, anxious, alert between two and five.

I can't remember the last time I felt well, joyful, energetic, slim. An image from my childhood arises: my mother washing her hair once a week in the sink and setting it in wire curlers. Late at night after she'd finished with the dishes or washed the kitchen floor, I'd see the tired look on her face as she stood in front of the mirror in her nightgown and pushed the pins into place. The clean, soft waves the next morning always surprised me.

Now I feel the weight of her expression set like clay on my own face. I can't remember what it felt like to ride four horses in an afternoon, to trot the mile-plus length of the ranch road, to ask Mud Pony to match his rhythms to mine. I can't summon the beauty of the hills where I ride, what it's like to leave the city and feel connected to the ocean, earth, and sky.

At night I dream that my mother is sitting alone in a room in an ICU, attending to a newborn foal whose stomach is pinched and tight. The foal is a milk-deprived orphan who will probably die. My mother won't lift her face to look at mine as I enter, but I can still read it. She's frozen, stupefied by the foal's demise.

I arrive at the ranch on a weekend evening just as my horses are being fed. It's too late and too dark to work, so after giving them their buckets, I head out on trail for a walk. I've been grading papers all day, and my stomach is sour and bloated from incessant snacking to stuff the tedium. I'm hoping a short hike uphill to get my heart rate going will help.

Just a hundred feet away, there's Rolando on the cremello, followed by Napoleon on Witch. It's too for me late to sidestep or hide, so I face him. He's summoned a lordly bearing, while I'm horseless and alone. He wants to know how things are going.

"We've slowed down," I say, "I'm just riding him in the arena—you heard I got bucked off before we left for the clinic, right?"

He nods.

How can I tell him I want Mud Pony to look to me when he is worried and not get so bunched up on his insides that he needs to flee? How can I tell him I want Mud Pony to follow the thought I offer him, to submit because he wants to, because he makes it his idea to cooperate?

"Just don't leave him alone," Rolando offers from atop his gelding, who frets and works his tongue under a thin, twisted bit. "I want to see," he says.

"Out on trail? In the arena?"

"Doesn't matter."

I know I'll never follow through. I want this on my terms. Rolando and Napoleon ride away and I head up the hill, unsure of my step in the twilight and fog.

○

After the encounter, I muster the determination to work Mud Pony at seven o'clock two mornings a week before I teach. Typically, José hasn't yet fed this early, so I fetch both horses from pasture and offer them three scoops of forage before we work. Saddles on, I walk them down the pasture row, over the creek, through the barn area, and past another row of paddocks and the three steer in quarantine. I set the palomino loose in the big arena on the other side of the ranch and take off her bridle, encouraging her to eat the grass that covers the midsection in a thin, green sheet. While I work with him, I notice how his feet hit the ground hard, revealing the resistance in his body. He reminds me of a distracted, chatty student, reluctant to change seats after being asked by his teacher. I release Mud Pony from the rope halter and ask him to turn in to face me, but it's a stiff, unyielding motion. I bend him around, put my toe in the stirrup. He takes a few steps. I hop with him, my foot still in the stirrup. He stops. I ask for another bend into me. He steps again and we move around in a circle until he finally offers to stand.

I release him and walk away so he knows that's all I wanted. He faces me with new interest. I smile, putting the toe into the stirrup once more, bending him, lifting myself up, patting his neck, asking his head to bend toward me, and he does. I pat him again, throw my leg over, settle into my seat, ask him to bend into my leg once more. For the first time, we ride in the same big arena with my mare loose. It's a short, easy ride, and after dismounting, I take off his tack so he can roll. I collect the palomino, put her bridle on, tighten her girth in two quick spurts, mount, and work her in the arena there with him watching.

Full of new strength and confidence, I ride the palomino back to pasture but leave him alone to stand in the arena. She's a delight—all I need to do is think *trot* and there she goes. *Maybe I can get one more ride on Mud Pony before his hay arrives? We've never done this before, but yes, I will ride him back to his breakfast as a reward.*

It will be challenging to get to school on time, I haven't had breakfast myself, I need to clean up, and I will probably chat with José, then make sure he's out of view before I change my clothes behind a trailer and drive back to the city.

Yet something inside me pushes for it—just one more ride. And because I want to meet that feeling and run with it, or let it run out of me until it's gone, I push past the rhythm of life at the ranch—the energy of collective eating, the grab and chew of hay—to meet that thing inside, to ride him *just once more.*

I hear Mud Pony call out as I untack the palomino in front of the pasture feeder, and I respond, "I'm coming. You'll be back here in a minute." She's sweaty from our work, and the flies burrow into the fur above her hooves where bits of manure have stained her yellow coat.

Mud Pony awaits my return, head over the gate of the big arena. He can hear the feed truck on its rounds. I bridle him, throw the saddle blanket over his back, letting the rope go just for a second, so I can reach for the saddle on the fence. He leaves, walking away and trailing the rope. The saddle blanket falls off his back and into the dirt. I growl with annoyance. What a chore this now seems. I collect his rope, his blanket, and this time, I don't let go. As I throw on the saddle and cinch it tight, I project reassurance, warmth, support. *We've already done our groundwork this morning. And since you've already been with me once today, you can get there more quickly.* We leave the arena and walk the path back to the pasture, pausing for a moment in the shade. I put my toe in the stirrup, ask for his eye to come around, lift myself up in the saddle. His head comes up. A sign it's unsafe to swing over.

I step down, one foot still in the stirrup, and pulse the rein to bend him around just as Roses taught me—then BAM! BOOM! A hard, blind explosion.

My jaw?! My leg?! Am I hurt? Can I move? Where is he? Doubled over, I fall to the ground. Sudden darkness except for twinkling fuzz above my left eye. I raise myself up and can now view where he went. Fifty meters away, there's Mud Pony with his head down, eating grass. I get up shakily and test my limbs. One hoof punched me square in the meat of my right leg. The other hoof glanced off the edge of my helmet then hit my jaw. I landed on my left elbow.

He doesn't raise his head when I go to him. Limping, sullen, upset, I snag the drooping reins and walk us back to the tack room, pull off his saddle and bridle, throw everything in a pile, set him loose in pasture, then sit in my car. It takes twenty minutes before the stars disappear from just over my left eye—*I thought that only happened in cartoons!* Now big sobs arrive, coming in heaves and gulps. When my convulsions cease, I drive to work.

While sitting at my desk in the department office, a large swelling grows under my left jaw. I crawl through three classes and sit stupefied through a faculty meeting. Now it hurts to yawn, to chew, to laugh. The next morning, I discover a bruise where I landed on my left hip after I broke the fall with my elbow and left thumb. My neck was wrenched from the blow, and it hurts to walk. The flesh of my right thigh, from midlength to crotch, erupts orange and blue.

Carter offers sympathy and kindness rather than the dismay and judgment I heap upon myself. I rehash the drama of that moment to him and anyone who will listen, enlisting their shock, bewilderment, pity. At school, a trusted colleague wonders if it's like being in an abusive relationship because I can't seem to leave this being who hurts me. But Carter doesn't think so. He observes that my narration of the incident ("He said, 'Fuck off! I'm outta here'") makes it seem as if Mud Pony were angry with me, that the hurt was intentional.

"He isn't mad at you," he says, "and he doesn't blame you. Animals don't do that. The kick had no more meaning to him than if you were poking him in his eye with a stick and he had to get away."

I relay Harry's probable translation of *what happened before what happened happened*: Mud Pony's thought wasn't with me. His mind was gone, and he was doing the best he could to preserve himself, to get away from the pressure. I want to reassure Carter, too, that I'm not going to get hurt again, and I recite the five new items on an improved, pre-ride checklist:

1. Don't be in a hurry.

2. Get him with you before you put your toe in the stirrup.

3. Don't be in a hurry. Breathe. Take care of yourself first.

4. Do your groundwork. Go slow. Work on the spots he shows you—like when he gets worried about the saddle or walks away.

5. Safety first. Don't be in a hurry. Accept that he may not be safe to ride at this moment. Stop. Go do something else!

Despite this resolve, I sink into self-inflicted mental realms of "duh" and "what were you thinking?" The morning he kicked me, I pushed through and neglected Harry's admonition about not sneaking rides. Yes, I ran with the part that wanted to do it all on my own. But for what? To get beaten up, stung, wrecked, helpless—so Carter could then comfort me?

I avoid the ranch for a week, seeking comfort at my writing desk, but the poke and shudder of a jackhammer at a nearby construction site spreads through the street, the floor, my brain.

How can I live more in the moment and not invest so much time and energy in futile plans? "Hope," said the writer Derrick Jensen in a recent talk at a workshop I attended, "is a longing for a future condition over which you have no agency." If he's right, I have invested hope in a horse whose instinct to preserve himself is greater than my ability to connect with him. To hope that he will someday be there for me is a setup for despair. *What if I give up this fantasy, the expectation that he or anyone will take care of me in the way I needed as a child?*

The jackhammering stops.

O

In high school, years after I'd stopped asking to ride horses, I pleaded with my parents to allow me to bring home a gray tabby kitten that was offered free "with all the corn you can eat," when we stopped at a farmer's stand on our drive home from church. For some reason, my mother acquiesced—maybe because she knew she couldn't give me a horse, but wanted to give me something? For nearly two years, I treasured the kitty with a pink nose that I dubbed Pierre in honor of my mother's French heritage. Pierre slept in the garage, but I would bring him into the house to play and cuddle. The rest of the time he roamed the neighborhood, and after dinner, I would call him inside by standing on tiptoe at the sliding glass door of our family room and shaking a box of cat food. One night, he stopped coming. Then he never came again.

It took me about a week to figure it out—and my brother confirmed it with the revelation of once having seen my father get rid of a litter of kittens by holding a bag over the exhaust pipe of the family station wagon. I knew my parents had either dropped him off at the SPCA or disappeared him. The fleas in the family room, cat hair on the furniture, cat mess on the rug...

I ran across the street and into the arms of Mrs. Burns. Hours later, I arrived home red-eyed and then sulked for days, refusing to talk or look at either of my parents. Finally, my father took me to Friendly's Restaurant. I sat across from him, scooping banana, whipped cream, and hot fudge into my mouth, as the cold and sweet carved a pit in my middle. I refused to speak. Losing Pierre caused me to go into hiding with my dreams and desires. I resolved to never ask for anything again, and when I yearned for an item of clothing or permission to go on a school field trip, I mulled it over for weeks and then stomached the shame.

I know now that longing and desire never leave, they simply take another shape.

O

A week later, he moves in the round pen at liberty with the saddle on but won't release any tension, lower his head, or let his breath go. I ask him, "How can I believe in myself when you do these things to me?"

Letting the tears come relieves some pressure inside, yet I still want him to witness my hurt. He stands quiet, still, alert. I put my hands on his belly, following the in and out of his breathing with my own as we did before. This time it comes in shallow, rapid puffs. For the first time, I consider what life is for *him*—separated from his herd, he's hypervigilant around humans, forever on alert.

I hope that one day my horse will let go of all his fear, his instinct to flee and leap away. I hope that one day we will find horse-human harmony, a relationship where we fully know and consider each other.

Am I deluded? What if he can't change? What if he's the horse I can't have?

What if I have been misled all these years by my fantasy? What if he never learns to connect with me, to turn to me when he's uncertain? What if this never gets easier? What if I get hurt? What if I must give up?

As a child, I don't remember ever crying or complaining. I sat quietly with my books and bothered no one, yet I always thought I was doing something wrong. I often told myself, "If only I could get better at this or that, if I could only be better, then everything around me would get better too."

Now, with my horse, I'm doing the same. I tell myself, "If I work with Mud Pony more consistently, if I get better at noticing the tiny things with him, if I figure out when to stop and don't rush him, if I do the groundwork before getting on him, if I can find another clinic to go to where I can confront my deepest fears... if I create new checklists and follow them, then things will get better, and it will no longer be my fault."

I believe it's all about *me.*

But what about *him?* He's a horse. His nature is to self-preserve, to flee, to be with his herd. *But he lost his mother and his safety when she broke her leg. When she lost her life, he thought he was going to die...*

If I give up my delusions, I am left with only his delusions. He *believes* he should be afraid. He *believes* he must exist in a state of high watchfulness. He *believes* he must be ready to leap and flee at any moment. And this state of alertness is so high-pitched that when he finally relaxes and gets that sleepy, heavy footfall, he can scare himself just by waking up. In all my training and work with him, it's been hard to see, to understand, and now I see it as if for the first time—all over again.

The prehistoric nomads of the Eurasian steppes used this word: *bhreg.* Now we who live in cities, who call them "civilization," say *break.* And now we lay open by breaking. We enter by force or violence. We penetrate with light or sound. We crack, divide, part. We fail or rupture. The human may break inside and out, but whatever's wild is not broken.

I want to return to the grassy steppes north of the Black Sea seven thousand years ago. I want to know how those humans got horses to accept them on their backs. I want to know why they chose to cooperate. I know the answer and yet it's unknowable. This is how the horse person of the Eurasian steppes got the horse to be with her: she saw him. She fed him. The horse felt safe. She asked him to break at the ribs and he did.

"So now," Roses says, "we connect his feet to his survival, to safety."

On a windy weekend during a lull between storms (now two weeks after the kick to my head), she leads us as we work inside the round pen. I'm walking next to him on the ground. Mud Pony is saddled and free to move wherever he needs. No halter or bridle. Nothing on his face.

"Draw him to you," she says.

I take two steps back and he swings around to face me.

"Now drive," she says, and I bring up the energy in my body, raise my right hand, and motion toward his hind end while making sure I'm pointing behind his ribs. He walks left, driven by the energy of my arm. With five feet between us, he moves in a circle around me as if we're two magnets pushing against a force field we've created. "Now draw him to you again," she says, and as I stop and take a step back, he turns in once more.

We repeat this dance of drive and draw, and later I'll think back to that first touch years ago, when Patti directed me to press and release. Touching him has become so familiar I've now forgotten what a marvel it once was.

"Can you see him leaving with his mind?"

He's out of himself, out of this moment in the round pen. I can see the subtle shift in his facial expression—worry, but the worry's taken him somewhere else. He's getting ready to bolt. Maybe a part of him already has.

"When you feel this," says Roses, "help him think about moving. Help him see that it's better for him to be with you, safely directed, driven and drawn."

I move him away then ask him to return. Drive and draw.

"How about you?" Roses asks. "Are you breathing?"

I can't speak but silently echo her question and await a response inside. *I think so.*

"Can you see what's happening *with his breath?*" *Maybe. It comes quickly. Like mine.* "Be there for him with your breath and heart." *Yes. I can feel those too.* "Again, draw him to you." *He returns and my heart swells.* "Now drive." *But he leaves and I grimace. Darn it, not again.* "It's okay, just help him move his feet." *Okay.* "Feel his rhythm. Feel your own." *Can I? How do I find it? Oh yeah, my breath. There it is.* "Now drive and draw him in rhythm." *Yes.*

"He's ready," Roses says. "Tighten the cinch and put on the bridle."

Now he stands with me, and there's no defense or sign of impending flight.

It seems so simple to put my foot in the stirrup and raise myself up, swing over, and reach for his other side with my leg. I sit deeply in the saddle, and for the first time atop him, I don't ask for anything.

As I sit, my breath flows down through my feet into the ground, the same ground he can feel through his body. From where Roses stands, she says she can feel how I'm breathing into his feet. Now my head expands like a big balloon, and maybe it'll detach from my neck, float away, and I'll be left a headless woman, sitting on Mud Pony in this therapy session where Roses has brought us step-by-breath into union. I fill my lungs, empty them, and I'm back.

This is the best moment we have ever had, standing together and feeling of each other. I can feel his back lift underneath me. I keep my hands still so as not to change anything. His head drops and he raises his tail for a fart that's more like a whisper.

"A release," chirps Roses, "good sign." She has not moved from where she stands just a few feet away. "Stay there, connect with your heartbeat. Feel your seat. Keep breathing."

This is the best work Mud Pony and I have ever done, to be still, yet still drawing and driving. This is the best breath I have ever taken, with my heart full between my legs, where he lifts the base of his neck and drops his head. He waits. I envision drawing and driving him in rhythm, my legs brushing against his ribs.

He groans and sneezes, letting the tension go with a nostril-flooding *fffflluuuuuhh.*

He let me in. For a few moments, I felt myself part of his body—ribs, neck, head, and shoulders. He released by lifting his spine, his tail, the whole length of his back, and then sneezing.

In the days that follow, I return to this sensation, and it's as if I were a teenager again, smelling horse sweat on the jeans I don't want to wash after being at the barn all day with Isabel. I go about my work with students, a half-smile on my face as I keep a glad rhythm.

I remember falling in love with Carter and our first surf trips to Santa Cruz, how the low tide at Cowell Cove sent friendly waves curling around the point. With water up to his armpits and a set re-forming near the beach, Carter stood holding the longboard, a sun-browned and beaten twelve-foot unit. As I got into position, and just before the wave crested, he shoved me forward.

Paddling fiercely, I moved from a push-up stance into a crouch once the wave was caught. I dropped only two quick feet down its face but felt a great force propel the surfboard's motion and me with it. Then it crumbled, and I stood triumphantly in the shallows as onlookers grinned and Carter applauded.

Something far bigger urged me forward on that wave, something that got its energy from prevailing winds, planetary forces, oceanic masses...

I rose to my feet on its fall.

· Eight ·

Winter deepens. With slap of rain and wind, dirt and manure make pasture a singular mix. Horse hooves sink into sludge containing things both known and unknown: seabird and bat guano, cow and chicken dung, arrowheads, old plaster, weathered molehills, wood chips, river sand, piggy banks, sawdust, moldy library books, nail cuttings, buckshot, oyster shells, coffee grounds, chimney soot, brown paper bags, knocked-out pipes, rotten pumpkins, shaved Brussels sprouts stalks, rusted hatchets, charcoal, wood ashes, ground bones, dead rats, horn shavings, lime, sphagnum, decayed pith, charcoal, eggshells, dog bones, leaf mold, pieces of glass, broken dishes—if only we could consciously compost our collective existence, how rich we'd be!

In our lifetime, might humans contribute to our planet's rehabilitation if we collaborated with this mud? Scientists have said that a quarter-inch increase of topsoil on every farm on Earth would lessen the effects of global warming by sequestering 25 percent of the carbon in the atmosphere. Greater and lesser miracles have occurred. *Why not this?* We could gather, mix, let it sit, then invite the cooperation of relatives from the animal and fungal kingdoms. Billions of hyphal tips with their smiling fuzz, millions of nematode mouth-holes, and workhorse bacterial conglomerates could then break down this matter into what matters: nutrients for soils fat as bacon, light as feathers, crumbly as cake.

It's a tender, hopeful vision of soil richness—these collective secretions, digestions, and excretions—a slow alchemy many never witness. Misunderstandings, therefore, abound. In 2006, Americans consumed spinach grown in the nearby Salinas Valley that was tainted by *E. coli.* Over a hundred people were hospitalized and three died; the culprit was found to be cow manure on the spinach leaves, so boarders were banned from riding the trails next to the farmers' fields. I remember my confusion during what became our final ride around the fields, when a worker waved frantically at us to turn around.

Horses had been blamed a few years earlier, even before the E. coli outbreak, when the creek that divides the ranch in half and empties into the nearby marine reserve was discovered to be carrying something that was killing organisms in the tidal zone. Our ranch, with its unsequestered manure, was suspect. The ranch was forbidden from spreading it on the trails, and the county threatened to shut us down unless we halted its flow into the creek. The ranch owner built concrete loading and storage pads, so a front-end loader could move huge piles of manure into enormous compost piles, which could then be easily loaded into a dump truck. Boarders separated shavings and manure and wheelbarrowed them into stations for removal.

It was later determined the contamination had been caused by construction of a neighboring housing development, but Jess, Carter's sister and ranch manager at the time, had already become the proud steward of several enormous and lovingly tended manure mounds.

Jess was also a full-time teacher at an elementary school, and she brought her inner-city students on a field trip to the ranch for a lesson on ecology. Pushing up her shirtsleeves and plunging a bare arm into a tower of decomposing horseshit, she allowed her hand to linger deep inside the mound. And, for effect, she described how warm it felt inside as she wiggled her fingers: "That's the microbes doing their job, eating the manure and turning it into the richest soil ever." Her students groaned in disgust.

Then she pulled out her arm, brushed off the leavings, and described how easily the detritus slid off her skin. "Things are clean in there, thanks to the microbes—it's all breaking down—see, it's not like poop anymore... my skin is dry, not wet."

Some of her kids shrunk back, but one or two brave volunteers took off their jackets, pushed sleeves to elbows, stuck out their tongues, and dove in. Grimaces of "Eeeew!" then smiles of "Aw, sick!" When the lesson was finished, dirt was no longer dirty.

The full moon appears just above the trees on a late winter afternoon. Is it the seasonal Hunger Moon or Wolf Moon here to witness my attempt to re-create that magic spot of release in the round pen we found with Roses only last week? Mud Pony stands quietly when I step into the stirrup and perch my weight just above his withers. Now I anticipate approaching the threshold of *feel* after those deep, connective breaths.

I resist the impulse to throw the leg over and opt instead to stroke his shoulder from where I stand in the stirrup. Two boarders appear with dogs, absorbed in their conversation as they head out toward the trail.

He's listening to me. I'm listening to him. We're together.

Taking a breath, I leg over, but accidentally brush his rump with my right toe. For a full second, I experience the sensation of my seat on the saddle before his lurch and leap. Desperate not to get thrown, I grab his mouth with one rein to bring his head around, but he runs right through my grip. I get tossed and land in a lump with sand in my mouth and shirt, acutely aware of the dog walkers laughing yards away. They missed the leap, the fall, and me on the ground like a roughly peeled potato thrown into a tub.

I'm nothing to him. I press my face into the sand then rise to look at him where he stands, frozen, tense, not bothering to flee from my approach. In previous collisions, kicks, bucks, and falls, I'd blamed myself, taken responsibility for my ignorance and lack of experience, felt I might be betraying him by pushing through and ignoring his feral nature, his traumatic history.

A cold, westerly wind kicks up from the sea. Now the moon is much higher. It's large and bright. Is it laughing? I grab hat, flag, and jacket, snatch the reins, kick open the gate, stare at him. Will he try to get by me? *You want out, don't you? Well then, we'll see about that...* He snorts and won't move. *Too bad. And because you jerked me around...* He skitters through. I yank him back to me with a punishing tug. *So what about your tender mouth or instinct to self-preserve. It's not my fault, Traitor.*

O

In my second year of teaching at a high school with a reputation for chaos and a majority of students designated "at risk," I knew, with a growing sense of helplessness, that I was failing my fifth-period class. Next door, Mr. X crushed dissent with humiliating tongue-lashings, and it was okay by him if certain troublemakers never again sat down at a desk in his classroom. He yelled at his students and relied on the pedagogy of drill-and-kill and speak-only-when-you're-spoken-to. There were none of the interventions and interactions I attempted: creative writing, group discussions, personal connections to a text, or reciprocal reading. He addressed each student by last name, assigned students to sit in rows in alphabetical order, enforced the rule of "keep heads and voices down," and relied on a traditional, chapter-by-chapter sequence of lessons in an outdated textbook.

A veteran of the district who had grown cynical and who was close to retirement, Mr. X. openly disdained my attempts to "save" the worst offenders. He'd wander into my classroom after school without my invitation and observe that I was a "hippie type." He scorned the couch I had in my classroom, where students crashed during lunchtime or after school to listen to music and hang out. I resented his attitude and felt that what I was doing was real teaching—at least I offered opportunities for students to express themselves both in writing and in speaking, I welcomed them at my door and started a hiking club to get them outdoors during club blocks. Then one of my students asked me to advise a new hip-hop club, which soon met in my classroom to play music and dance.

During the hottest week of the spring semester, frustration and restlessness pervaded the school as students roamed the hallways before, after, and during class. It was as if staff and faculty were too hot to be bothered. In my classroom, fifth period began right after lunch with two students launching themselves over my desk in a tussle. Another swiped the warm-up exercise from the overhead projector and hid it, faking ignorance. Then the class clown entered, wrapped in packaging tape and performing a robot dance, causing the class to explode with laughter. Of course, he upstaged me. Against my protest, another student shouted with sarcasm, "Why don't you yell at us like Mr. X does?" Then a student in the class, a leader who was usually cooperative, cast forth a string of complaints about the heat, pleading for me to open the door and provide ventilation, as the windows didn't open. I shook my head. Too much noise in the hallways.

"It's hot in here," someone joined in, shouting.

The sarcastic boy spat at me, "I hate this class."

I gulped. That hurt more than anything.

"You want some air?" I challenged. "I'll give you air."

I lifted a metal chair and with one leg, punched through two panes of a sealed glass window. Shards pierced my hands and wrists. Feeling no pain, I stood in front of my students with a new sensation of clarity, or was it relief?

I set the chair down. For the first time all year, they were silent. Apparently, I had become even more fearsome than Mr. X. The transparency was delivered to the projector. I cleared a space around the broken glass with my foot, grabbed some Kleenex to stop the bleeding, and began the lesson.

No staff or faculty member knew what had happened until a week later, when the JROTC teacher overheard two students talking about the incident. He questioned them and took their statement to the principal. I didn't know it at the time, but the group of administrators who called me in for questioning had just found out that the district was planning to close the school at the end of the year due to low enrollment.

"What were you thinking!" the principal groaned, slapping her palm against her forehead as I sat in front of the administrative team. There was nothing I could say in defense—my actions were unacceptable, reprehensible—and I was sent home on leave as an investigation was conducted. The union rep recommended that I not meet with any administrators without her. As a temporary teacher with an emergency credential, I had no recourse but to look for another job.

Two weeks passed. After each student was questioned and the investigation concluded, the assistant superintendent gave the okay for me to return to my class—on the condition that I attend anger-management training and receive an official write-up in my file. The week I came back, I kept a low profile and didn't make eye contact with anyone in the main office until a guidance counselor stopped me and described what had happened during the student interviews. To my relief, he grinned and shook his head, "They questioned twenty kids, and each said the same thing: We were talking. She got mad. She broke the window. She gave us some air."

I apologized to my fifth-period class and promised I would never do anything like that again. For their part, they were less rambunctious and more respectful, but I overheard some of them betting on whether I would get "crazy lady" again. For the remainder of the school year, they called me "AC."

O

My newfound knowledge of *feel* no longer feels like power, but fragility. I wish someone could free me—or even fire me from Mud Pony. Might I exit via a new job or a different horse? But I know there's no such luck. I prefer to be the stuck one, the holder of his history and conditioning, the responsible parent for a potentially dangerous and formerly feral child. However, I've got options: to let Mud Pony live out his life in pasture and focus my riding desires on the palomino... or sell him to Rolando.

I envision the latter: he'd train Mud Pony to dance, to be a parade horse. He'd stick a gag bit in Mud Pony's mouth and snap whips at his newly shod feet. It would be a dramatic and mechanical reckoning—hardened muscle would bulge unnaturally at the front of Mud Pony's neck, and I'd watch with horror as over time, his body and spirit would wither from unnatural stress. I'd hear the rattle of the knacker's truck, its loose, head-high panels creaking down the ranch road. At a trimming clinic, during the dissection part, I'd fish through a garbage bag full of cadaver hooves and find his feet.

Outside our window in the schoolyard at 8 a.m., a feral cat lies on a white rag at the doorstep of Bungalow 2. He doesn't bother to stalk the pigeons mere inches away, pecking at the grass growing tall between the cracks. Carter says he's probably dying. "I've been watching him for days—he's hardly moved." But when we unlatch the window, the inert feline lifts his head. The pigeons fly away when Carter launches a carton filled with water out the window and it splashes on the asphalt. I rummage through the cupboards for a can of tuna or sardines but find only a package of powdered milk.

All day I stare out at the schoolyard and watch the cat's belly rise and fall. The table is stacked with essays. I could procrastinate on the piles I need to finish grading and go to my horses, but instead I hide indoors.

I'm left to my own wanderings in between the focus I give to each student's developing ideas. They've been groaning about the length and complexity of the assigned novel, *Invisible Man*, and now, how to write an essay about its motifs, but they've hung in there as I've encouraged them to discuss each episode of the epic: a surreal battle royal and racially charged sexual encounter; a psychopathic professor; the unnamed narrator's existential crises; his participation in organized activism, speech-making, riots, and the burning of dilapidated, disease-ridden buildings. A rape fantasy scene. The ravages of racism in both the North and the South. What, they asked me, does this all mean? And during the narrator's penultimate epiphany, after he has just seen his friend being shot to death, time slows, and a flock of pigeons rises above him and dives in synchronized movements, catching the light with their bellies as they roll in midair. The author highlights these pigeons for a reason, I told my students—what is it?

I wracked my brain for meaningful connections and then distributed framed photos of our pet pigeon. I told the story of our life with Chad and how she flew away one day out an open window; how most people seem disgusted by these birds and call them flying rats; how pigeons are no more flying rats than people are... *but we're the ones who name them, who make that meaning. We're animals who can define our own existence.* The narrator discovered he could act with free, conscious choice despite being used, mistreated, dispossessed by a punishing and racist society. He realizes freedom when he goes underground to create a life on *his* terms.

Each essay struggles to define itself. Much of my students' thinking is inchoate, but I find strong insights and moments of brilliance. On the day students handed in their essays, one student brought in cupcakes, each decorated with an iced pigeon.

I broke a window in my classroom not because of Mr. X, a stifling hot day, or a chaotic school, but because I was locked up inside. Floating above unnamed reservoirs of anxiety, insecurity, fear, I braved the world as an observably functional adult, barely concealing my anxiety and rage, for I often felt put upon by forces I couldn't name. I loved my job and wanted to prove myself, but in a desperate fashion, as if my self-worth depended on it. After shattering that glass, I became even more terrified of failing and told no one (save Carter) what I'd done. *Why was it easier for me to forgive my students than myself? Why is it now so hard to forgive Mud Pony?*

The constriction inside my chest increases when I see his parked stance and concave spine like an old-fashioned walking horse in a halter class. He's tight through his ribs when I tie him at the post. And when I get the broom to sweep the rubber mat he's standing on, he snorts and pulls the line taut. He would strangle himself in the effort to escape if I didn't stop sweeping.

The ranch is bustling with activity. It seems everyone has something to say about him. "How's he doing?" they ask.

"He's a chickenshit," I snarl.

More people stop and watch. "Look how tense he is," they say. "Look how tight the skin on his belly."

Their gaze intensifies my humorlessness and vitriol. I want to spit on them.

An hour after wrestling with his lower limbs during a hoof trim, he still hasn't taken a breath, and his neck remains hard as a pile of stacked bricks—it's the fallout of his flee and my fall, but even more than that, it's everything between us: *he's a traitor, and I'm a sucker.*

Early this morning, Carter left to work with a graphics client, and I sat on our bed, shuffling my tarot deck and laying the cards face down in the shape of a Celtic cross. When I got to the final card, I asked, "What will my future bring with Mud Pony?" And then, I drew the Death card—reversed. A sharp inhalation—of all the cards to draw!

The accompanying description in the booklet read, "Slow change or no change at all. Narrow escape from serious harm." I envisioned the long road ahead—or no road at all. Could it mean that I am able to change *but he cannot?*

I push against the Death card. I let him loose in the big arena and chase him with a lunge whip as he throws up clods of mud and grass, raises his tail like a flag, blows and snorts. This causes the nearby paddock horses to startle. Everything about him is SO MUCH HORSE.

He finds a patch of grass growing in the middle and puts his head down. Something stirs in me at his flagrant attitude, a rejection. *Oh you won't change? C'mon then! Show me who you are!* I throw the rope at him. He spurts out of reach. I chase him around the arena until he's blowing and sweaty. This is not effective training. I am running him from the feelings I myself want to flee: hurt, frustration, shame, failure.

"Get away!" I shout at him, but I'm yelling at myself too: *I don't want you to see that I don't know what to do, that I don't believe in myself enough to help you. Flee from me! Get out from under my ugly self! Get away from my fuck-ups and failure! You will never find comfort! You will never be safe! You will never be who I want you to be!*

Later, after his coat is wet from effort and exhaustion, he plunges his nose into his grain bucket, down then up, watching for my intrusion just like he did on the day we trailered him to his new home. *Slow change or no change at all.* In the waning light, I tug on his muddy, clumped mane with my fingers as the clouds begin to gather into vague masses. My fatigue settles into a blankness after the tantrum. I want to fall asleep clinging to him and wake up as someone else.

He licks the bottom of the bucket.

Back in the city, I notice a slowed rhythm. I buy a chicken taco at the corner taquería and eat it with roasted salsa, tortilla chips, extra salt, and squirts of fresh lime. I'm sitting at a table against the wall with the stack of *Invisible Man* papers I've been carrying everywhere in a brown bag. The chicken is warm and tender, and the clumps of black beans are filling. Facing the door, I notice a woman my age with curly brunette hair past her shoulders enter and walk past where I sit, hands thrust deep into her magenta trench coat. There's something strange about the way she looks straight ahead as if to avoid anything in her peripheral vision. I mimic her mannerism, suppressing the urge to turn my head and follow her motion. She walks to the bathroom and out of my line of vision. Now she reemerges, walking slowly, but this time she's got a half-finished burrito in her hands. *Where did she get that? I only saw her enter and exit the bathroom.* She eats and walks in a deliberate yet respectful way—out of the taquería and onto the street.

I finish my taco, grade one essay, and start another. Then she's back, walking in the same slow manner, hands in pockets, eyes up, without any eye contact. She stops at the trash bin at the front of the restaurant, reaches in, fishes around, and pulls out a remnant. Now, instead of visiting the bathroom, she sits at a table near the door. She seems to be playing the part of a customer who gets to eat a burrito inside the taquería. Her fingers are long and graceful as they hold the butt of the burrito and its peeled foil. She takes a bite and then closes her mouth and eyes, slowly chewing with care. Rice and beans spill onto the table. She ignores this, and when she's had her fill, pulls a napkin from the dispenser, wipes her mouth, and leaves crumpled napkins and food scraps too. She rises and walks out the door, hands in pockets. The manager behind the register lifts his head and meets my gaze. He moves from his post to wipe up the mess.

For weeks, Mud Pony comes to me in my dreams. I've forgotten him and he's been hobbled for days in a winter creek on the hilly grounds of a suburban corporate park. I finally arrive, he's assumed the shape of my younger brother, shivering and hungry. The water rises and threatens to submerge him. He pulls away as I reach out to him, but I glue myself to his neck and pull him out of the creek. I'm sobbing, wretched and at fault. In another dream, he's been in a stall for days covered with a thick blanket. Now he's no longer cold but sweaty, feverish, and shrunken to the size of a toy horse. I take the blanket off and he stretches—first one hind leg then the other, like a dog. His gut is tied up from dehydration. I pour water on his back and he grows to normal size.

I go quiet around Carter and he asks if I'm okay, tries to comfort me, but I can't let him in. On weekends, I spend hours napping, prepping, and grading, rarely leaving our apartment. As I alternate between sleep and work, I try envisioning something positive, but nothing emerges. An atmospheric river has dropped rain on the coast and snow in the Sierras, and for two whole weeks, storm after storm follows. The horses find shelter under a tree and stand together. That's the image I need to connect to. Without going anywhere, I transport myself to the herd's great, patient stillness. It was not a problem for them to wait in the dark for their hay. The rancheros are watching out for them too.

What I first wanted from Mud Pony now seems far away. It's the dream of a child who no longer exists. To smell or see without getting to taste or eat is an old, familiar feeling. And it's not enough to look up at the stars at night and know the light we see is from a source that may no longer be. I am saddened by what I can't have yet still reach for it through that sadness. It's a strange heat. At least it's better than the coldness of nothing, the stillness of *no reach*.

Carter says I don't have to turn my longing into something bad. I can just have it and love Mud Pony as best I can. And I love how he loves even my longing.

I teach my students the Latin root of the word *desire*, meaning "from the stars." I ask them to write about their own desires and consider what it means to reach for the stars but know they will never get there. "Which is better?" I ask, "To have the desire and never have it fulfilled or to have no desire?" And then I ask them to find these references in the play we're reading, *A Streetcar Named Desire*. They are amazed to find *stars* and *desire* scattered like seeds throughout the scenes. "Did the writer plan all this?" they wonder.

Near the climax of the play, Blanche says, "The opposite of death is desire." Most of the students have scorned her mannerisms and manipulations until that moment, but then they get why she made the choices she did. I tell them that we all do this in some way, wrap our lives around our desires and hold on to fend off what's inevitable—hurt, sickness, disappointment—we all go through something. Some give up. Some never let go.

O

Driving south on the coastal highway to the ranch, I envision another sort of exit. A teacher is returning midyear from maternity leave, and I could propose she take my classes. *Wow, could I really do this—opt for a semester of leave? Or what about exiting the classroom altogether?*

These ruminations are interrupted by the engine light on my dashboard, which suddenly blinks on. I've lost all power and the engine's dead. Gliding downhill, I turn on the flashers, tap the brakes, and ride the winding shoulder, hoping no stray cyclist or abandoned car sits there. Eventually, I slow enough to set the emergency brake, stop, put the car into first gear, and crawl out the passenger side.

My car is parked mere feet from all those who barrel down the hill, and it shudders as they speed past. *Narrow escape from serious harm.* I sit cross-legged on the shoulder of the highway for an hour, waiting for a tow, looking at the hills along this stretch. There are condominiums and bright blue Eichlers at the top. Ice plant and rhododendron bushes thrive at their feet. Car after car. A cop whizzes past without a glance.

At the garage, my mechanic tells me the car is dead—the timing belt snapped, then its forward motion and spinning steel wrenched the engine out of alignment. He could put in a new engine, but glumly, I realize I don't have the money and sign over its shell to the junkyard.

○

Without any missed connections, the one-way bus trip from my door to the ranch gate takes two hours, including a mile-long walk down the ranch road. I try to make good use of the time, rereading the novel I'm planning to teach for the last unit of the semester, Remarque's *All Quiet on the Western Front.* I sit between teenagers both on the train and on the bus. Even translated, the language is deft, visceral, disturbing. My stomach churns when I read about a battle in the trenches where horses scream as their guts spill from gaping wounds in their bellies. Around me teenage boys mock each other and curse the fog. I'm unsettled by their restlessness and unarticulated anger. They are bored, agitated, full of profanity. They wear sports jerseys, boxers peeking out of saggy pants, and jewelry. They ogle the pubescent girls, who stand next to the driver. These boys could lay waste to themselves and others like the soldiers in this book. I want to reach out to them, but they frighten me.

We spill off at the Lottie Mar bus stop. The boys don't yet scatter. A man seems to be waiting for them. They call him "Forty." There is a quick exchange. They cross the wide boulevard to the beach across from the strip mall. On a school day, they might carry binders, books, or backpacks, but on weekdays or weekends, they carry only their phones. I've herded hundreds just like them from one end of the school year to the other but will never know whether any of the things I taught stuck. Some responded to my efforts, took the risk, and learned something. Many could not.

I imagine a day in their lives: they taunt each other, smoke weed at the beach, drink coffee at Starbucks, and dare each other to steal Doritos from Safeway. There's rage barely concealed behind a scrim of disdain. I sense it because I, too, know hurt, defense, reaction, the need to belong. But even when I broke the window to get my students' attention, they didn't give up on me. Maybe it's because they saw my frustration, helplessness, and anger. They, too, wanted more order, structure, and safety. *Perhaps, just like Mud Pony, my students keep me honest.*

I sit on the bench next to a woman wearing a waitressing uniform and we continue our wait for the connecting bus. She stares at our feet where stray grackles peck crumbs and points at a bird that's missing a foot and has a stick for a stump. Another has a leg with eruptions that look like cauliflower. I go back to my book.

Finally, the 17 arrives. Few passengers continue the hop over Devil's Slide to Moss Beach, so it's easy to grab a window seat and marvel at how closely we ride the edge of the cliff above the sea. On the mile walk down the ranch road, everything is gray or green or brown. There are new shoots of grass. I drop down next to the creek that borders the ranch road. By the time I reach the pasture, my heart has begun to lift. I'm greeted by the neighing and excited trembling of all the horses on the row of paddocks that border the pasture. *It's been so long since we've seen each other!*

In the aftermath of a foggy wind, the sky is the same monochrome gray as the ocean, and I can't tell where one ends and the other begins. Eucalyptus pods and branches cover the ground. Mud Pony and the palomino stand next to each other on a mound above the muck and behind the pine tree, which offers some shelter during the rain. This has probably been their spot for a couple of days, and I imagine they have not yielded it to any of the other herd members. I call out and they lift their heads. Mud Pony calls back, shifts his weight, and pushes the palomino out of the way so he can be the first to descend the short, steep slope, walk through the mud, and meet me at the gate. She follows. Last night, I had a dream she was down and fevered, her hind hoof ripped open to reveal the coffin bone. I got out of bed and moved to the living room couch so the image would unstick.

I put three scoops of forage in their buckets and add supplements. Both horses are caked with mud. His mane is matted with wind braids. I spray detangler on the brush then directly on his hair. He snorts when he sees the bottle. I ignore his reaction, finish the task, and put him back in pasture so I can focus on the slight lameness I saw in the palomino's walk on my last visit.

Fortunately, she moves without hesitation, and I don't sense any heat in her hooves, although they are fetid from standing all week in the mud. I clean and trim them. My tools are dull, but the horn is soft. White flakes soon cover the ground like snowfall.

On my walk out the ranch road to the bus stop, I pause to look at a horse sleeping on its side with hooves as delicate as a doll's feet attached to a hunk of ribs and belly. I marvel how these feet supply all movement, all health to this inert being—and how much weight they hold! Four hours of sleep a day in twenty-minute REM increments seems only a bit of rest for such a big body. I wish I could place something on his belly to watch the up-and-down motion—a rubber ducky or a bowl of soup. Another herd member stands nearby, watching.

I continue walking. Four or maybe five cars slow down as they see me. Darkness descends. A truck stops after passing by, and the driver, a ranchero I don't recognize, asks if I want a ride. I thank him but refuse. I wait for the bus at the corner street stop, pull my book out of my backpack, and reenter its world under the soft yellow glow of a streetlamp.

○

The morning is bright and cool at seven. I want to drink in the air next to a quiet pasture with my horses, but instead I stand with Carter at our kitchen window and look out on Mission Street and the abandoned schoolyard, observing sky, light, wind, street, pigeons. As if on cue, the construction crew that began yesterday at 8 a.m. renews its noisy barrage.

I can't connect to the hours I spent with my horses yesterday. I can't remember the song I sang to Mud Pony when I first rode him with Rolando. I can't connect to how I told him, "I'm here for you. I'm not going anywhere." Right now, if Carter asked me to find his pulse or massage his back, I would need a map. *I'm out of my body. How do I get back in?*

January winds stir things up inside me I didn't even know were there: how I dislike hearing Carter crunch his toast on the couch; how the herk and jerk of the bus offends my body; how Mud Pony can't suffer me to rasp his feet. I reenter my sensations through grand, self-important irritation. With every flap of a trailer cover or swing of a tack room door, he snatches his foot away, and I'm left to follow his hind end to the length of the lead rope, around the tie post, back to the rubber mat where the dance begins all over again. He will not relax his head and body except when I stop and scratch his neck, shoulders, and withers; then he drops his head, but only for a second.

Later that night, I dream I'm inside the pasture with the palomino and I can't get to the gate, for she's kicking at me and blocking my exit. She's surly and threatening and I'm afraid of her. "You can't have what you want," she says. "Just because you want something doesn't mean you can have it."

This root I have grown since infancy, the root of flowering wrong, is still a dormant tuber at my core, hiding its thick bottom in darkness and dirt. I carry it around like an invisible medicine ball or enormous tumor. I hunch at the middle. My steps are slow. I'm now growing a new root, but this old burl is thick, scabby, embattled. I want my organs and blood to have a different set of memories. I wish my spleen would not worry. *I wish my colon were not such a workhorse hitched to a plow.*

As we're working in the round pen during our monthly weekend lesson, Mud Pony kicks out at Roses when she drives him around the pen. Roses rattles the flag at him, but not in a mean way. He erupts into a gallop with the puffery of an arched neck and raised tail. I admire how Roses, like Harry, is never reactive. When she shakes the flag or chases him, it's never done as an outburst or with a shaming tone, but as a straight meeting of the horse's body with the correct amount of pressure, not too much.

Roses pronounces, "Even though only a few short months ago, you were riding all over the place, that's simply not where we're at." During a pause where we stand together and let him catch his breath, she adds, "But there's no reason to believe we can't get there again."

I offer her my water bottle, but she shakes her head.

"Remember, when he can break at the ribs it means his thought can come around and be directed by your leg, or the pressure on his mouth or at his side. Don't forget that a horse that's 'broken' isn't broken in spirit. A broken horse yields his ribcage. This is a horse who has not given you that."

By the end of our lesson, when I see him accept the saddle without moving off, when he lifts his back to it, takes a breath, and allows my foot in the stirrup, a part of me believes her. *Maybe.*

After we finish, I return the length of the ranch road to the bus stop. I'm restless and walk a single block to the town's only corner store to gaze for a long moment at the brightly wrapped colonies of Hostess, Nabisco, and Nestlé stacked carefully next to the cashier. I choose chocolate-coated donettes and a box of animal crackers. I save them for the bus ride, selecting a seat on the left side so I can look at the ocean. The donettes are more texture than taste—a gooey, hydrogenated paste. I eat them all, then eat half of the animal crackers before studying the packaging. An image of snarling tigers in caged compartments on yellow wheels, yet the animal I put into my mouth is an amorphous woolly sheep. The junk snack gives meager satisfaction. Instead of energized, I'm now bloated and large, as if I now heft an inflated life raft inside a rib cage that can barely contain it. I sit with the discomfort and try to reassure myself: broken is not to be fixed but where everything is found.

○

The hills are still green from the winter rain, but ever since the dry space of several weeks between storms, there's a coat of dust under my feet on the ranch road. The pasture herd spends much of its day mouthing the hard, sandy pack of the hill for the grass sprinklings, which patch the slope like topiary growing a new coat. When I arrive in the late afternoon, they're grazing at the hill's zenith, having made a clockwise sweep of its slope. I call to Mud Pony and the palomino, and they raise their heads. I move around the tack room and hope they will come down when they hear the grain land in their buckets. But at this time of year, they do no such thing; they linger, put their heads down, continue to nibble.

Finally, I unhitch their rope halters from the pasture gate and make my way up the hill, alternating between switchback and straight up. Sometimes I wobble and worry I might lose my balance and fall—the footing is loose and uneven. I smile at how the horses stand above me, nonchalantly watching my clumsy ascent. When I reach the mare, I offer a carrot and pull her halter round cheek and poll. Mud Pony, grazing many yards above her, finally raises his head, nickers, and drops down the steep slope with the ease of a backcountry ski bum. I leave her standing there with the rope over her back and climb and fetch him just above where she stands. I halter and lead him to her, then ask her to move ahead and down the slope. On each step of the narrow trail, both horses stay with me. There's his warm breath on my neck, the lick and chew of his relaxation. I am positioned on top of the dock of her tail—she could flick a fly from my face. I let her choose our path.

Suddenly I know this to be the most comforting place in the world, stepping, picking, descending, sandwiched between my two barefoot horses. If I were at the pasture gate, I would be curious to watch how the trio snakes its way down the hill, how the rest of the herd follows in a line, how the human does not flinch or struggle or direct but nudges and follows, how the rest of the herd now wants to rush ahead.

When we reach the bottom, we stand aside and allow the other horses to pass and careen down the steepest section, tossing their heads when they reach the bottom and exploding into a joyous gallop. I look up and see a high, full moon in a royal-blue sky. Once, my mother picked me up at school in the family van and for no reason at all, there was a box wound with gold string on my seat—with a gasp, I realized it was for me. Nested in tissue paper was a lime-green skirt with ruffles and lace and a top with a green ribbon to match. A slight lift in my mother's face. A gift.

O

Rolando rides the cremello out to the PG&E road, passing nearby as I work in the round pen with my horse. I sense his gaze.

He will never know that I am rearranging my life to better care for this process. He may never understand that this is all I may get right now—a right eye, lowered head, lick, and chew. We leave the round pen. I look up. He's gone. Perhaps I was too harsh to think Rolando would abuse Mud Pony if he owned him. Everything I know of him suggests he would be both caring and careful.

I run a hose on Mud Pony's legs, then tie him at the post and go to work to finish yesterday's trim. I marvel at the perfect feet he was born with. An oval of dead sole can be peeled off with my fingers like a thin layer of fat on a cold bowl of bone broth. I don't even need a hoof knife.

The chickens are clucking and stinking it up behind me as I work. One puffed-up hen refuses to stop venturing into the cardboard boxes in the corner, where she probably wants to lay an egg, but a clutch of bigger hens launches the attack when she gets too close. There's blood on her head—it's been pecked raw, and on one wing you can see the roots; they went for that too.

I hear Harry's voice: "Have patience, focus, wait, you'll make it." The best teachers get inside you like this. They give you everything they've got because they believe in you, and that belief gets stamped on your heart. *I can pause before I swing my leg over and before I ask him to move. I can wait for Mud Pony to lean into me rather than flee. I can wait for him to take a breath, and the years I wait will become the many breaths we take together.*

Someday he may feel reassured by my presence. I've got Harry's belief in me and my willingness to follow and find it inside myself; I, too, can wait and notice.

O

After the early soak, it's now become the driest winter I've ever seen. Dust devils hover above the ground in flat spots. Sometimes the moisture closes in, and I think I can taste it, but then the clouds from the north recede and hover over the ocean horizon rather than drop their moisture. The horses look puffed up, and their legs seem swollen from the dry air and static heat. The palomino has marks on her hind end above her tail—the chunks of her underlying caramel-colored summer coat that were ripped out months ago by another horse's teeth have been filled in by ashen-colored, winter hair. Her rump looks like the aerial view of a recently harvested cornfield, with broken stalks and patchy areas that were missed by the machine. The dirt in the pasture has gotten hardpacked and unforgiving from confined horses standing around. It needs to be refreshed with aeration, water, and compost.

I watch and listen and don't think of the future. Without the freedom of a car, I am not with my horses as much as I would like, but when I arrive, they come down the hill to greet me. Of course, there's nothing for them to eat, having nibbled it all down to dust. I ride her and pony him close by my knee up the hill, and the tall, dead grass has broken ends that rattle when we brush against it. Stepping through shrubs or grass there is much sweeping and swooshing and crackling. Everything seems to be on alert and awaiting something—the ground, the grass, the dust, the trees, the sky. Even the deer with a broken leg I spy in the eucalyptus is standing at attention. I see him before the horses perk up their ears. It's a young buck with stubs for horns like a Halloween devil. He limps loudly on three legs through the crackly duff, retreating into the shadows of the trees as I stand there with the horses. Coming down the big hill over the harbor and highway, two golden hawks shriek. I see them in a pine tree, agitating the heavy lower branches. One flies off with a snake dangling from its talons.

In the early hours of the morning as I lie on my back, I hear the blood swoosh through my ears in an even gait. I swallow once then twice, just to feel how smoothly the muscles at the back of my throat open the passage, then settle back into rest. And my nose, the tip of it, alert and sensitive, ushering in the air that flows down the throat into my lungs, which lift and lower at their own pace. Each organ of my body is an instrument, and the heart is their conductor, orchestrating purpose, direction, and tempo. If this conductor could dance, she would lead me in the graceful steps of an estampie. She raises her arms and the organs lift themselves; the liver opens its mouth and the stomach waits for an empty, silent note to rumble; the blood fans out and through, washing over everything in its path.

As I lie in bed, my horses stand side by side in the darkness on the bottom slope of a hill. They stay clear of the shadowy trees, so they can hear their guts churn. Their nose tips flare with each inhalation. Their eyes roll back in their sockets when they yawn. When they inhale, I exhale. When they shift their weight, I curl up on my side. When they sneeze, I stir. We are together—all our bones, organs, and blood—sleeping, secreting.

Rising, I look out our kitchen window. Two teenagers bounce and sway on the Mission Street sidewalk in rhythm with the body-rattling bass of a parked car. A woman in spandex with a pregnant bulge takes baby steps as she jogs. Later, I exit our apartment and approach the top of our stairs above the gate.

There's neighbor Darren, a tall, broad-shouldered woodworker, exiting the building just before me with his five-year-old daughter, a mischievous sprite who rides a pink bicycle through the hallways. She reaches up, and without breaking stride, he lifts her in one motion to straddle his neck. There they go, crossing the street into the late winter sun, perfectly attuned to their carry-and-ride. He wraps his hands around her shins. She extends her arms and hands to the sky, increasing her papa's height. His joy and pride seem to grow with each step of holding and honoring her playful request to be taller than him.

Darren is a quiet person to whom I rarely speak, but his parental gesture conveys amazement, tenderness, a message far more powerful than casual chitchat. I follow them for a short distance and then turn into the alley, where I suddenly gasp and choke, caught by a fit of weeping. A hollow pain through my middle. The sensation of something taken or severed. Little and littler. A nameless thing.

To have parents who once attended, then imploded, withdrew. *To have a child, to have been a child.* Though they now seem like strangers, I know it through and through: *I was loved. Am loved.*

◯

I've never seen a school full of students rise from their seats to applaud one of their teachers, but then I've never seen a school say goodbye in this way. I've been so busy, I haven't even thought about my departure until now—when I told my students I was leaving at the end of the semester, I was shocked that they even noticed or cared. I'm flushed and flustered as they usher me to the stage to stand in front of the school. I had forgotten how these students gave me their willingness to be vulnerable, to follow me on a path they couldn't navigate, to take the risk of being beginners. *Then they hand me flowers!* Four of my former students get up to speak, and they mean what they say because their praise is mixed with the ambivalence they felt for my teaching at the start:

"Last year, I didn't understand what the heck she was teaching us in the fall, but then I woke up in the spring and realized I could write."

I'm leaving the comfort and security of this school to unearth my deepest junk, to confront the trapped feelings that herd me from lesson plans to paper grading. I'm unsure how I will sustain a life over the long term, and I don't have another job yet, but I know I want to write and to ride. Carter, who has reinvented himself countless times—most recently as a sculptor and graphic designer—assures me I have my intelligence, skills, and experience. He says I can take this with me and do whatever I want, find something that will support my inner rhythms. I want to lead or be part of my own herd, even if that herd is just the two of us and my horses.

In the early afternoon, after I administer the final exam to my last class, he picks me up at school, and I stash shopping bags full of books, exams, papers in his pickup. "You're a quitter," he says as he hugs me and kisses the top of my head. "I'm so proud of you."

We drive down the coast alongside the late January sun. I'm wan and chubby from nonstop sitting, grading, and eating over the holidays. An hour and a half later we arrive in the parking lot at Año Nuevo State Reserve and blink into the low sun, flat ocean, blue sky, and mild offshore winds. It's strange to expose my skin. On a guided hike to the elephant seal rookery, we can't see over the dunes except for the top of the old lighthouse keeper's residence, once converted to a research station for scientists and now inhabited by sea lions and elephant seals. I wish we could go out there and see them sprawled across the old linoleum of the kitchen floor. Maybe they are wedged into cracked, peeling hallways or resting on the stairs on their way to the second floor. Maybe their layers of fat roll over the edges of the bathtub, or maybe they have stuffed themselves in a closet.

Our group chatters incessantly as we dig into the deep, soft sand and climb the dunes. Irritated by the talking, I find myself part of recent unemployment or disability crises, extra shifts at the hospital, loads of administrative paperwork, career changes, and classes. Someone observes for the hundredth time that it's a beautiful day, but all talking stops when we reach the first bull.

Conserving his energy for weeks at a time before he returns to the depths to feed on squid and fish, he lies there with all two thousand pounds of his flesh. A giant's toddler has pushed mud and sand into a rude log with his massive hands—this one has the schnoz of a cartoon character but not the fatty proboscis of a full-grown male. His eyes are barely open, and we see only dark slits atop his bulk. The elephant seals are not afraid of us. The guide explains that their only natural predators on land are grizzly bears, and now, of course, the only grizzlies in California are on the state flag.

We leave the lone bull and climb the dune to an overlook where more enormous lumps rest up against each other—a harem of females with the alpha male in the middle and stray beta males at the fringes, waiting for an opportunity to challenge. The guide explains how they scarcely move in the heat. One digs into the sand with a side flipper to find the coolness beneath and sprays the sand over them. I never knew how far these seals travel—thousands of miles to Hawaii and up to the Aleutian Islands. The deepest dive measured by scientists was five thousand feet. I imagine how in the ocean they must glide with the ease of jumbo jets in the open sky. How strange to be so powerful and fast and agile in water and be so still and clumsy on land. Yet they move quickly, too, when needed.

The alpha bull, who is easily twice as large as the one-ton Percheron mare I used to lease and ride, chases another male by raising up half his bulk so his giant flap of a nose falls up and over, then lunges his entire body toward it, pushing from back to front and moving more like a snake or bear with rings of muscle pushing rolls of blubber. The guide tells us that these seals are directly related to bears, and I can see why—I recall films of grizzlies on display, fighting with lightning-fast bulk and jerk as the rolls of muscle and fat on their back propelled the strike of a paw.

A soundtrack accompanies our hike. Before we even saw the seals, we'd heard a series of metallic gurgles like the sound of an emptying drain. The resonating chambers of enormous sinus cavities serve not just to regulate temperature in their bodies but also to call, signal, and warn. We hear a bull covering a female and pushing the others out of his way then the chattering and crying of pups who lie like black Labradors next to their mothers and could easily be crushed. There's the familiar crying of gulls, which walk nonchalantly among the beached sea elephants, looking for bits of placenta to gulp. They accompany the adult seals and their spawn like a group of shrieking demons in Dante's vision of hell. But is this the ring of sloth, lust, or gluttony? All familiar human sounds or compulsive pulses of English have finally stopped.

Carter and I take a different route back once we have left the restricted area. We walk along a hard-packed strip of beach with the yellow cliffs behind and the sun dissolving into blue. It spreads a soft orange and pink glow over the waves. Mars appears as the brightest point in the sky. We sit on a log between two bulls that breathe in and out every ten to fifteen minutes. Tonight, as I fall asleep, I shall think of these great seals on this beach underneath the planets and the stars—unmoving except for the infrequent blasts of air through their noses.

We hike back to the car in the dark and fly up the coast road, the ocean on our left like an endless swath of blue crushed velvet. We arrive at the parking lot of a strip mall, sit in the booth of an Italian restaurant next to the other land animals. We eat slowly and too much. We'd like to sleep here in the booth, but we lay down our cash instead and sleepily make our way to our vehicle. I suggest we stop at the ranch on the way home to visit the horses.

The palomino is finishing the leavings from the nearest feeder when we drive up, and she makes a rumbling sound in her throat in anticipation of treats. She is large, furry, golden. The moon has not yet risen. I don't see Mud Pony but call to him, and he appears from nowhere as if finding a new shape in the dark. They close in, butting us with velvety noses and licking our hands with warm tongues. We hug their necks, kiss their noses, dangle our arms over their backs. We want to feel all of them—their mammal warmth and sharp whiskers. Have they been swimming in the deeps of day, night, sun, moon, wind, herd, hay? This could be someone's dream or another planet. The horses are closer kin to the elephant seals than we are, and what I really want is to be part of all herds: seal, horse, and human.

· Nine ·

Mara was for sale in the months after her owner died. She stood in a paddock, suffering the endless, stifling insistence of a blanket too much of a bother to remove, underneath which festered a greasy, fungus-patched coat. She had a left leg that wouldn't straighten and a reputation for dumping riders on trails. But when Petra set her loose in an arena, she ate up the ground underneath her. "She's got a big engine," said another onlooker. My toes curled. I doubted the flimsy railing could contain her if she decided to leave.

Petra told me she wasn't looking to buy a thoroughbred, especially one over twenty years old, but there was something about the way the mare looked at her: "She seemed to need me," she says, rinsing a trio of grain buckets. "Plus, she's got the sweetest disposition of any horse I've ever met." She didn't know the mare's owner, but I did. I'd met Guinevere long before the diagnosis of stage IV cancer, when her hair hung down to her waist over her expensive britches and she was secretly referred to as "DQ" or "dressage queen" by several boarders. Guinevere never actually said it, but her unsolicited opinions made it clear to everyone that she thought her three thoroughbreds were superior to the mixed breeds at the ranch.

A couple of months before her death, Guinevere gave away her two other thoroughbreds, but she held on to Mara. "She's worth the most of my three," she told me flatly, "over thirty thousand dollars—but nobody will buy her."

I didn't ask why, but probably it was the mare's age, temperament, or injuries. Of course, I didn't know Guinevere was so close to the end—she'd been in remission for years—and after this encounter, it took me weeks or maybe months to notice that she didn't come around anymore.

One afternoon I walked by the sand arena where she was lunging Mara. As I paused at the rail to marvel at the mare's beautiful, springy gaits, Guinevere nodded, then said in a husky voice, "God got something right when he made thoroughbreds."

In her life, both before and with Guinevere, Mara had successfully evented and completed advanced dressage tests, but newly abandoned, she acted like a horse who'd never been exposed to much of anything. Petra said she bolted or gnashed her teeth every time you took her outside her paddock. Her saddle fit poorly, and she had calcifications on her spine where it had pressed over many rides. She had scars inside the elbow of that crooked left leg—probably from landing on a fence. The hair on her withers had turned white from where the blanket had rubbed the skin raw, and if you touched her neck, ribs, or heart-girth area, she made as if to bite. ("Air-shark!" Petra warned.)

Petra didn't ride Mara. Instead, she took her to equine bodywork clinics and learned how to move her gently around the arena with ace bandages wrapped loosely from shoulder to hind to shoulder. She took her for short walks; she administered healing herbs and treatments (electromagnetic blanket, acupuncture, chiropractic, massage). Megan also worked on her, and over time, Mara became a successfully rehabilitated horse—one of her "star pupils."

Mara's coat has gone from dull to shiny in the eight months Petra has been caring for her. She's bright and interested; she's walking calmly and no longer looks older than her twenty-odd years.

Carter told me that once, on a whale-watching tour off the Monterey coast, he had the incredible fortune to encounter a blue whale that surfaced just a few feet from his boat. It leveled one enormous, unblinking eye at the passengers, prompting Carter to question who was watching who.

The way Mara stands there, offering her gentle, wordless presence, makes me small in a big way—like the watery gaze of Carter's whale.

○

Leaving the classroom to find a new calling initially felt exhilarating, liberating. It's still a wonder to wake up each morning and realize I've shed the responsibilities of stewarding five sets of students through a year's worth of curriculum. Released from anticipating the ten thousand unknowns of what they might do with my offerings, I'm no longer on the constant lookout for activities to make class material more accessible or engaging; I'm finished with observing their responses (or lack thereof) and pivoting in response; and best of all, I'm free from the tedium of administrative minutiae that comes with being part of a large institution.

Now I move more slowly, standing for minutes that become hours and looking out the window as teachers walk to and from the elementary school around the corner, laden with guitars, papers, and boxes. I watch the changing light and the weather. I linger over meals. Most days, there's no place I must be. Of course, I miss the anchors of meaning and much of the busyness—I've lost the daily connections with students and faculty. I no longer have stories to tell Carter about a horde of new faces and their daily dramas. But maybe there's learning and connecting enough with my horses and Carter.

I'm drawn to Mara, but it's a different sensation from the elation I initially felt with Mud Pony. Mara has less mystery. She's bred from hundreds of years of careful selection for hunting, running, racing, jumping, with a tattoo on her lip and papers to prove it. She's been feted, shown, and ridden by dozens of advanced riders. Petra tells me the vet who evaluated her for the sale said Mara was clearly well cared for, her legs regularly hosed with cool water after each ride to banish inflammation, so there's little arthritis as is typical with horses in their twenties. Plus, her conformation—the overall proportions of skeletal and muscle shape—is beautifully balanced, near perfect.

O

How can my horses achieve calm if I clench my jaw at night and wake with fear?
How can I inspire straightness, forward, and a joyful spirit in them if my body is

slumped, tight, or crooked? How can I listen when my hearing is jumbled, when I can't stand the void inside, when everything shouts, "Be full, get full, fill it!"

My dictionary defines *Mara* as a sinister being. She's the fount of the French *cauchemar* and the English *nightmare*. In German, she's *mahrt* for mare, an evil spirit from the underworld. In Old Irish, she's *marah*, death or plague, but today I see only a chocolate coat and a black mane and tail that make the white star on her forehead pop. She's a big girl—both broad and tall—"more warmblood than thoroughbred," a trainer told Petra.

"Maybe Selle Français," says my friend Sarah.

"She looks Irish to me," responds Roses.

I feel like a kid on her, maybe one of my former students? *Perhaps I am Mara's student?* Sure enough, she stands still for me to mount then walks off with calmness and confidence when I gently press her belly with my leg. It's the faster gaits that wind her up, and as we begin to trot in the arena, I sense her tense and electric with the wide eyes of a jackrabbit. When we slow the tempo after some invisible stream of worry rises, she finds calm again, but I don't trust it—at a walk, she's with me 90 percent; at the trot, maybe 50.

A sudden ambition stirs as we amble along within the confines of the round pen. "Let's go out on trail," I call to Petra, who volunteers to spot us on the ground. We head out, finish the gentle slope of the PG&E road, then cross the levy and head for the farmer's field to make a short loop. I ride every step as Petra leads on foot. So far, Mara has been calm and attentive, and I say hey to Petra, that this is a good place to turn around, but as we head home, Mara is suddenly running underneath me without covering any ground, just like I would in a dream where I flee from a stalker but remain fixed in the spot where I stand. Ignoring my voice and seat, Mara tries to bolt through the bit. I hold on to my balance and her mouth. The reins carve red lines into my hands.

My fear hasn't outrun me yet—not like it does with *him*, where the squall picks me up and drops me like a branch. He totally leaves, while Mara is still half here. *But unlike him, I believe that half of her.*

Petra steps off the trail to get out of the way, but I ask her to return and fist the rein just under Mara's chin so I can safely dismount. I'm amazed that even in her anxious state, Mara knows her job—she pauses and waits for me to get off. But on the ground, she can't contain herself, and it wouldn't be surprising if Petra or I got knocked to the ground in one of her bursts. She calls out to the other horses at the ranch as if she had been lost at sea and the current is pulling her out.

"Yes, we are going back," I tell her, "just not like this." On the ground, I circle her in one direction then the other, trying to stay out of her way. It would be safer for us both if her circles could be bigger with more room to move, but we didn't bring a longer line.

Thirty minutes and two hundred yards later, we enter the ranch, our shirts plastered to our backs with the heat of our effort and Mara as wet-sweaty as a seal in the shore break, her brown coat now flecked with foam.

I know I'm no Lord Buddha, triumphing over the demon Mara, the one who challenged him with all the forces of doubt, craving, passion, and temptation. The Buddha was able to sit still through it all and call the earth as witness with the fingers of one hand. I stumble through, barely feeling the ground under my feet. Mara both exhilarates and exhausts me—maybe she is more like Mud Pony than I thought. Released to the safety of her paddock, her mad flight ceases.

The next day we're back at it. I'm hooked with the zeal of a murder mystery addict, who can't set the book down between chapters. "You will focus on me," I tell Mara from the ground as I push her around the round pen, making it a contest, "even if I have to slap the flag a million times in the air or on the ground. I *will* get your attention. You *will* give it to me."

Wait a sec, is this really tit for tat because of what happened the other day on trail? Maybe Mara fears me (and the flag as an extension of my arm), and maybe I seem aggressive to her—like all the riders she has known, the ones I previously condemned.

Frustrated, I exit the round pen and put her away. I walk the ranch road to the bus stop. I'm glad we paused, for I got too big and couldn't see what she offered. These are tiny, subtle actions, like a mouse reaching one paw forward, like a hawk turning its head, like a dove lifting one wet wing. It's not the barking of a dog or the hustle of a busy street or the crack of a branch about to fall. Rather, the offer is a mere ripple, a vibration from a song that's fading in the distance.

At home, I read my notes from the Harry Wittsom clinic over a year and a half ago. I see the blind courage and desire it took for me to swing my leg over Mud Pony on that day and get bashed against the round-pen rail. But then I reread what happened over the course of that week. Something better awaits if I can help Mara find the places where she feels good with me.

"The problem," Harry said, "is that most of you weren't raised by my mother. When she said yes, you knew you would have all her power behind you to get what she promised. When she said no, you knew nothing would change her mind, and there was absolutely no arguing about it. Imagine this kind of security. It's the same thing you need to give to your horse, to get him to feel safe with you and look to you when he gets in trouble."

Here we go again. Human expectation and desire are irrelevant to Mud Pony and Mara, who leave due to physical or emotional wounds that never fully healed. They think it's still happening and I've got to convince them it's not. Fortunately, horses don't lie, deny, or hold grudges.

Petra tells me Mara's registered name, "She Gives Kisses." *Maybe I can learn to receive them.*

O

With a huge stride and frequent, sudden spasms that interrupt for un-known reasons, Mara reveals her mystery, ducking or whirling like a bee got inside her guts. Lucky for me, she doesn't seem to care about flinging me from her back like Mud Pony. Even as she tries to flee the claws of an internal, infernal beast, I'm able to stay on. Eventually it passes. It's as if she knew part of her job is to keep me there.

"Rhythm," Roses calls from the gate, "will reassure her in a way noth-ing else will." So she encourages me to *da da da da* my own tempo at the trot. Dancing girls cancan their heels in an exuberant hall in Belle-Epoque Montmartre and the audience throws their voices into the brass band's jam. Mara moves into a speedy trot as I sing.

There it is.

I stop wondering what I'm supposed to do and surrender to the rhythm that moves through and between us: Feet to Seat to Hands to Mouth.

"Good, now notice her beak," Roses says. "People think when a horse is flinging foamy saliva from the mouth, it means they are relaxed, but actually it means the glands are constricted, so the body overcompensates. All we want is a nice white outline of the lips."

Sure enough, Mara's lips are covered with a shallow layer of spittle. As if on cue, my own salivary glands release and the drool gathers in the back of my mouth as if my favorite salty snack had been set before me.

Roses calls me over at our lesson's end. "This mare is going to help you with Mud Pony. They are so similar."

And I tell her how I felt the same thing come up in me on Mara's back as I did when I was riding *him*: the uncertainty of getting too heavy with my cues or not cueing enough. *Mara will help me find that place in myself where rhythm and its reassurance lie. She is going to help me believe in my own deep voice, my own strong roots, my heart that wants to sing through his feet.*

O

At the ranch, I joke with Bunny, another boarder, that without a car, I'm all set for time travel to the nineteenth century, since I own a bicycle, two saddles, and two horses. She asks me what I've been doing for work, and I describe "my new job at the ranch's new nonprofit branch—getting Mara restarted under saddle." But to my relief, a few temp jobs have come my way and two students need help with essay writing. I've found work scanning tax returns at a law firm, ghostwriting articles for a corporate headhunter, writing website content for a hairstylist and professional bios for a chef and a musician, compiling research for a local professor who is often on the road... all this arrives in a seemingly magical way by letting the world know I'm available.

Similarly, the rewards for showing up for Mara are noticeable after just two months. She now not only looks to me but can tolerate the tension of being asked to perform. Her huge movement underneath has cracked open the stuck parts of me. Could she help me cast off this old skin? I have few excuses now. I can't say I'm exhausted from paper grading, teaching, or planning. My confidence is growing. But why do I persist with Mud Pony or Mara when there are others like the palomino who offer themselves in such a willing and easeful way?

I ask Roses what she thinks of my choice. "It's the Herd... you want all of it—the whole horse."

O

Every night for two weeks, a stranger has been sleeping in a corner of the schoolyard on a wheelchair ramp. As Carter and I brush our teeth each morning, we look out and watch him get up. He relieves himself behind the portable classroom, gathers his blankets, stuffs them in a garbage bag, and stores it in the space between the upper and lower slopes of the ramp. Stiff and achy, he stoops to adjust his socks, which have fallen to his heels. Then he shuffles out of sight. Some days he sleeps longer and Carter worries that he isn't well. Sunday mornings he's not there at all.

At the same time our house-less neighbor rises each morning, my horses pace at their feeders, waiting for hay. Without any warning, spring seems to have vanished and become the season of dust; manure dries fast and gets broken into flaky pieces by hard feet. By nine o'clock, the herd munches contentedly at the feeders as Carter and I eat hot buttered toast.

Why is there ever any need to feel bad about myself when my horse is there on four strong legs, eating hay, sleeping, climbing the hill, descending, watching the light shift through all phases of moon and sun? What a gift I have been given to be able to think of you, dream of you, know you! Why is there any need to ride you when I can write you, then arrive to find you just where I last left you, head raised, ears pricked, as if you had been looking and listening for me all along?

Wholeness, equilibrium, rest, and safety. This is the place where we are both one and many, someone and everyone. Whether the herd is a group of horses split into paddocks or living together on a hill, they sleep while others stand over them. Watching is more like feeling—the hill, the light, the temperature, each other. They respond to the direction and strength of the wind. They shift their focus for the arrival of rain or hay, the presence of humans and other animals.

I consider Mara's personality. She is not a herd leader or bottom horse, but the middle mare who moves with ease at the center. To ride her when she's calm is like sailing on a big ship—smooth and floaty even through the turns. She rounds her body and picks up her neck at its base like the prow of that ship.

"She could be a butterfly... or a whale," I say to Roses.

"She's water, so never try to contain her. Just move with her."

I think *we*, not I. My self becomes *us*, both leader and follower, directing, but not containing. The energy exchange between us like two ends of a river, source *and* mouth.

Mara counts on the routine of the ring with its predictable circles and corners, but when it's time to go on the trail or walk through the barn area, she continues to get upset and disorganized. Suddenly, rogue waves rise inside her. There's no more routine, and the person on her back is a mad stranger reining her in, not a trusted leader. Just like Mud Pony, she must move her feet to find safety.

So I let her.

Sometimes I dismount and we work with me on the ground, my two feet moving with her four. I draw her to me when she goes away, getting the hip on my side to yield. Then we walk on and she does it again, but "You're not in trouble," I say, "you just need to push that shoulder over." *There it goes.* She's listening to me for two strides, then she leaves again. Every time she speeds up, I redirect her without containing the momentum. The result: she never works herself up into the frenzy of the last few encounters. She goes away but then returns. I remind her where her herd is. *It's me, Mara. I'm it.*

Now my job is not to let the river fall down a cliff but to keep it on even terrain. If she doesn't stop when I stop, I don't punish her for it, just move with her, pretend she's Ginger Rogers, while I'm Fred Astaire.

But if Mara is water, Mud Pony is wood. Her movement is fluid, dynamic, while he's solid, hard, stuck. How can I help you, you trunk, you knot, you thick root? How can I help you soften? You are the smallest horse in pasture yet your shoulder is so solid the others never cross you. All you have to do is shift your weight in their direction and they back off. *Someday when*

*you decide to get with my idea of things, we will be a forest that moves through a
mountain. I must find the groove into your grain so I can smooth and soothe your
hard, unbending frame.*

○

My relationship with Mara deepens even more, for I can now navigate the
anxiety and fear that rise from a source I can't see. When someone standing
at the rail inadvertently waves their hand and she leaps, or when the chickens flutter and squawk in their nearby pen and she twists her whole body
away from them, I'm moved to thoughtful action, not reaction. I take hold
of my reaction, reach down through my own contraction to hers: when she
startles or begins to get wound up, when she no longer listens to me, I'm
ready. I bring her head around, ask for her hip; she gives it, then I tap-tap
to get that shoulder. And she's no longer thinking about the raised hand or
the chicken pen.

The steady seat I provide Mara grounds me in a joyful and unexpected
fashion. Back in the city, I stop and talk with Thai in front of his store. He's
taking a smoke break as workers carry boxes of produce through the narrow aisles. I greet the veiled women who recognize me and will soon stand
behind the counter of the head shop next door to sell lottery tickets, beer,
cigarettes, hookahs, and snacks. Then there are the commuters lost in their
cellphones who stream on and off BART; the droves of uniformed students
who descend from the 22 Fillmore or 14 Mission bus lines; the man from
the shipyard with enormous, calloused hands who carries home groceries
for his family. The students in uniforms throw their heads back, laugh, and
make fun of each other. The man from the shipyard studies a list. It's a scene
I usually avoid, but right now I can stand in the midst of it, not to simply
tolerate it and push by but to observe, to appreciate.

Ready to go up, I hold our building's gate for a pair of women with tod-
dlers in tow. Gold teeth flash from wide faces as they enter before me. Then
I hear Lou's voice booming from his second-floor office, where he helps
ex-felons find jobs. I'm ready to match his friendly hello when he appears

on the landing.

I cook vegetables and meat that I've bought from Thai as I wait for Carter to get home. Boneless, skinless chicken breasts get tender in butter, coconut milk, and white wine. I chop herbs for the finish.

I'm alone in the quiet of our kitchen, and from this not-too-busy space of my life, a memory surfaces. In ninth grade, Cathy Schmidt was one of the popular girls, but unlike the others, she smiled and waved to me at both school and church. I chose not to reciprocate her friendly gesture, even though I liked Cathy and wanted to be friends. During lunch period, while Cathy gossiped with our classmates, I snuck my food into the library and combed the stacks.

The summer before tenth grade, Cathy and her whole family died in a house fire—Cathy's body was found at the front door, where she had succumbed to smoke inhalation before she could unlock the deadbolt. The other family members died in their beds. At the funeral mass, there were four coffins at the front of the church. My classmates sat in the first pew, holding on to each other and weeping, but I sat behind them, in between my mother and brother, with a rigid body and throbbing head, imagining the inside of those coffins. Cathy, Mr. and Mrs. Schmidt, brother Rudy— like the ash-burnt people of Pompeii in the twisted postures of their final, fiery moment.

I turn off the burner. No longer hungry, I long for Carter's return. How I wish my mother had not missed this opportunity to comfort me, to hold my hand and tell me it was okay to cry. How I wish I had been able to re-lease a flood from my insides, one that would have extinguished that house fire. So much stuffed inside seems wadded up, stuck, unresolved. *Can I let it go? I don't want to miss my chance again. Who knows what the future will bring or how long we have to do anything?*

I can pound and pound to get what I want but pounding without un-derstanding is dull frustration. Now, because *how* I do things is as import-ant as what I do, I'm thinking more about my approach. So much time is re-quired for things to coalesce: a conversation with a neighbor, a smile from a stranger on the street, a safe classroom, a student's trust, a soft horse, the magic of a new sculpture, a nourishing meal...

I wait for the thing to become itself, whatever it wants to be in this mo-ment. And if I don't shirk away from the thing reaching for me, all I must do is return to this moment and wait. Planning won't bring me the safety or control I long for—what I want cannot be controlled, and if I could control it, I wouldn't want it.

○

I gallop up a hill on the palomino ponying Mud Pony. At first he stays alongside, his head at my right thigh, then he tries to pass her, but she warns him with flattened ears. Now she's increasing her stride, running through the bit, taking control of our trio. The saddle slips to one side as she leans one way and he goes the other—oops, I never did tighten that cinch. Today I'm just a passenger, a passive one, and I laugh and go with it. *Why not!*

As we reach the crest, I get flung upon her neck, lose my balance and Mud Pony all at once. In the next second I've fallen to the ground and my palomino (like the well-trained horse she is) has stopped in her tracks. The ground is soft, and this can't even count as a fall—it's more of a bubbling over after I got shook up. *Ha! There goes Mud Pony, running away, tail lifted high and streaming.* Getting away on trail has happened so many times, he's become an expert at dragging the rope to one side without stepping on it.

I stand without bothering to brush the dirt or leaves off or find where I might be hurt. *Ha ha!* I just told my friend Bunny that I've never fallen off the palomino and when Bunny rides her, she'll have no problem because this mare is bombproof. I tighten the cinch and remount, careful to lean over and hold the opposite stirrup leather so the saddle doesn't slip from her sweat. *She stands still and waits for me—such a good girl.* There Mud Pony goes down the hill, then stops and looks back at us, screaming a high-pitched whinny. "Hurry up," he seems to be calling, but the closer we get, the more he moves away from us, and the more excited the palomino gets. She wants to chase him. Her ears are flattened against her head—"cow-y" is what horse folks would call her.

More laughter as we gallop down the hill parallel to his path, and I hope to cut him off at the bottom so he doesn't trample the Brussels sprouts in the farmer's fields or clatter into the barn area and startle horses and humans. I want no one to hear I've fallen off her or lost him, but who cares anyway, I'm laughing so hard. The palomino races toward him once more. I realize how easily the saddle could slip, how I could fall yet again, and that makes me laugh even harder, but I decide against that option and concentrate on tightening my stomach muscles and keeping my belly button between her ears. How pent up I've been these past weeks! This morning as I sat on the sidewalk waiting for the bus, I turned my head and a muscle in my neck went into spasm. I winced for minutes after, pushing on the pained spot until it passed.

Now we're close, but I'm both surprised and relieved to see him at the bottom, suddenly blocked by Rolando, who has emerged mounted on the cremello. He swipes at the rope but Mud Pony evades him, swerving just as he gets within reach. Rolando smiles, repositions his horse to block the escape, and Mud Pony finally stops and puts his head down to graze. *Ha ha* I slide off *her ha ha* go to Mud Pony smile at Rolando. *Ha ha* all relief and burst and spill.

Within a day or two of falling off the palomino, I fall much harder off the much taller Mara. She unexpectedly ducks one way and I go the other, ending up on my back in the sand, slightly shaken and minimally bruised. I don't get back on because I must leave to catch the bus and work with a student in the city. Petra tells me that afterward Mara refused to eat. It was as if she knew she'd done something wrong. She stood in the corner of her paddock with her head down and her eyes dull.

I don't dare tell Carter what Petra said. He is forever disagreeing with me when I tell him what a horse thinks or feels—"You're anthropomorphizing again," he admonishes—but with *this* mare, it may well be true.

I've often caught her looking at me when she thinks I don't see her. She is so expressive. I can see it: her face and body register pride, dignity, offense, pleasure, apathy, anxiety. Carter is somewhat mollified when I tell him that perhaps I *look* for all that in her and so *find* it, or perhaps I'm now getting better at reading her by paying more attention to these things in *me*.

Despite being prepared, the next time I ride Mara, I get surprised by her duck and swerve. My hands jerk her head around and I erupt, yelling,

"Knock it off!" as if she's doing it *to me,* consciously provoking or unseating me the way my younger brother used to push me off the swing in our backyard so he could claim it as his own. I want to spank her with the whip, but I hold back. Underneath my ire, I know what's there—fear.

Roses motions us to stop. She reminds me that Mara is my teacher, helping me learn how to be with *him.* "There's no reason for you to get mad at her when she reacts," she says. "Plus, when you react, you're just giving her a reason to react again. She's just being a horse: she can't help herself—yet."

"This mare *really* likes you," encourages Petra, who's watching next to Roses. "She's trying to do what you want." I'm relieved Petra is being supportive without getting huffy or protective of her horse.

I calm myself and talk to Mara. I tell her that both Petra and I are pleased with all the progress so far, how she has become a working horse again. I breathe through my whole body and I vow to take better care of all our feelings, especially our fears. We take a break and walk around the ranch. I suddenly notice how my stomach hurts, how I've been holding my heart in my mouth. There's a lump in there. Somehow, I need Mara to be what I want for *me* without thinking about *her own needs*—but truly being with her means I must hold *both* of us, and this includes the trust she is beginning to give me. *Maybe I can't choose what I fear, but I can choose what I do with it. But first, I can allow myself to feel it.*

A few days later, I'm on her back on a windy morning, and I resolve for us to stomach the empty parking lot with its stand of creaking, crackling eucalyptus. I want to lean in to whatever emotions come up—for both of us. And sure enough, on two occasions, she spooks at nothing obvious and must gallop back to the ranch. This time, I don't get upset or angry with her. I don't yank on her mouth. I clamp my thighs to her sides and press my navel to my spine. I go with it, bending her to one side as she tries to force her way home. I stand up in the stirrups and lean on her neck to speak directly into her ear, "It's okay, it's okay."

One ear turns back. She slows. We snake trail up, down, around the parking lot until I can finally bring her to a halt. I check in with her. And I notice how secure and stable I feel in this saddle since we added shims and adjusted my stirrups. I'm no longer sitting like I would in a dressage saddle, but in a forward position meant for moving with a horse over a jump. I am there with her, using my whole being rather than the petty part of me that wants to make it her fault.

When I can ride that icky stuff, Mara returns. And sure enough, there she is, on try number three at the scary place, *with* me, checking in, calmer. She returns home with a lowered head. As we approach the tack room, Petra, who has just arrived, observes Mara to be newly confident, soft, and "pleased with herself." On the ground at her side after untacking her, I offer a carrot, and on a whim, put it between my teeth and crouch, extending it toward her nose. Mara sniffs it. Then delicately, gently, she puts her own mouth around the opposite end. I open my mouth to relinquish it, and she relishes the treat.

"Princess lips," observes a beaming Petra.

I'm beginning to understand the difference between my horse and Mara. He so easily reverts to his wild state, while Mara is inclined to search for human connection *before* fleeing. She and I seem to have a way to communicate, a language, while he and I have only our untamed feelings.

But maybe I'm still not accepting who he is, for I suffer and fret over his ungiving, wooden limbs. Later, when I place his front hoof on the hoof jack and offer a carrot as a bribe, my strategy remains a ruse, and he snaps the hard plastic stand back, knocking it into my calf. I simply limp away, then try again. He does the same thing to my other calf. I walk gingerly on the ranch road to the bus stop, hoping someone will give me a lift.

As I sit on the bus, I comfort myself by thinking how my grandfather would put a chocolate bar between two pieces of bread and hand it to me for an after-school snack. It pleased him to see my enjoyment. One time, I stood next to him as he made an omelet, breaking eggs into a pink glass bowl and pouring the yellow bumps into a pan with a pool of foaming butter. He palped the yolks with a wooden spoon and smoothed them into soft folds, producing a warm and runny goo that made my nose wrinkle.

"There," he nodded, firmly and deep-voiced, "is good."

And it was. He sat with me, smoking as I ate. Whenever he coughed, I imagined the dark, cracked walls of his lungs falling apart in wet chunks. The throbbing in my calves lessens.

O

Late spring surprise: thunder and lightning. Last night, the feral cat crouched on the edge of our roof like a gargoyle and then hid like all the other critters in the schoolyard, humans included. More flashes and crashes. Fog follows, then more rain—a warm storm from the south. The air gets fresh and newly broken, salty. I praise the new morning with its high fog and low blue sky.

I take the bus to the ranch and see as if for the first time the crowded human habitats from the window—so many carbon-copy houses, each with a square of brown lawn in front. These could be family graveyards or a dead salesman's dream. The disabled, the elderly, the mad, the ill, the unemployed fill every seat on the bus. I gape at how insensitive the bus driver is, how he cuts corners, speeds, careens, punches the brake. He is not feeling of his vehicle and jerks us around. I shift in my seat, trying to find a comfortable place to view the ocean bubbling in its own restless stew.

I regret to think that I have ridden horses in the same way. How uncomfortable and maddening to be moved around by such heavy, full-of-force fingers. What an ogre! This bus must be angry underneath its driver. At last, I arrive at the ranch and approach the tack room with its adjoining coop for chickens, ducks, roosters, doves, rabbits, pheasants, quail. This is no quaint menagerie behind our tie posts but another sort of madness, a fenced asylum. One chicken holds the remnants of a dripping, broken egg in her beak and the others chase her around the yard, each vying for the yolky ooze while three ducks stand together and quack a chaotic, jumbled counterpoint. This same trio searches for water to gulp and dive into, but they have only a plastic feed tub with a puddle of brown water from a cracked hose. In a separate cage within the yard, a pheasant pecks a baby quail's down until red. The shed where the chickens lay eggs smells of too many in a few square feet. When I enter the adjoining tack room, a wood rat with a scaly tail clambers over the seat of my Western saddle.

Riding the palomino and ponying Mud Pony on trails softened by the new rain, we move at an easeful, pleasant walk. Thousands of pumpkins dot the field orange. Workers in the distance bend over patches of green. A few honeybees buzz around a set of wooden hives. I give the palomino a hint for where we're going next with a slight bit of leg pressure.

On the bus ride home, I stare at the ocean on my left because I don't want to see what lies to the right: strip malls and endless rows of cheaply constructed houses on the hills. The coast used to be so beautiful to me—a refuge from the concrete dis-ease of the city, and a jewel of a place after growing up in the grid of a suburb. Suddenly I'm squeezed from my insides. *Where may I stretch? Where can I rest?* This is an old feeling, so old it goes back to the clearing of the ancient forests in Europe and the building of factories there for twentieth-century wars. My grandparents had a modest plot in an Alsatian village with chickens, bees, cows, and a garden. After the war destroyed everything, they were able to let it go and build a new life across the ocean. I, too, moved across the continent to a far shore and found new, dramatic beauty. I lived in its city, got spoiled by it, now see it to be spoiled too. The horses are so beautiful in body, mind, and spirit, but they stand behind fences in large groups, mouthing their manure when they run out of hay. And humans rush to and fro in metal boxes on asphalt strips: malls, offices, corporate parks. These are fenced in as well.

I sit on the bus, sliding back and forth in my hard seat as the driver once again wrenches wheel, gear, and brake. I go where he goes.

O

I hoard books, old magazines, curricula, outdated teaching materials, binders, readers, journals, clothes, canned goods—all because I anticipate the single, important occasion I may need them. Our shelves and cupboards and floors are crammed full. Now I'd like to drop some of the weight to let in something new, but what if this item or that will serve me or come in handy someday? Amidst the piles that crowd our apartment, I look helplessly at Carter, who says I don't have to pay attention to these feelings of scarcity and anxiety, "Just have 'em. Know where they come from, observe them, but that's all."

Nice try. Won't he help me go through the mess, sit with me and help me decide what to throw out? Instead, he points to where I can set my stuff in "clutter spaces," places where I can stash as much as I need without worrying about it while keeping other surfaces clear. Now the books, binders, folders, and files that represent many years of classroom teaching have been added to what was already there. He leaves me to sit with it.

As I shuffle papers and boxes, I wish I were elsewhere, with my horses and Mara. They stand, eat, move, and sleep except for the occasional interruption of humans who ask to be carried or, in the case of my horse, to be ponied on trail. There is no excess, no clutter, no space to clean. The hay they eat becomes manure, which turns into dirt.

Both the past and future weigh on me. How can I let both go and allow something new to enter? I wish I could afford to send my horse to Roses for extended training at her ranch inland and farther south. I could then commute there as if going to school, since it will be as much my education as his. Roses once reassured me that horses have memories like elephants and won't forget what you've taught them, good or bad. He could sit in a pasture for five more years and we could then pick up right where we left off. For now, all I can do is focus on the process with Mara. I turn back to my piles and sigh. At least there is no expiration date on our education.

○

Mara lowers her head as I ride her in S-curves across the arena. Her body and eyes are soft; she sighs. I make slight marching movements with my arms and legs, and she picks up a trot, imitating my rhythm. Then I brush my outside leg against her side, suggesting the next gait, and she accepts my offer, stepping up into a smooth canter, assuming a balanced, vaulted shape. I bring my energy down and she does too—thrusting out one front leg into a trot.

I am humbled by her whole round being and big, dark beauty, how she searches for me, how she pays attention to my every move. When we leave the safety of the sand arena for another part of the ranch, the trouble comes up and she is no longer soft but edgy and anxious. Her shape gets ragged, her movement uneven. She can no longer stand still or walk forward in a straight line. Her mind is back at the tie post where she gets groomed and eats the snack Petra has prepared, or the sand arena where she connects with me, where she rolls and strikes out playfully at Cat, who lies in the sand.

I have some idea of the depth of her troubles, but I pay no attention. I let all her layers rise. *May they all come up and out. May we face them together. May she do what she needs. May she move as she wants.*

We walk back to her stall and stand there as she gets calmer. Then I point her head away, and we walk down the aisle. She wants to turn back toward her paddock, but I insist on going forward. When we reach the big back arena, she frets, but much less than before. When she finally takes a breath, we walk back to where she wants to go. It's slow progress to move forward, circle, and stand—then repeat the whole thing.

The next day we go the same route, work and circle and stand in the same places. She's a different horse—calm and relaxed. She eats the grass and releases her breath at the places where she could only fret and trample the day before. Only once or twice over the course of an hour does she startle. I stay there but keep out of the way. Delight rises in me to have helped her make this shift. We all need a safe place where we can let the trouble rise—a paddock, a bed, a tie post. There, we can hold it, touch it—and let go.

Now I am keeping Mara in my body for the rest of the day and evening, and into the next day. And when I don't ride her, I still do. Years ago, I gave up surfing when I got Mud Pony, but I can still know what it's like to ride waves or a mare all day and into the night as they carry me into my dreams.

○

The apple is so big I need two hands to hold it and I pull off the sticker and place it in his bucket as he stands tied to the post in front of the tack room—head high, hind legs splayed. As soon as he sees me drop it in there, he lowers his head and neck to investigate. He takes a huge bite, lifts his head to look around, and the other half of the fruit falls to the ground. He leaps at the thud, then snorts and looks as startled as if I'd just thrown the Western saddle on his back and climbed on. Gloopy strands of apple froth dangle from his mouth. He fears the fruit—its weight, what he desires to eat. I cannot take it personally when he fears *me*.

He finishes his grain and I sweep up thick, sticky clods of cobweb in the tack room. They cling to the damp corners of the walls whose thin plywood defends the ducks and chickens and my tack from winter wet and summer dust. Both seasons live in this shelter along with saddles, bridles, grain, jars of unopened applesauce and molasses, apple cider vinegar, shampoos and slickers, supplements and medical supplies. There are layers of bandages and palliatives sitting in plastic containers.

Rats slink in and out of all corners and leave their dried turds everywhere. I sweep with the broom and dustpan, coughing at the dust I raise. Many spiders are dislocated. Soldier beetles wake up on the wood floor and find themselves scrambling at the feet of a chicken, then lifted by a beak and gobbled down. I take a break every now and then to breathe the outside air.

The ravens have left the ranch. I haven't seen the family of four croakers in a few months. Today the sun is out and warming the mud, which puddles into a thick goo. Mud Pony has been lying in it and I scrape his caked coat with a shedding blade, releasing clouds of dirt and dust. I touch and circle and massage him. I rub the muscular ridge under and between his front legs. And then—it's as if I had pushed a button on a mechanical toy. He immediately lifts his back and lowers his head—in yoga they call it a cat stretch. On all fours you lift your back, raise the belly, drop and dangle your head from the base of your neck. *This feels good to him!* To see my horse in such a state of relaxation is a revelation—for once he is not troubled by my touch.

○

The cremello has been moved to a neighboring ranch and there has been zero activity in front of Rolando's trailer for many weeks. No horses being worked or groomed, no gathering of vaqueros. On my commute down the ranch road a few weeks ago, I caught sight of Manolito playing alone on his Big Wheel, going back and forth, grinding the rocks underneath on the gravel road.

Turns out I'm one of the last to hear: Rolando's been taken by police and now sits in the county jail, awaiting his hearing for something he did or didn't do. Even if he's not convicted of anything, it's likely La Migra will deport him.

Rumors of a love affair, confrontation, betrayal by the ranch boss, and a dramatic arrest in the middle of the night bounce around the ranch. José is visibly upset. He's angry at Rolando for messing around, messing up. He's angry at those who called the police. I wonder how long Rolando will sit in jail. I shudder to imagine the frustration, the trapped feeling of one accustomed to being outdoors all day. What a waste of his strength, generosity, knowledge. I'm suddenly helpless, then empty—as if Rolando were one of *my* students who failed, then fell.

O

This morning as I step out into the street, I look up at the sky and catch sight of the biggest, most beautiful morning moon against blue I have ever seen. Its crags and juts are so crisp, I want to follow it all afternoon until it falls in the sea. But then it's gone, swept behind a bank of fog. People on the street swirl around me.

Later, as I walk up the road toward the pasture, Cat comes trotting toward me, her black tail snapping back and forth over her tan body like a kite flying over a sandy stretch of beach. She rubs her face on my leg. I pick her up and she burrows into my chest and gently sinks her claws into my arm. Petra and I have been giving her lots of praise for killing the rats in the tack room.

Today at the canter, Mara is speedy, unbalanced, and leaking out the shoulder on her left side. I turn her, but the more she turns, the faster she seems to wind herself up. I'm afraid she might fall, and I don't want to go down with her. But I don't want to yank on her mouth either. I center my seat and gather up the reins. I want us both to be safe. This seems to work, and she transitions down to a trot, then a walk. She immediately wants to leave the arena and walk to her paddock, which I allow her to do, following her lead. *Does gentleness and release from a human still seem new to Mara? What is it like for a horse to know her rider is listening when they didn't listen before?*

Back at the tack room, I see Cat carrying a freshly killed rat. She lays it down then licks it, walks away, returns, licks it some more. Before long, she's gnawing on its eviscerated body. A soft clump of purplish innards has been flung two lengths of a cat from where she feasts in bright red.

○

This is not how I have been taught. I know straight, calm, and swing. I've learned from Roses to not force the horse's head, neck, or mouth into a frame but allow them to be straight and relaxed, to feel the hind end propelling you forward. You give the body room. You help the horse find the freedom it already has without bridle or rider, and your touch is the connection that shapes the horse's thought, their offerings of softness. And what movement a horse can have!

Harry has described how a horse "can be so light in your hands, you can move him around like a fly in an empty room." I think of the flies that make ragged circles in our apartment, and how I direct them out an open window with the motion of my hands.

This seems backward—Roses is telling me to *increase* my contact with Mara—and as soon as I do so by shortening the reins, she gives. Then *I* give.

"But don't dump her!" Roses shouts. "She gets lost. Give her the contact. Allow her to lean into it."

It's as if I had learned some new words or phrases in a language Mara already speaks, for she's responding, both giving and reaching for the contact: "Yes, yes, say more," she says. This is a voice she knows, this steady stream of words and phrases from my hand and seat. She meets my hands, gathering, rounding, collecting. I can hardly believe the lightness that comes from the feel on her mouth.

I imagine she looks like all the horses in the photos I've seen in magazines—huge, rounded, with a satin sheen—and the reins a straight line from her mouth through to my elbows, all the weight and muscle of her under my straight, proud back. It's a strange lightness, born of domestication, but there's something wild in it too. I've rarely felt such a floaty sensation on any horse. It seems we're starting it all backward, moving from what's hard to soft. Maybe *boundaried* is a better descriptor.

"In two months," Roses says, "we'll let up a bit and see how she responds. And then maybe in four months, you'll be here." She reaches for a rein to show me, indicating a surprisingly longer length.

I'm puzzled, so she illustrates by standing at Mara's shoulder and holding one end of the rein while I hold the other, pretending she's rider and I'm the horse's mouth. She asks me to feel what it's like on Mara's end to be held in contact with the rein and then suddenly released.

"What happens when I suddenly drop the contact? Can you hold it?"

I shake my head. I have nowhere to go when Roses the rider drops me.

"For now, we've got to start with where she is and what she knows. Otherwise, we're just letting her loose upon the world, and despite her age, she's too emotional and undeveloped—we can't do that to her. It would be like putting a five-year-old into third grade before kindergarten. She'd be lost. She needs the support of the contact to find balance before you can float it."

Petra arrives at the gate to watch.

"Hey, do you recognize your mare?" I ask, sitting the trot in a rhythmic, one-two one-two as I pulse and release, pulse and release. For Mara, this contact has clicked the on switch to a past life of training and eventing. She gets excited to do something she knows while experiencing the old insecurities that accompanied her on that path. When Roses, now sitting at the arena gate, reaches into her pocket to quiet her mobile phone, Mara swerves and leaps, exploding in a "poof" that I laugh at and easily contain and ride. "Go ahead," I say, echoing Harry, "have a fit—you'll feel better." If I were afraid or unaware, if my leg and seat were less melted into her side and back, if I didn't have the past months of riding her under my belt, I'd be in trouble. My ability to sustain these meltdowns without punishment is a relief to her, and so is the new sense of contact between us.

At the canter, Mara still leans heavily on the left shoulder like she's going to fall over, and I'm amazed how Roses wants me to increase the contact even more. *What the...? How is that possible? Am I just pulling on her?* No, at this level I am helping her rebalance her front end. She needs the outside rein and a bit of inside leg and enough inside rein to keep her from going down, but she's bunched up in this one spot at her shoulder as if the ligament, tendon, and muscle were stuck to each other, fused and unable to work in tandem. After all, Petra reminds me, Megan found hard knots of scar tissue deep in there.

Her body requires so much of me—to melt my back and elbows into steady, comforting rhythms, sink my calves and seat, offer contact with both reins and a bit of inside leg. I ask her to move off that shoulder but hold her with everything I've got, and with my heart too. And she responds to my intention—for a few strides she is not bolting away or running to her stall. She's not finding an excuse to freak out or duck. She's not bunched up in that left shoulder and leaning precariously to one side. Before I fully understand what's coming, she collects herself at the canter. The movement is so big and tumbling and light, I find myself laughing and giggling, and my happy spasms move in rhythm with her three beats. Her weight has shifted back onto her hind end. I move her like Harry's fly.

When we stop, I'm smiling wide and breathing hard. I can't wait to see what we collect together next.

○

Carter and I have been shaking our heads for weeks at the newly posted signs under all the second-floor windows of our building: ATTENTION: DUE TO RODENT SITING ALL WINDOWS ARE TO BE SHUT AFTER DARK. NO EXCEPTION! We both thought it a ruse by Uncle Leo, the ex-cop and super who lords over the hallways, monitoring the sound levels from the rock bands in the basement's walk-in freezers. In a building where people used to shoot up in the hallways, we're fortunate to have someone keep watch at the entrance. He tells the dealers to move along when he sees them at street level, and now is apparently defending against mouse invaders after seeing one leap through a window.

Carter says Uncle Leo made that all up. "Mice don't need to leap," he laughed. "They get in any way they can."

And yet, one morning before breakfast, Carter tells me how last night, when he was watching TV after I went to bed, a mouse jumped through the window next to the couch and sat there in front of him on the floor. Astonished, Carter kept still. Then it scurried under a shelf.

In honor of this mouse visitor and Uncle Leo's flying-mouse warning, Carter spends the next afternoon creating stickers of a friendly, furry creature with wings, which he affixes to the hallway walls under each sign. Now we laugh to think how we've brought Uncle Leo's mouse into our home.

"Our new roommate!" I say.

We discuss places to put a live trap, and Carter exclaims, "I want to be that mouse, leaping bravely into a new world—no predators, and all the food I can eat! A whole new life."

O

I set Mara loose, and she stretches into the length of the big back arena, eating it for breakfast! The stiff webbing in her left shoulder is loosened by that gargantuan gallop. I take a photo with my phone, then see on my screen that I missed her entirely. It takes a good twenty minutes for her heart rate to come down. And I wonder if this isn't a good time to ride her, but I do it anyway. She's now so sweaty and pumped I need to tighten the cinch two holes more than usual, and despite the race-proud look in her eye, she listens when I mount and then ask for a walk, trot, halt, back, lateral movement.

She gets anxious whenever we get near the gated end of the arena and calls out to other horses, but she still listens when I remind her that I'm here. And I use our new language of contact. I cluck and gather the reins an inch, ask for a bigger trot. Then the canter begins—not just in her feet, but in the cradle of my diaphragm where the upper and lower halves of fascia, bones, and muscle meet. She sense that tiny shift even before I squeeze with the outside leg, offering an easeful lope. It's the calmest and most balanced

I've ever ridden her at this gait. She's not running from me as she has in the past; she's cantering *with* me—side, top, and bottom. Her magnificent shoulders and neck are the dip and lift of a crane, her rear light and nimble like a deer's. Maybe she could go forever on this smooth pathway, but I want to keep the ride easy, not push for anything more, so I think *trot* and she transitions from three beats to four.

No horse has ever required this of me or made the request in such a queenly manner—with all the nobility of her being. I resolve to study and ask her, then do it again, to stretch and imagine my way to new pathways in my body. Hips that hang open to absorb the shock. Balanced, loose bones from my skull plates to my toes. I suck up Mara's back and legs into my own and she moves in a round, light way as if I weren't even there.

I don't tell Carter or anyone else how high I felt riding Mara today. For some reason, I want to keep it hidden, protected. Even if I could share it with my teachers—Rolando or Roses or Harry—I wouldn't. The sensation is so delicious it makes me giddy, and I'm suddenly afraid someone might take it away. What new life will take shape in Mara when she is able to fully communicate with me, as I feel her back rise underneath me, as I urge her toward collection and extension, as we ride through to lightness? What will come through her? What will she give? *I want to let flow whatever I can stand to feel. I'm swinging the door open, allowing my heart to be as big as it can to receive her.*

○

As I brush Mara and get her ready for our lesson, Petra dumps chopped vegetables into her black rubber pail—dandelion leaf, bits of curly parsley, shredded beets, carrot, red cabbage, whole oats, parsnip. She spoons pureed flaxseed on top then scoops rice bran pellets and mixes it all together with water using a dirty spoon. She sets it in front of Mara, who eats it lustily, dreamily, with her eyes half open.

I tell Petra how yesterday my chiropractor looked at photos of me riding Mara and said I must position my knee over the second toe in my stirrup, and from there, the psoas—a muscled band deep inside the big ball and socket of the hip—will open and relax and not grip and clench. Then the leg will not tense, the knees will not tighten. I will be moving from the whole leg and can thus allow my back to be open to a neutral position. My spine will lengthen. My head will float.

Roses teaches me how to position for the trot on Mara in the forward seat of the all-purpose saddle if I move my hips like the pop singer Shakira. "You still have a neutral spine," she says, "but your legs are up here, not back there and under you like you would be in a dressage seat."

We switch back to the dressage saddle to illustrate the point, and it's a different sensation with my legs now under me, but my body thinks I'm still in the forward-sitting saddle.

"Keep thinking Shakira," she calls. "Now you can open up those hips."

And she's right. I can wiggle my hips with four legs underneath me.

At the canter I gyrate in slow motion from the corner of one seat bone to the other, responding to the rhythm of Mara's footfall, and she slows the canter to a tight circle, a canter pirouette. I picture warriors on horseback, merging with their horse like centaurs. From this deep-rooted position, I could close my eyes, eat a meal with knife and fork as I sit in the booth of a diner, or throw a spear. And when the wind picks up leaves and blows them across our path, Mara leaps, but I hold our spines steady without effort, legs wrapped round, sitting lowrider style with the driver's seat pushed all the way back. I'm revving its big engine, and in cool, laughing fashion, proudly drive that Ford Mustang down Mission Street.

O

As I leave for work, I discover my bicycle missing. Its sliced cable lock hangs forlornly on the banister at the bottom of the stairs. Unfortunately, Uncle Leo's nighttime security check didn't catch the event. I am devastated by the loss—how long will it take me to save and replace it? Carter listens when, empty and bothered, I return to him at the breakfast table, and then later I tell everybody who will listen—Thai; Lou; Kumar, the security guard at the bank. My brother who lives in Mexico writes me an email, telling me about his most recently stolen bicycle.

"Bikes come and go," he writes. He sends a photo I've never seen before—me as a four-year-old on a red tricycle in bare feet. I always imagined I was slumped or hunched as a child—I often still see myself this way—but there I am, perfectly balanced, a perfect plumb line from ear to shoulder to hip to heel. I wear a long white shirt with a ruffle that comes to midthigh. I scream in delight, eyes squinting at the sun. My toes grip the outside edges of the pedals like a young chimp. I turn the handlebars with a bend through my whole body. *Why did no one ever tell me I looked so fierce and spirited? Why did it never occur to me that even as a four-year-old, I could reach into the sky, pull down the moon, and crawl across its pocked surface?*

Later, infused with sadness and gratitude, I trim my horse's feet and marvel at their lovely and amazing shapes—the intersection of cone, dome, and triangle—a sacred geometry the same as the arch of a Romanesque church, the flying buttress of a Gothic cathedral, the bow of a monk, the lowered head of a horse to its morning hay. Here comes the sun. Our earth arcs round its fire. Light and blood are the same—life moving in its own flashes and spurts.

O

Awake at 3 a.m., fretting about my stolen bike, my horse, my life. *What am I doing? Where am I going? Will I ever be able to ride Mud Pony again? How can I arrange to visit Rolando in jail or get a note to him?* All things seem held in an unpleasant stagnation, but then an unexpected rainstorm begins, and I envision Mud Pony, the palomino, and the rest of the herd standing in a sheltered spot under the pine just at the hill's rise. Raindrops pelt their backs and roll down their flanks. They lift their heads, shift their feet and weight, but they do not get upset or run. No horse rails against the dwindling light. None concern themselves with the dying wind or rain. They sink farther into the mud, they get wet, they wait, they rest, they accept. "We were once fish," they say. "Now we live on both land and water. We breathe in to receive the rain. We breathe out to give it back."

The night after my grandfather's funeral, I slept in his bed, amazed to think of his body in the ground while mine stayed warm between his un-washed sheets. I could still smell his cigarettes, aftershave, dragon breath—and felt his face kiss my cheek all grizzled and tickly in the mornings. As a child, I once slept between him and Grandma in their bed. When I couldn't stop coughing, he found my hand and offered me a warm, slimy lozenge from his own mouth. In this same bed after the burial, I comforted myself by imagining the two of us as toads, sitting side by side under a stone.

How can I find that comfort now? How can I reassure myself when I the longing arises and it's so much bigger than anything I can imagine or resist? No wonder it's hard for me to rest or sit still. I foster a constant, underlying state of agitation, unable to stand in rest as the horses do. And even when I do rest, I persist in believing the search for something new or better will satisfy me.

But there's truth in rest, that is, once I finally accept it. By force of their bulk and goodness, contact with my horses moves me from a place of despair and neediness into stillness and peace. Even hours after being with them, I am content to be quiet with myself, to stare at the lights from the street on the wall until my head gets so heavy, I can't hold it up, and I sense their big movement and stirrings. When I wake again, and it's still cold and dark, I comfort myself by feeling their calmness. We are both held and cared for by some force more powerful than gravity—maybe gravity's grandparent.

· Ten ·

When the judge rings the bell, Mara and I enter the arena. For our first training-level dressage test, we trot a crooked zigzag to the center, a preview to our comedy of errors. Our musical accompaniment should be a hurdy-gurdy tune: her hind end angles to the right as we halt for the salute; when I ask her to walk, she breaks into a trot. Most of the test is supposed to follow the arc of a circle, but her movement is so big and hurried, I must cut the corners, so our circle becomes a square. On the straight length of the arena, when I ask for a working trot, she canters. Then, on the downward transition to a free walk, she jigs and veers off the track; throughout the test, we overshoot the markers where we are supposed to turn or transition to another gait.

After we end in the same spot where we began, the judge exits the box and calls us over. Another clownish moment—we tower over her and her scribblings attached to a clipboard spotted with unicorn stickers.

"In dressage," she says in an even, serious voice, "we practice *even* gaits—did you know your horse is *uneven* behind and probably lame?"

I contain myself and pretend to listen, thank her for the feedback, and leave the arena. I'm greeted by Petra, whose smile fades when I tell her what the judge said. It's as if I were riding one horse, but the judge saw another. Later, when I receive the written comments, I note how they mark only where we fell apart, and how a year ago we could not have even walked next door, let alone warmed up in an arena with seven other horses trotting and cantering in various directions, and then make it through a test. The judge's claim is not to be believed, not after all the bodywork, rehabilitation, and careful riding. No, the crookedness the judge saw reflects her emotional state, not her physical one.

The judge didn't see the bigger picture, the many months of groundwork and how Mara learned to reinhabit a body ridden by a human. She didn't see our insides or the *feel* we've found with each other. Mara used to be a huge, forbidding presence, a dark ship I was drawn to but afraid to board for fear of unsafe passage, but gradually I came to know her and to trust our work together. At the outset, I couldn't just *know* this—I had to sit with the unknowing and surrender to it. Now I find that she is smaller and I'm bigger.

○

Walking the ranch road after getting off the bus puts me in a watchful mode more in rhythm with the horses than driving. I note the speed of clouds, the motion of treetops, rabbits hovering where the bushes meet the road, and a hawk hanging in the sky. I see how the hills are turning yellow, the grass is disappearing, and the dust has a different smell and taste than a month ago. As I reach the tack room in front of the pasture, the herd is spread out along the fence eating their morning hay. I set my backpack down and roll a wheelbarrow to Mara's paddock. As I enter, she leaves her hay to come stand with me, first presenting her head and then the dock of her tail for me to scratch.

After mucking, I lead her to the tie post in front of the tack room and brush her. I'm using the softest brush, but she has "non-allowed areas," as Petra calls them. Mara gets a cranky look, lays flat her ears, and flings her head and neck back in warning, communicating an old discomfort. I pull on my britches and boots and gather my hair into a ponytail underneath my helmet while she eats her horse cookies, rolled oats, carrots, and supplements. I lay the pad and saddle on her back and tighten the cinch slowly— one hole on either side, walk a few steps, then two holes, walk a few steps, then three more holes. I remove her halter and ask her to open her mouth for the bit with my left hand, thumb, and forefinger, pressing gently on the bars of her mouth while holding the browband with my right hand just in front of her eyes.

She opens her mouth with ease, and I lift the headstall over her ears and lay the metal on her tongue. I fasten buckles at throatlatch and chin and then straighten the headstall across her forehead, gently pulling her thin excuse for a forelock over the leather browband. I put on gloves and grab a whip, pull the stirrup leathers from behind the irons, walk her on my left to the blue mounting block, and mount the block and then Mara, pulling on the opposite stirrup leather as I press my left boot into the left stirrup so the saddle doesn't shift with my weight. I throw my leg over and sigh with gladness.

○

After successive days of work, Mara deserves a day off, so we turn our gaze toward Mud Pony, who stands at the tie post after eating his grain in his typical head-high stance, legs splayed, as if on the lookout for a moment of possible escape.

"Let's try something else today," says Roses. "A whole new approach with him that may offer a different way to be. We're going to help him before he reaches his red zone by talking to his stomach. You know where I got 'red zone' from, right?"

"That dog whisperer guy. We're predators establishing our lead in the pack?"

"Yep. Think of a word that you don't usually say or hear, and I want you to use that as your cue to bring his attention to you whenever you notice him thinking about leaving."

"Something in another language..." I muse. The Spanish word *mira* (look, over here) occurs as a possibility, but the edges of its *m*, rolled *r*, and "ah" sound aren't strong enough. "How about *écoutes?*" I ask.

Roses echoes the word in a perfect French accent. "We're also going to use the carrot as positive reinforcement so he really gets it, remembers it, and looks for it. And once he shows that he's with you, you'll stop and offer him a treat, but you're going to feed it to him at the corner of his mouth so he doesn't mistake your fingers for the treat."

Before we go to work, we clear a space on the bench outside the tack room, cut carrots into pieces, and accumulate enough pieces for soup. It's warm enough to wear just a hooded sweatshirt, and I put a handful in each of my pockets. The saddle, says Roses, will help him know we're in work mode. There won't be any attempt at riding today—we'll do everything on the ground.

I approach his back with the cantle across my right hip while holding his rope halter in my left hand. As I get near, the stirrups swing ever so slightly and he jumps sideways. I keep a firm hold and pronounce, "Écoutes!" He stops and I feed him a carrot coin, which he grabs in a big hurry, almost taking my fingers with it. Approach with the saddle. Again, he leaves. "Écoutes!" I feed him another. He blinks, licks, and chews. The saddle goes on, he blinks, licks, chews. "Écoutes!"

"You waited a bit too long there," Roses says. "Give him the treat right after you've noticed him blink or chew and you've said the word. For now, help him make the connection by tapping on his shoulder and presenting the carrot."

I put the saddle down, tap twice on his left shoulder, and offer the carrot at the corner of his mouth. He swivels his head, hurriedly snatches it, then resumes his vigilance. Putting the saddle on and tightening the cinch take awhile and at least half of my carrot tokens as we stop each time for rewards, but he never flees and seems to be thinking about it a lot less. Working on the line, it's a lot of energy to push him to maintain a trot, probably because of the tension through his body.

"Call to him," says Roses, "but don't do anything else. I want to see what he does." No response. "Just as I thought… he doesn't know his name."

I freeze, flummoxed—as if I've discovered the separate, secret existence of a close relative. *When I got him, I never even asked if he had a name.*

"Écoutes!" Roses shouts. She laughs and throws a carrot piece at my shoulder.

He drops his head, snorting, yet looks more relaxed. "Écoutes!" I call and he halts for the treat. Although he's responding to the reward, I notice when I ask him to increase his speed, his tension increases too, and he moves counterbent in both directions, his head pushing outside the circle. And sometimes I too get pushy by thinking about what he *should* be doing and what I *want* from him instead of what he *is* doing.

As if she were already inside my head, Roses calls out, "Think dressage!"

My mind can't comprehend, but my body does. I get straighter and calmer and more balanced as if I were sitting deeply in a saddle. My weight shifts back to my heels as if I were riding. I stop chasing him and I picture "bigger trot," as if I were on Mara, and sure enough he increases his length of stride in front of me.

"See how much training he's got in him?" says Roses. "See how much he knows? We can't expect perfection from him. All we can do is create a world and invite him in."

○

My uncle picks me up at the train station in downtown Sacramento and bends down from his six-foot-four height to kiss my cheek. His voice is low and breathy. His mustache tickles me. He's aged so much since his illness I barely recognize him. The truck is parked across from the downtown station on a busy, one-way street where people drive well over the speed limit. We sneak through the bent portion of a chain-link fence. I haven't seen him for many years, but now I remember how he does things with a great sense of adventure, like a rebellious, adolescent version of my father.

He hands me the keys. The truck he wants to give me is even more beautiful than he described on the phone. Parked under the cool shade of a tall maple, the '95 Ford 150 XLT with mag wheels glows with a faded coppery color that reminds me of a saying about the weather: "Red sky at night, sailor's delight." It has the rectangular, boxy shape of a vintage model, and its trim and paint job are in perfect condition. It has the original chrome mirrors and bumpers, and my uncle added rows of steel cleats alongside the bed for tying down or covering cargo. I imagine all the things it might carry: hay, camping gear, saddles. It's got a tow ball, super cab, and art deco wheel covers. As quiet and smooth as a Cadillac, it's the most beautiful truck I've ever met. I imagine driving it down the ranch road and past the vaqueros, who will give me the thumbs-up.

My uncle asks me if I looked at the return train schedule when I was in the station. I say no, no reason to. Why? He says he won't let me take it away with its personalized license plates: QMCUSN or Quartermaster Chief US Navy. The letters stand out against an image of Yosemite Valley at sunset—Half Dome's shoulder turns away from the viewer in rose-colored light, and the image blends with the truck's warm bronze tones. He's visited there countless times. Next week, he will tell me he cried the first morning he looked in his garage and saw the truck gone.

Prodding me gently into the driver's seat and guiding me through the dashboard's switches and gauges, he talks proudly about the engine and other features. His voice is gentle, not the curmudgeon's growl I expected. I adjust the mirrors and seat and put the truck into gear.

He wants to eat lunch first, and so we stop at a diner. He laps up turkey with gravy and mashed potatoes and has difficulty controlling his limbs as we sit in a booth and I pick at my salad, but I pretend not to notice. At least twice, he bends down to pick up a fallen menu for a waitress or a candy wrapper dropped by a child. In the hospital waiting room, he catches the eye of a stray toddler and makes googly eyes. In between mutterings I can't understand, he giggles with the receptionist at her station, the nurse who pokes him three times in the attempt to draw blood from one of his veins, and the woman at the front desk of the DMV. Suddenly I want him to tell me everything. *Why is my father the way he is? What do you remember about me as a girl? What was it like to navigate carrier ships at sea?*

After we finish the business of transferring truck ownership at the DMV and getting new plates, he asks me to stop at the mall so he can bring home a Chick-fil-A sandwich to eat later for dinner. In the living room of his bachelor pad, he pulls out a thick manila folder with the truck's maintenance history. His house smells of mothballs. There are piles of papers everywhere. He finds me a wrench and I remove the license plates. He tells me he is going to have to move out of this house, and he will need some help. Then there's something he doesn't say, but I know it: the disease is increasing.

Driving back home as the sun begins to set, I notice how quiet the engine, how big and safe this truck is compared to the compact cars I've driven or owned. I skim over the torn, bumpy pavement of the right lane where the loaded semis tear up the asphalt. The truck has helped me hatch into a larger, more powerful body, and I look beyond the freeway to the rich green of restored wetlands, the golden hills spotted with dark dots of grazing steer, the shadows of clouds on the bay.

O

The wave no longer needs to mount, crash, and end on the shore. It can allow its vibrations to retreat and join up with the bigger body of the sea. I'm no longer a presence to irritate or annoy Mara. I know the crunch or crumple in her body that precedes the buck or the leap and I move it through her by helping her move through it. She walks, trots, and canters without pain or worry. I sense her playfulness underneath, the desire to move in ways I don't know much about. Maybe she wants to jump fences cross-country or perform advanced dressage tests in front of an audience. With Roses' guidance, I ride the fast-moving river she offers. Now I'm fully riding her heart in tandem with mine. I crawl inside its big, open dome. I do not fear her—I *feel* her.

Her movement gets unexpectedly big so often that each session in the arena becomes an improvisation where I explore the many possibilities offered by her crunching up, tensing, or exploding underneath me. Roses has taught me that the half-halt or cue to rebalance (e.g., tightening my core, giving pressure on the inside leg while pulsing the outside rein) is going to be different depending on what she offers. Like listening to a sequence of songs on a shuffle setting, I accept what's offered rather than attempt to contain her momentum using a halt, backup, or tight circle. I redirect and help her balance with the outside rein. I allow her to move out of a tight circle into a big curve. I ask her forward and lift my hands into the contact, riding ten feet in front of her nose. I count a rhythm and become her conductor. When she spooks, ducks, or veers from the rhythm, I keep a steady beat and ignore any outburst or spasm. Now I know we'll make it. I stroke her neck lightly with the whip to bring her focus back to the work. I pulse the outside rein and inside leg. I alternately bend and release her shoulders at the canter. She responds and releases.

All these are not measurable benchmarks toward a goal but a series of discrete listenings with co-respondings bringing us into balance. I don't confine her. I gently remind her. Sometimes she suggests something new, and I both feel and hear her insides.

O

It's far more convenient to cry in the super cab of my new truck than in the cramped seat of a bus, where I suffer the incessant click of the turn signal, the whoosh of the brakes, or the wobbly jerk of each pause or go. This morning I learned that my uncle was moved into a nursing home, and he said it was his final stop. At first, I try to stuff an onslaught of guilt and then don't, relieved to be both safe and sad, to dislodge the hard-packed feelings inside as they shift to sorrow. I change the station on the radio. Every classic rock tune or pop song brings a new flood. I know what Carter would say: "Bring it—whatever it is... crack it open." He and I have talked about how we sometimes cry not just when we're sad but when we're loving the moment so much and watching it pass even as we feel everything in it.

Strange how we do the same things every day our whole lives without noticing or appreciating—eating, sleeping, working, commuting, reading, writing, riding—and there's hardly anything new that seems to emerge. Maybe that's one reason people have children, to live daily with constant change. Maybe that's why I lasted as long in the classroom as I did, reveling in the promise of new names and faces at the start of every school year—it never occurred to me that I would grow older (because each new class never did), and then years passed, and I looked in the mirror and saw my age. *What did I miss?* Maybe that's why fear, crisis, drama, and trauma become so compelling—there's a break or rupture in the routine—an accident, an act of violence, a disaster, a change that enlivens and energizes, delivering the new and unexpected. Only then do we wake up from our trance and discover. *Is that why I'm so drawn to Mud Pony and Mara?*

I don't want to miss any of this, so I let it come—waves and more waves— one loss connecting to all losses—my parents and the years of estrangement between us—the students I cared for, nurtured, taught—the ones I couldn't help or couldn't reach—and those I did help but who never knew—my aging mare—Mud Pony who can't let me inside his heart... Rolando!

I think of the comfort I sought going across the street to Mrs. Burns when I was a child, and how every evening Carter and I tell each other about our days and share our discoveries. I remember an encounter with my mother on the day I left home. After saying goodbye, I realized an hour into the drive that I had forgotten my address book, and from a phone booth at the entrance to the Pennsylvania turnpike, I asked my mother to bring it to me. She complied and, after a brief exchange, watched me run from where she sat in the family van down a grassy slope to the car that would put three thousand miles between us. Now, after all this time, the space between us becomes something else. Across a continent, I open my heart and sense something of what she must have felt to see me leave. *She cared for me, worried about me!* Strangely, this seems like a release—and I sense an "us" I couldn't find before.

○

In Spanish, my mare is assigned the color *palomino,* meaning "like a dove." The Latin root means *pallére* or pale, and *palumbes* or ringdove. As a spindly, alabaster newborn, she came from the belly of a tall chestnut mare and stood up in the fog on a summer morning. They named her Tia's Ghostly Spirit.

I call her Spirit—from the Latin root *spiritus:* breath.

In fall, winter, and spring, she's ash, sand, and dirt. Her coat dulls as it thickens, and her mane and tail become the color of a used washrag after I take her saddle off and she rolls not once but three times, vigorously wiping her face and neck against the ground as she lies on one side, then balances on her spine with all four legs in the air, swishing her tail back and forth, before she crashes on the opposite side and begins again, getting the sand in every damp, joyful crevice. There's folk wisdom behind this—you can spot a good horse by counting the rolls; each side she rolls on adds another hundred dollars.

Spirit rolls once more, sits up, sets her front legs at a 45-degree angle, and pushes herself up with her hind end. She pauses for a moment, as if to assess her own satisfaction (or monetary worth), then shakes herself from head to tail, blinks, rolls her eyes, then yawns.

In early summer, she glows splendid cream and dark honey with a flaxen mane and tail and caramel body. By her birthday on July 3, she displays brindled hocks, dappled shoulders, and silver spun through the white of her tail. I watch her pause in between bites of hay to amble over to the water tub and dip her head. She's the only horse I've ever seen twitch her ears from flat to forward with each swallow as she drinks. I laugh quietly because I don't want to let her know how funny I find her bouncy bunny ears—Spirit must be granted dignity, for majesty such as hers lends delicacy to even a trough full of larvae and algae slime.

Accordingly, she has never been a mare to cuddle with. Spirit does not move into human space for connection or comfort the way Mara does. But recently, I've discovered if I pour warm herbal tea from my thermos onto a paper towel and then gently wipe her eyelids, she lowers her head and softens into my touch, relinquishing the crust that has hardened in the corners. She and Mud Pony stand next to each other all the time in pasture. Although she's considerably taller than he is, her shape—from the highest point of her hind end to her head—is an easy, gradual descent. He's a hard climb up the steep part and often seems bigger than he is.

For years, I have focused on him, but Spirit has been there all along, a shadowy figure more background than fore, the one who carried me when I forgot I was being carried—the type of horse described as worth her weight in gold, and "the kind," as Harry would say, "that fills in for you." She's surefooted and calm, forward and willing. I've done everything with her I once dreamed of as a child—camping trips, trail trials, dressage tests, team penning—*but maybe I didn't dream big enough.*

I ride Spirit for the first time in a long while and appreciate her softness and even rhythms. I have not been able to honor or appreciate her greatness, her gentleness and subtlety, until now—he and Mara have been so big and showy. They drew me, compelled me with their power and athleticism; I preferred the abandoned and traumatized, the charismatic and dramatic. But now I see Spirit's consideration and care, how she waits and watches, thinks. She is contained, quiet, and so *easy.*

Mud Pony brought me to Mara and Spirit, and all three have taught me this: Spirit's wide back is the inside of my mother where I rested sound as a young fish. I floated there, kicked out at nothing, sucked my thumb. Spirit reserves that space inside her, a quiet I can't name, a longing so big I can barely whisper it: *Can I take her shape so Mud Pony and Mara feel safe?*

We behold a fancy, a reverie, something otherworldly when we first commend our passion to another sentient being. We don't know it, but if we have the courage—to ask, to open—we find where we begin.

Post

I once asked Harry, "If I ride a horse out on trail, and they rush when we head back so that I have to stop, count to twenty... but then they rush again, should I consider them really *with* me?"

Now I have my own answer. Riding the flow of the horse's focus underneath, being aware of its changeability below the fluid nature of our own attention, the idea of "getting somewhere" or "being with" is no straight line to the moment of blissful achievement. The question is not *is he with me?* but *am I with myself?* And when I am, what do I notice?

Progress is always happening and going nowhere. Progress is a circle whose center is everywhere. In our attention to the moment, it increases and decreases with unhurried, sustained lengthenings of concentration.

On my drive to the ranch, I catch a glimpse of a crystalline sea out the passenger side. How still yet energetic the ocean, like the surface of a gem with the sunlight catching its edges. Wet-suited surfers occupy the rough entrance where the waves break.

As I walk toward the pasture, I notice how the horses don't wait for me. They are with themselves, and I am learning to be more like them in the way they observe and respond to even a rustling in the scrub. Mud Pony raises his head as he catches a whiff of something—could it be me? His voice is a trumpet. He's covered with dirt and hair fuzz, which is the same as his sleep, which is the same as the sun.

All is process left to its own passage. That's the wild in him. And I can never approach head-on, but alongside. I call to him, then press my lips together, humming a song I didn't even know I knew. That's it. When a new member enters the herd, everything shifts toward finding a settled sound. The herd hears and is heard by all. Anything damaged or estranged becomes whole by being part.

Author's Note

Mud Pony was distilled from daybooks, clinic notes, and journals during a decade of training, teaching, and trail riding. For the sake of narrative, time is compressed or rearranged in several chapters, and the names of most humans and horses have been changed or composited. Tom Dorrance's *True Unity: Willing Communication Between Horse and Human* was an essential source for understanding his concept of feel. References to the evolution of horses were drawn from Stephen Budiansky's *The Nature of Horses: Exploring Equine Evolution, Intelligence, and Behavior.* I utilized Martha Olivo's pamphlet *Healthy Hooves: The Bare Facts* and notes from her lectures on barefoot trimming, which she presented at two clinics. Olivo's teachings included references to the work and research of Dr. Hiltrud Strasser, specifically *Shoeing: A Necessary Evil?* I attended a talk by author Derrick Jensen at the California Association for Teachers of English (CATE) conference and cite his quote from that event. The 2001 *San Mateo County Boundary Study,* prepared by the Peninsula Open Space Trust, refers to specific flora and fauna of the coastal setting of the book as well as the timeline of Spanish and Mexican land grants. *The Ohlone Way* by Malcolm Margolin was a source for descriptions of wildlife pre-European colonization. *Bad Indians: A Tribal Memoir* by Deborah A. Miranda includes historical accounts of the horrors of the California Missions as well as the impact on surviving family and descendants. I utilized *The American Heritage Dictionary of Indo-European Roots* to describe words used by the people of the Eurasian steppes over 5,000 years ago. Linda Tellington-Jones' techniques for healing touch with equines and the use of her TTouch exercises provided inspiration as did the *Giant Rider-Waite Tarot Deck.* For Bible study at the Bible Horsemanship Clinic, I source from the *Saint Joseph Personal Size Edition of the New American Bible,* a book my father bound in leather. W.S. Merwin's translation of Antonio Porchia's verse in the epigraph is found in a bilingual edition of Porchia's *Voices.*

Acknowledgments

This book would not exist without the many horse and human friendships fed by riding trails on the Northern California coast. I am grateful to Jess, Patti, Sarah, Kathy, Curly, Mojave, Wings, and Tia's Ghostly Spirit (amongst many), for all the adventures and fun that inspired early drafts. Bows of gratitude to Robert and Desiree Yarber and the Morris Graves Foundation for two retreats in solitaire at Morris Graves' sunny studio on The Lake, and to the San Francisco Arts Commission, for a Cultural Equity grant. I relied on the guidance of writers, teachers, readers, and editors, especially Gail Sher, who showed me the path of the imagining ear; Diane di Prima, who cautioned me against taming anything wild; Melissa Stein, for shepherding me through revisions with a keen eye, light hand, and good humor; Paula Dragosh for her gracious and invaluable proofreading expertise. I benefitted from the wisdom of Teacher Consultants from the Bay Area Writing Project, especially Judy Bebelaar and Harvesting women Marty Williams and L. M. Quraishi. Special thanks to Barbara McCann, for rehabilitating Mara in body and spirit and inviting me to be part of the process, and to Vicky Golub for her enthusiastic love of Tia's Ghostly Spirit. Over the years, I've benefitted from the help and support of several teachers and trainers, especially Harry Whitney whose kindness, patience, and humor astound me. Pam Vilchez has been my principal teacher of *feel*, and I am grateful to her for extending her teaching to the realms of therapeutic horsemanship and healing. I am indebted to Nancy and Mac Burns, and Jennifer Galilea, for giving their support, generosity, and love of animals when I so needed it as a child. Great thanks to Richard Moore and Douglas Moorhead for the deep listening they offered, and the same to my soul sister Amanda Capehart. David Fought gave freely of his gentle, untamed approach to life and love of rain, mud, and all things interconnecting and meaning making. Profound thanks to the land and sea, animals and people of the Bay Area who bestow a refuge suffused with light, abundance, and beauty. And finally, all the horses who inspire us to be braver and more generous than we ever thought we could be.

About the Type

This book is set in Cormorant Garamond, which was created as an open-source font by Google's team of type designers and foundries based in Mountain View, California. Earlier Garamond fonts were designed by Robert Slimbach for Adobe (1989 Adobe Originals). These contemporary digital versions have their roots in the innovations of Claude Garamont, a 16th century punch cutter, typesetter, and publisher based in Paris. Monsieur Garamont (ca. 1480–1561) was one of a half-dozen master artisans of his time to cut types in the more modern 'roman' or upright style that displaced the blackletter or Gothic type which had been used in early French printing. M. Garamont was also one of the first independent punch cutters to specialize in type design as a service to others, rather than working in house for a specific printer. M. Garamont's original typeface, with its subtle, graceful strokes and ornamentation may well have enchanted 16th century readers, who were likely drawn to its informal, handwritten feeling. Readers of Garamond fonts in the 21st century, however, may register a more elegant, formal, or fanciful impression.

CPSIA information can be obtained
at www.ICGtesting.com
Printed in the USA
LVHW021738030523
746011LV00002B/370